PRODUCT DISCOVERY THINKING

BCS, THE CHARTERED INSTITUTE FOR IT

BCS, The Chartered Institute for IT, is committed to making IT good for society. We use the power of our network to bring about positive, tangible change. We champion the global IT profession and the interests of individuals, engaged in that profession, for the benefit of all.

Exchanging IT expertise and knowledge
The Institute fosters links between experts from industry, academia and business to promote new thinking, education and knowledge sharing.

Supporting practitioners
Through continuing professional development and a series of respected IT qualifications, the Institute seeks to promote professional practice tuned to the demands of business. It provides practical support and information services to its members and volunteer communities around the world.

Setting standards and frameworks
The Institute collaborates with government, industry and relevant bodies to establish good working practices, codes of conduct, skills frameworks and common standards. It also offers a range of consultancy services to employers to help them adopt best practice.

Become a member
Over 70,000 people including students, teachers, professionals and practitioners enjoy the benefits of BCS membership. These include access to an international community, invitations to a roster of local and national events, career development tools and a quarterly thought-leadership magazine. Visit www.bcs.org to find out more.

Further information
BCS, The Chartered Institute for IT,
3 Newbridge Square,
Swindon, SN1 1BY, United Kingdom.
T +44 (0) 1793 417 417
(Monday to Friday, 09:00 to 17:00 UK time)
www.bcs.org/contact

shop.bcs.org/
publishing@bcs.uk

bcs.org/qualifications-and-certifications/certifications-for-professionals/

A highly practical guide for building products with AI, without losing the human touch.
Jamie Bartlett, *Bestselling Author of 'How to Talk to AI: (And How Not To)'*

In a world besotted with technology, outcomes and speed, *Product Discovery Thinking* is a book built on the three key factors needed to create great products which are people, problems and possibilities. It is a step-by-step guide, informed by decades of experience and deep research, which is easy to apply to any situation, company or category.
Rishad Tobaccowala, *Author of 'Rethinking Work' and Former Chief Strategist and Growth Officer of Publicis Groupe*

So much is written about product discovery, but *Product Discovery Thinking*'s refreshing honesty is what finally makes it land. Evidence-based decisions are one thing; having the backbone to say no when the evidence tells you to is another.
Annie Moss-Quate, *Founder of Product Assembly and Senior Consultant Product Manager at Herd*

Product Discovery Thinking is fantastic. It's accessible, well researched and full of relatable examples. It highlights practical models and shows that discovery and creativity still need structure and discipline.
Christina Lovelock, *Tech Author and Director of Catch 22 Consulting Ltd*

As AI accelerates output, the real risk we face is building the wrong things faster. Paddy has spent years teaching teams to slow down and ask better questions first ... and this book proves it.
Vincent Mirabelli CBAP MBB PMP, *Principal Research Director at Info-Tech Research Group and President of the IIBA Toronto Chapter*

Product Discovery Thinking is a rare book that successfully combines strategic thinking with practical action. Packed with real-world stories, proven frameworks, beautiful stories, powerful analogies, compelling visuals, practical templates and hard-earned lessons, Paddy Dhanda distils decades of experience into an essential guide for anyone seeking to turn ideas into valuable outcomes. An outstanding work of deep thinking, expertise and craftsmanship.
Boby Jose, *Author of 'Test Automation: A Manager's Guide' and Test Strategy and Transformation Leader*

Regardless of what you do for a living, if your work involves generating and/or evaluating ideas and making better decisions involving 'people, problems and possibilities' then I would highly recommend this new book. Filled from start to finish with engaging and entertaining storytelling, powerful real-life business examples, a wealth of valuable tips, and a host of whimsically creative visuals, this innovative book will capture and hold your attention. From the first page to the last as you 'discover' how to better leverage your human skills and maintain your humanity in a world where it sometimes feels like the robots are taking over.
Todd Cherches, *CEO and Executive Coach, BigBlueGumball, Adjunct Professor, NYU and Columbia University, and Author of 'VisuaLeadership'*

An essential guide to the product discovery mindset for solution builders. It proves that moving beyond copy-paste frameworks is key to deeply understanding client problems and delivering bespoke outcomes.

Jahanger Hussain, *Director of Product Solutions, Decoded*

A book that should be on every IT professional's shelf. It reminds us that technology is a means to solve problems, not an end in itself, and shifts our focus from solutions to understanding both the problems and the dynamics that shape successful outcomes. Ackoff's classic elevator example captures this perfectly, while the author's practical experience provides techniques readily applicable to real-world challenges.

Daniele Gianni, *Enterprise Architecture, Service and Project Management, EU Agency*

An insightful and highly practical guide that moves beyond frameworks to the mindset, behaviours and culture needed for valuable continuous product discovery. One you'll return to throughout your product career.

Annie Birchall, *Lead Product Manager and Digital Transformation Specialist, Methods, an Alten Company*

I can't think of a better person to lead a product discovery journey than Paddy, building foundations, providing the tools and leading onwards to mastery in an ever changing world. I loved Paddy's narrative and Grant's visual style; a perfect product package.

Ben Walder, *Author of 'The Visual Agile Coach Playbook', Enterprise Change Leader*

Product Discovery Thinking is arriving at an excellent time where there is a need for organisations, not just Agile teams, to recognise the importance of human intelligence and human-centric roles in the age of AI. A highly recommended read for product teams, business partners and leaders.

James McConnell, *BCS Accredited Trainer, AI Pathway, Duco Digital Training*

A refreshingly honest guide to discovery, blending human judgement, mindset shifts and practical tools. It reshaped how I think about risk, ideas and the messy politics of product work.

Harpal Lidder, *VP, IIBA Toronto and Business Analyst, MiWay*

From spotting real problems to reading stakeholders and asking sharper questions, Paddy turns discovery into a practical toolkit any product role can use immediately, a genuine playbook, not just theory.

Erivan de Sena Ramos CBAP PMP, *Business Analysis Lead, Esri Australia*

Clear, practical and very human, this book turns product discovery from a buzzword into a daily practice for anyone who needs to understand users and find the most fitting solutions.

Iurii Gomon CBAP CSPO, *Founder, The Passionate Business Analyst*

PRODUCT DISCOVERY THINKING

Human skills to launch valuable ideas in the age of AI

Paddy Dhanda

bcs
The Chartered Institute for IT

Published by BCS Learning and Development Ltd, a wholly owned subsidiary of BCS, The Chartered Institute for IT, 3 Newbridge Square, Swindon, SN1 1BY, UK.
www.bcs.org

EU GPSR Authorised Representative: LOGOS EUROPE, 9 Rue Nicolas Poussin, 17000 La Rochelle, France.
Contact@logoseurope.eu

Paperback ISBN: 978-1-78017-7304
PDF ISBN: 978-1-78017-7311
ePUB ISBN: 978-1-78017-7328

Ebook available

British Cataloguing in Publication Data.
A CIP catalogue record for this book is available at the British Library.

Publisher's acknowledgements
Reviewers: Helen King, Hannah Pearson-Coats
Publisher: Ian Borthwick
Commissioning editor: Heather Wood
Production manager: Florence Leroy
Project manager: Sunrise Setting Ltd
Copy-editor: Gary Smith
Proofreader: Andy Cook
Indexer: David Gaskell
Cover design: Alex Wright
Cover image: Shutterstock/Alones
Typeset by Lapiz Digital Services, Chennai, India
Illustrations: Grant Wright
Additional illustrations: Pavan Dhanda
Printed in the UK by Hobbs the Printers Ltd

FSC www.fsc.org MIX Paper | Supporting responsible forestry FSC® C020438

CONTENTS

FIGURES AND TABLES

AUTHOR

Paddy Dhanda has led Product Management and Agile practices at one of Europe's largest technology training providers, shaping human and AI-powered product skills for some of the world's best-known brands. His career spans more than two decades across software engineering, business analysis and product management, within sectors including insurance, banking, telecoms, and consulting.

Along the way, he led a community of practice of over 2,000 business analysts at a global investment bank and co-founded The Visual Jam, a community dedicated to visual thinking and the human skills that boost creativity, communication, and collaboration.

Paddy went to one of the worst-performing high schools in England and describes himself as a professional introvert who became addicted to conversation through his podcast, which was nominated for Best Content Creator at the Creative Industry Awards. He is also an international keynote speaker and guest lecturer on the University of Birmingham MBA programme, where he helps inspire the next generation of leaders.

FOREWORD

It's never been easier to build products. With modern technology, anyone with an idea and a laptop can create software and launch products at hyper-speed. It's exciting, but also troubling; as building gets easier, so does the risk of 'product slop' and failure.

There are few people better to help us navigate this age of acceleration and experimentation than Paddy Dhanda. He's spent over two decades leading software engineering, business analysis, and product management. More importantly, Paddy has a rare blend of curiosity, experience, openness, enthusiasm, and clarity, not to mention an inexhaustible appetite to learn new things. His personality shines through on every page, as it should, because these very human attributes are precisely what we need right now.

In *Product Discovery Thinking*, Paddy explains that while AI can help us build at super speed, it means our human skills are more important than ever: careful listening, patience, and asking questions. Making good products is not about mechanical delivery; it relies on the more human discipline of understanding people, their problems, and the possible answers before we start building. So prepare to get informed and get uncomfortable - in the best possible way.

Jamie Bartlett
Bestselling author of *How to Talk to AI: (And How Not To)*

ACKNOWLEDGEMENTS

Thank you to Kal, my beautiful wife, for putting up with way too many evenings and late nights while I have been glued to my laptop. This book was only possible because of your patience and belief in me, just as every step of my career has been. You are my rock behind everything I do.

To my children, Arjan and Pavan, thank you for your constant mockery throughout this journey. Arjan, for asking me, more than once, are you nearly there yet? Pavan, for your help with the illustrations. Seeing your work in print is one of the proudest moments of this whole project. I hope, when you are both older, that something in these pages will be useful to you.

Thank you to my mum and dad for guiding me when I needed you. I will always be grateful for everything you have sacrificed to give me the opportunities you never had.

A special thank you to Milo for keeping me sane and healthy throughout this journey by insisting I take you out for your daily walks.

To everyone who shared their stories and insights throughout the book, and to all my colleagues at QA Ltd who have supported me.

Grant Wright, my dear friend and partner in visual crime, for the brilliant illustrations that have brought each chapter to life.

And above all, almighty God, for every step that has led me here.

INTRODUCTION

> *'It was discovery at first sight.'*
>
> ***Paddy Dhanda***

MY GREATEST DISCOVERY

Four hours after meeting her, I asked her to marry me. I realise this is a strange way to begin a business book. You may have picked this up expecting to read about customers, experiments, stakeholders, AI, frameworks, and the messy business of launching better products. But stay with me, because that moment taught me something I only understood years later.

In Indian culture, arranged marriages are still part of the tradition, although the modern version is often very different from the way it is portrayed in the media. It is less about two strangers being pushed together and more about opening a door and then letting two people explore the possibilities.

At the time, I had spent most of my school and university years buried in books, so dating had never really been part of the plan. I have traditional Indian parents, and like many parents from that generation, education came first.

Then, one day, a good friend called and told me about someone he knew. He thought we might get on. I remember feeling nervous about it, but we agreed to exchange numbers. That led to a couple of phone calls and a few SMS messages.

This was long before WhatsApp and fancy dating apps, it was just my trusted Nokia 3310 and good old-fashioned conversations. After a couple of weeks, we decided to meet. I drove four hours across the country from Ipswich, where I worked, to Bradford, where she lived. When we finally met, the conversation seemed to flow naturally. We talked about our families, our education, our values, our hopes, and the kind of life we imagined for ourselves.

At times, it probably did feel like we were interviewing one another, although in the best possible way. Every question was an opportunity to be curious, and with every answer, we discovered new insights. We were trying to learn enough to make an informed decision, and by the end of those four hours, I knew enough to make the biggest decision of my life.

WHAT IS PRODUCT DISCOVERY THINKING?

The biggest decisions in life are rarely based on complete certainty. We do our best with the information available to us. We listen, ask, notice the small signals, pay attention to what feels right and what feels off, and weigh up what we know against what we don't. At some point, we have to decide whether we have learned enough to commit.

That same pattern sits at the heart of product work. Every product decision asks an organisation to commit something valuable. Budget is the obvious cost, although it is rarely the only one, because teams also invest their time and energy.

The trouble is that many of those commitments are made too early, before you have learned enough to feel confident in the decision. Think about what usually happens in your organisation when a senior stakeholder demands that you build their features. Or a leader gets excited about a new technology. Maybe a competitor launches a shiny new AI tool, and the organisation feels the pressure of FOMO to respond. Suddenly, we feel compelled to help and do what we were always trained to do, deliver an innovative solution, even if we haven't quite understood the problem properly.

This is how good people end up building things that do not create value. It's not that they are careless. They are usually under pressure, working with incomplete information, trying to be helpful inside a system that rewards certainty and speed.

The alternative I want to offer is a practice that builds learning into our work, so we are no longer forced to choose between speed and good decisions. I have come to call this practice *product discovery thinking*, and here is the definition I will use throughout this book:

> *Product discovery thinking is the discipline of learning relentlessly about people, problems, and possibilities, so we can make better decisions before committing valuable time, money, and effort to a solution.*

Let me break that definition down so you understand the rationale behind it. I use the word discipline because, unlike everyday discoveries that often happen by chance, like finding the food we enjoy most or realising which sports we are good at, product discovery takes a more structured approach. It is a discipline backed by tools and techniques that have evolved over the years, many of which I will introduce you to throughout this book. All of those tools are designed to maximise our learning so we can build better insights, and we have to be relentless because everything around us is moving at such a pace. If we treat product discovery as a one-off activity, we leave ourselves exposed to being overtaken by our competitors.

The next part of the definition focuses on the three Ps: people, problems, and possibilities. These are the most important things we are trying to make sense of. If you think about any product or invention that has ever existed, it began with a problem that someone was experiencing. The interesting work then becomes imagining the creative possibilities for solving it, and that is only possible if we have a deep understanding of the people we are building for.

Finally, discovery is an investment in time, money, and effort, and that investment should be reserved for the decisions that genuinely warrant it. If we are about to make a significant commitment, whether that is a year of a team's time or a substantial amount of money, then the cost of getting it wrong could break the business case for building it in the first place. That's when product discovery thinking becomes our tool for managing risk.

WHO IS THIS FOR?

Throughout this book, I will use the term *product discovery thinker* to describe the people doing this work. That's you, by the way.

To be clear, product discovery thinking is a capability, not a job title, and an increasingly critical one to develop. Whatever your current title, building this capability means championing user needs from spotting problems through to landing on a solution people genuinely value.

The work pulls together skills that usually sit in separate professions, which is why no single role can fully prepare you for it. You investigate problems with the curiosity of a researcher, while also facilitating group thinking, the way a coach would. Alongside that, you need to influence decisions in situations where you may not hold formal authority, and often without the luxury of clear answers.

Many of the books I have learned from on this subject are excellent, but most have been written primarily for product managers. I believe that product discovery runs through every product role, including product managers, but applies just as much to business analysts, product owners, UX practitioners, engineers, and founders.

I would go one step further and say this book is also for people who have never set foot inside a product team. We are entering a world where anyone with an idea and a laptop can build their own product, whether they work in marketing, finance, sales, HR, or any other function outside the technology department.

Although this book draws most of its examples from the world of digital products, the core principles are applicable to any kind of product or service.

My aim was to write an accessible, easy-to-follow guide for anyone who wants to practise product discovery, regardless of the path you have taken to get here.

THE DISCOVERY JOURNEY

I have organised the chapters into three parts that build on one another.

Part I is about laying the foundations for product discovery. Before you reach for the tools, these early chapters look at the role that failure plays in product work and make the case for why discovery is needed. We begin with the most hated paperclip in software history, then explore how other professions outside the product world use discovery in their daily work, including how Liverpool Football Club signs some of its best players. Then we will see what watermelons and hurricanes can teach us about managing uncertainty. I introduce you to the ghosts of product risk that can haunt your product unless you spot them early. We end Part I by discussing the importance of safety in your team culture, and how one organisation pours champagne every time a project is killed.

Part II is where we walk through the product discovery thinking process, rolling up our sleeves with the popular tools and techniques, along with the mindset shifts needed to become an effective product discovery thinker. We start by learning where to find problems, beginning with a Manhattan office tower that wanted to speed up its lifts, until someone asked a better question. From there, we look at how to understand user needs, and you will meet the team that was struggling to sell their milkshakes. We then turn to generating and assessing ideas, where I will tell you about the author who made a bet to write a story in no more than 50 words. We look at how to test our ideas before committing to them, including a simple tool I use to design better experiments. We finish by introducing a set of popular frameworks, some for short bursts of intense learning and others for building discovery into the everyday rhythm of a team. For each of them, I provide guidance on which one to use in different situations.

Part III is about mastery, and by mastery I mean the human side of the work. We begin with stakeholders, who are far easier to work with once you stop trying to manage them and start trying to read them. We then look at what it takes to facilitate a room well, with a little help from Eleanor Roosevelt, who helped delegates from 58 nations navigate their differences around one of the most famous documents in history. We explore how to ask better questions, and you will see how one badly worded question cost a retailer nearly two billion dollars. Santa then shows us how to present our ideas with impact, and we close the book by looking at how to build a discovery culture across your entire organisation.

You do not have to read the book in order, but if you are wrestling with a difficult stakeholder this week, go straight to Part III and start there. If you simply want techniques you can start using immediately, then jump to Part II. I have written each chapter so that it can be read on its own or as part of the wider set. My only suggestion is that if you are new to all of this, the journey from Part I onwards will give you the right foundations to get started.

You can also visit my website at www.PaddyDhanda.com, where I share podcast episodes, templates, and a regular newsletter, all focused on the human skills behind great product work.

THE RISE OF HUMAN SKILLS

I have put the human side of the work at the end of the book, in Part III, but I want to explain why it is a core theme. Product development is going through a generational shift, and you cannot have a conversation about the future of our work without talking about artificial intelligence.

In the space of a few short years, AI has made the act of building products faster, cheaper, and easier than at any point in our industry's history, which leaves a different question that's on every product professional's mind. If the act of building is no longer the hard part, then where do product people now create value?

The answer, I believe, sits in the work that AI cannot easily do just yet. For years, the industry has described these as soft skills; often, it felt like they were nice to have, and somehow optional. But soft skills are hard.

For that reason, I think of them as essential human skills. They run through every chapter of this book, but we go much deeper in Part III.

Before we begin

Years ago, a four-hour conversation changed my life. Fast forward to today, my wife and I have built a beautiful life together with our two children, and a slightly chaotic puppy called Milo.

I cannot promise that this book will lead you to the love of your life, but the same instincts that helped me that day, the curiosity, the questions, the patience to listen and learn, are the same ingredients required to build a product discovery thinker's mindset.

I have poured in over two decades of mistakes, lessons, and stories, along with insights from more than 200 experts I have spoken to while writing this book. To back up the key ideas, I have drawn on research studies and a rich set of behavioural insights. If even a handful of these ideas change how you approach your product work, then the late nights and hard graft will have been worth it.

The best growth happens when you step out of your comfort zone. So, as I say at the start of every episode of my podcast, pull up a chair, grab a samosa or two, and make yourself very uncomfortable.

PART I
UNDERSTANDING PRODUCT DISCOVERY

1 WELCOME TO THE FAILURE ECONOMY

'Curiosity killed the paperclip.'

Paddy Dhanda

THE INFAMOUS CLIPPY

'It looks like you're writing a letter. Would you like help with that?' That sounds like something a modern AI assistant might say today, but in fact it was a feature built almost 30 years ago.

Let me rewind to 1997. Blur and Oasis were still battling it out at the top of the UK music charts, the Spice Girls were telling everyone what they really, really wanted, and *Titanic* was making waves at the cinema. Meanwhile, Microsoft was busy launching Office 97, and tucked inside was an animated paperclip officially called Clippit, though to most of us he was better known as Clippy.

If you ever had the joy, or should I say the pain, of working with Office 97, you will definitely remember Clippy. He would pop up on your screen offering to help, whether you wanted it or not.

Figure 1.1 Clippy offering to help

The most famous failed feature

Microsoft had been inspired by some fascinating behavioural research from Stanford University, which showed that people treat computers much like they treat other people.[1] We project emotions onto them and even respond politely without realising we are doing it. The team at Microsoft turned that insight into a feature of the Office 97 suite, and the goal was to make technology feel more human, with Clippy on hand to offer advice whenever we needed it.

From a technical perspective, Clippy was surprisingly cutting-edge. He ran on an early, rule-based form of natural language processing and a user-intent recognition system known inside Microsoft as Lumière. Rather than learning from data the way modern AI models do, Clippy relied on thousands of handcrafted rules to guess what you might be trying to do.

There were early warning signs when Microsoft's own focus groups raised concerns about the character's male-oriented design, but they had a bigger problem. What the team had missed was that people were not looking for company while they worked, they were looking to get things done.

Picture yourself at your desk, racing to hit a tight deadline. Every time you settle into the work, an overly friendly colleague leans over with another piece of useless news or advice. That was the effect Clippy had on users. Every time he popped up to offer help, the software paused whatever you were doing, and there was no easy way to switch him off.

That might have been tolerable the first few times, but eventually the interruptions became a real nuisance. Clippy insisted on helping even when you didn't ask for it, and in doing so, Microsoft broke a basic rule of user experience. They created friction between the user and their desired goal.

Users rejected the feature because he constantly butted in and offered help they had not asked for. Despite Microsoft's investment in animation, behavioural psychology, and hundreds of design variations, he failed. *Time* magazine even named him on its list of the 50 worst inventions ever made.[2] Eventually, Microsoft embraced the negativity, releasing Office XP under the tagline 'Now without Clippy!' a rare example of a brand celebrating the removal of a feature and marketing it as a selling point.

Clippy may go down as one of the most famous failed features in software history, and yet Microsoft Office became one of the most successful products of all time. For millions of us, it is now woven into the fabric of modern work. As of February 2024, Microsoft 365 held around a 30 per cent share of the global office software market and generated roughly $49 billion in revenue.[3]

The real lesson Clippy teaches us is that even the most talented product teams can build the wrong thing, and as it turns out, they do so far more often than we realise.

THE COST OF BUILDING THE WRONG THINGS

There is a real pride in seeing your requirements turn into features in a live product. We tell ourselves we are helping people solve everyday problems and write case studies about the successful launches, while those of us who live on LinkedIn shout about them to anyone who will listen.

But how often do we stop to ask how many of those features are never actually used? The honest answer is far more than most of us would guess. Research found that 80 per cent of features in the average software product are rarely or never used, and they add up to an estimated $29.5 billion in wasted development costs.[4]

To put that into perspective, you could strip out roughly four in every five features from your backlog or requirements document, and most users would never even notice.

Zoom out from individual features to whole products, and the picture becomes more troubling. Depending on whose research you believe, the failure rate of new products sits somewhere between 40 and 95 per cent. Even if we treat those figures with caution, the message is hard to ignore. Close to half of everything we build ends up creating little or no value.

What strikes me most about these numbers is how rarely our industry admits to failure at all. I have interviewed hundreds of candidates for product roles over the years, and not once have I seen a CV that proudly lists the products that flopped. Yet, if the data is right, failure is not the exception, it is business as usual.

Compare that with other professions. Imagine a doctor hiding a misdiagnosis, or a lawyer leaving the case they lost off their record. In medicine and law, studying what went wrong is part of how people grow and improve. In tech, we still cling to the belief that every product we ship has to be a success story.

Figure 1.2 Too many features

THE LAW OF MARKET FAILURE

Alberto Savoia, a former engineering director at Google, has spent much of his career trying to understand failure and, more importantly, helping teams avoid building the wrong things in the first place. After leaving Google to work in startups and innovation consulting, he was invited back because the company wanted to understand how failure was holding back its ability to innovate.

After years of research, Savoia concluded that product failure was so widespread and so predictable that it deserved a law of its own, which he named the Law of Market Failure:[5]

> *'Most new ideas will fail in the market – even if they are competently executed.'*

This distinction is important because products fail for all kinds of reasons. Some fail for technical reasons, such as buggy code or poor marketing. Others fail because of a flawed business model, where the numbers never quite stack up.

But the most common failure of all, and the one this book focuses on, is the lack of market need. This is when you build the product perfectly, ship it on time and on budget, and then find that your users never needed it. Clippy is the perfect example, because the technology itself was never the issue.

More recently, Clubhouse, the social audio app that everyone seemed to be talking about during the pandemic, was valued at its peak at $4 billion.[6] Just a few years later, its user base had dwindled to a small, niche community.

Search 'biggest product fails of all time', and you will get millions of results, an endless trail of post-mortems for products that were full of promise and never delivered, most of them quiet victims of the Law of Market Failure.

THE RISKIEST PROJECTS OF ALL

Of course, most of us do not work at startups or on glamorous consumer apps. So what happens when you work on a large enterprise IT project, a new internal CRM platform, or the replacement of a creaking legacy billing system? These programmes are usually treated as essential to keeping the business running day to day. They tend to be complex to deliver, and their development plans usually stretch across years.

If you are early in your tech career, you might reasonably assume that an industry this mature would have learned to deliver these projects well by now. The odds, though, are stacked against you before you even begin.

Researchers at Oxford University published a global study of more than 11,000 mega-projects across 126 countries and 23 industries, worth $4.6 trillion in total, spanning everything from construction and defence to energy, healthcare, and tech.[7] Led by Bent Flyvbjerg, it was one of the most thorough studies of its kind, and the team set out to discover which kinds of projects are most likely to fail to deliver on their original plan.

On the face of it, the numbers for tech do not look too alarming. Only around 40 per cent of IT projects run over budget, compared with 100 per cent of Olympic Games, 97 per cent of nuclear power plants, and 75 per cent of hydroelectric dams. The danger is what happens when IT projects do go wrong, because they tend to completely spiral out of control. Among the worst performers, the average cost overrun was more than 450 per cent, the highest figure in any category in the study. The researchers concluded that IT projects are not just risky, they are the riskiest of all.

When Universal Credit built the wrong thing

I experienced this during my consulting career, when I worked on the UK Government's Universal Credit programme, one of the largest Agile transformations in the world.

It was an ambitious attempt to replace six different benefits with a single payment. Financially, the business case made perfect sense. The estimated delivery cost was £2 billion, to be rolled out by 2017, with projected annual savings of £2.2 billion on fraud and administrative errors.[8] So it would have paid for itself within just one year.

I was stationed in the north of England for over six months with talented consultants from all of the big consultancy firms. While we faced big delivery challenges because of the complex nature of the work, the bigger failure was the lack of focus on the people who would use the system. Claimants were locked into a fully digital process, even though many lacked stable internet access and basic IT skills. The system was 'digital by default', leaving vulnerable people effectively excluded from accessing their benefits.[9]

To make matters worse, claimants had to wait five weeks for their first payment. For families already struggling financially, that was simply too long. It pushed people into debt, rent arrears, and even homelessness, with food bank use rising by 30 per cent in areas where Universal Credit was rolled out.[10]

By 2015, the government's own Major Projects Authority confirmed that Universal Credit had been reset and its projected lifetime cost had climbed to £15.8 billion.[11] The team had built a system around a set of assumptions that turned out to be wrong, and no amount of careful delivery could rescue a design aimed at the wrong problem.

High-profile examples like Universal Credit reflect a wider industry trend. Research into large digital transformations found that 70 per cent fail to deliver what they set out to achieve, because their intended outcomes are poorly defined from the start.[12] Only 40 per cent of organisations bother to define those outcomes before they begin, which means most teams launch major programmes without ever agreeing on what problem they are solving or what success would even look like.

THE OUTPUT TRAP

You might expect that organisations with heavy governance and rigorous processes would have found ways to avoid these risks. In my experience, the problem is rarely too little structure or oversight. More often, there is far too much of it, and the projects fail because the whole system is set up to reward the wrong behaviours.

Ask a few different product teams how they track progress, and you are likely to hear very similar answers. Most measure things like velocity, or how many story points the team got through this sprint. Others count the number of features shipped and releases deployed.

These are all measures of output, and on the surface that seems perfectly reasonable, because surely more output means more progress.

The trouble is that output tells you nothing about whether you are building the right things. A team can ship 50 features in a quarter and still deliver no value at all to its customers. Melissa Perri, author of *Escaping the Build Trap*, describes this as one of the most dangerous traps in product development.[13] Organisations become so fixated on shipping that they lose sight of why they are building in the first place, and the goal shifts from creating value to simply staying busy. This leads to what John Cutler calls the 'feature factory', a team that runs like an assembly line, churning out features without ever stopping to ask whether they solve real problems.[14]

Worse still, all those extra features can actually make the product harder to use. Psychologists Sheena Iyengar and Mark Lepper ran a now-famous experiment in a Californian grocery store.[15] On some days, they set up a tasting booth with 24 varieties of jam. Other days, they offered just 6. The larger display drew more interest, with 60 per cent of passing shoppers stopping to look, against 40 per cent for the smaller one. The surprise came at the checkout, because only 3 per cent of the people who saw 24 options bought a jar, compared with 30 per cent of those who saw 6.

Similarly, every feature in your product is another jar of jam on the shelf. Building more does not mean people will use more. In the early days of search engines, Yahoo's homepage was crammed with news headlines, stock tickers, shopping directories, and dozens of category links, all competing for your attention. Then Google arrived with just a text box and a search button, and the rest, as they say, is history. Sometimes less really is more.

The alternative is to measure outcomes, the changes in behaviour, or business results that show whether your work is genuinely creating value. Did people adopt the feature? Did it cut the time they spent on a task? Did it increase retention or satisfaction?

But the difficulty with focusing on outcomes is that they are far harder to measure than outputs. You can count the features you shipped on the very day you deploy them, but working out whether those features actually changed anyone's behaviour takes sustained effort long after release. That is one reason output metrics remain so popular, because they provide immediate gratification when you hit the target.

THE ACCELERATION PROBLEM

If the system already rewards output, what happens when we start building at turbo speed? AI has passed the point of no return, and its adoption is only going to grow. Tools that once took years of training to master are now accessible to anyone with a laptop and an internet connection.

As a Gen Xer, I have had the privilege of living through four transformative technological waves. Desktops let us work from home, the internet connected us to the world, mobile gave us access on the go, and AI is now accelerating the sheer pace at which we create and innovate.

Each wave opened up new possibilities, and each one brought new ways to fail. For all the hype, even AI products are far from immune. Research suggests that more than 80 per cent of AI projects fail. That is roughly twice the failure rate of technology projects that involve no AI at all.[16]

Take Humane's AI Pin. It launched in 2023, the brainchild of two Apple veterans who had helped shape the iPhone. The Pin was a wearable device that clipped to your clothing and projected information onto the palm of your hand. It meant that you didn't need a screen since it was a voice-controlled AI assistant intended to replace your smartphone.

I remember watching one of the early launch videos and feeling a strange mix of excitement and doubt. Part of me admired the ambition, a product bold enough to ask whether we even need a phone. But as the demo went on, another thought crept in. Did I really want this? It looked like one more gadget to charge at night, and one that expected me to talk to it in public. Now, I have spent enough mornings on the London Underground to know that it would take a very brave commuter to break the silence on that train. Surrounded by people buried in their Kindles and newspapers, it is about the last place on Earth you would want to start talking to a gadget on your chest.

In February 2025, Humane shut down sales completely and sold off most of its assets.[17] It was one more reminder of how easily product people get swept up in the excitement of the latest shiny technology, chasing a problem that never really existed.

Democratising development

Traditional software development demanded years of study to master languages like Java, which is why only a relatively small group of specialists could ever do it.

A new wave of 'vibe-coding' tools has removed the barriers to building software and given rise to the 'citizen developer'. These non-technical builders are reshaping how software gets made, and analysts expect them to outnumber professional developers by four to one in large organisations.[18]

The term 'vibe coding' was coined by Andrej Karpathy, co-founder of OpenAI,[19] and it caught on so fast that *Collins Dictionary* named it their Word of the Year for 2025.[20] The idea is that you no longer need to learn complicated syntax. You go with the vibes, almost forgetting you are coding at all, simply describing what you want in plain language and letting AI generate the software for you. The shift is so dramatic that Microsoft's chief technology officer, Kevin Scott, has predicted that in the future as much as 95 per cent of all software code could be written by AI.[21]

In many ways, vibe coding mirrors our natural creative process. We express an idea, picture it, refine and iterate, and once we are happy, we ship it. If you work in an Agile team, this will feel very familiar, because we already experiment early, gather feedback quickly, and iterate often. The one real difference is that this is Agile at supersonic speed.

Ideas that once needed teams of engineers and months of coding can now be brought to life in minutes by almost anyone. It is now so simple that even little humans can do it.

When I vibed with my son

It was a Saturday afternoon, and my 13-year-old son was slumped on the sofa, glued to his phone. Like most teenagers, he was watching YouTube videos of other people playing computer games, and it struck me how much of his generation's digital life is spent consuming rather than creating.

It had not always been this way. When he was younger, he used to spend hours drawing his own comics. He had a whole series he called *Dolphin Adventures*, hand-drawn on folded paper, and he would show them off with pride.

Figure 1.3 *Dolphin Adventures* comic, drawn by my son

Somewhere between then and now, the creating had stopped. So I opened my laptop, loaded up Replit, a popular vibe-coding app, and asked whether he fancied building a game of his own. As a passionate gamer, he immediately accepted the challenge.

For the next four hours, he let his imagination run wild. Then, grinning from ear to ear, he proudly showed me Dolphin Quest, his very own game. The best way I can describe it is a cross between Pokémon and Minecraft, set in a 3D underwater world patrolled by giant fish.

It was a genuinely special moment. He had not spent years mastering the art of game design or learning how computer chips work. He simply had an idea and brought it to life through his own creative thinking.[22]

The rise of product slop

Building at speed has a darker side when we lean on AI too heavily. When creation becomes this effortless, there is a real risk that we grow lazy and start outsourcing our thinking to the machine. The danger is that we accept the first thing it hands us, without ever questioning it or bringing our own creativity to the problem.

Researchers have a name for this side effect. They call it 'AI slop', the flood of low-quality, machine-generated content littering the web. Think of it as spam for the internet, and it is becoming a serious problem. One large study analysed 65,000 articles and found that more than half of all new content published online is AI-generated, and this figure is growing.[23]

The one dollar podcast

We are already getting a taste of things to come from the creator economy. In 2025, a startup called Inception Point AI began flooding the podcast world, producing more than 3,000 episodes a week across some 5,000 different shows.[24] Each one costs almost nothing to make compared with a traditional human podcast, at just $1 an episode.[25] In some weeks, the company accounted for around 1 per cent of every podcast published on the internet.

This is the slop era at its bleakest, an endless churn of hollow content that mimics human connection while feeling completely empty. As someone who has spent years making my own podcast, I find this hard to watch. Behind every good episode are hours of work the listener never sees, from researching guests to carefully editing the best bits. Watching that creative effort get replaced by mass-produced AI slop made for just $1 is hard to stomach.

If we repeat the same mistakes as the internet, we are at risk of flooding the world with mundane and uninspiring products, or what I prefer to call product slop.

LANDFILL OF TECHNOLOGY

In many ways, the technology industry reminds me of fashion. Every year, around 100 billion garments are produced, and roughly 92 million tonnes are thrown away.[26] That is the equivalent of a full rubbish truck of clothes every single second. The damage does not stop there, because it reaches into polluted rivers, billions of wasted litres of water, and huge amounts of carbon pumped into the atmosphere.

Technology has its own version of this throwaway culture, except that our landfill is invisible. Instead of heaps of clothing, we leave behind unused features and abandoned apps. Every unused feature still has to be stored and maintained, and just like the fashion industry, this all adds unnecessary strain to the infrastructure and the environment.

Martin Fowler, one of the most influential voices in software engineering, calls this accumulated cost 'technical debt',[27] a term borrowed from finance to capture the way shortcuts and unused code accrue interest over time. Unlike financial debt, though, technical debt is largely invisible. Bit by bit, bugs become harder to fix and teams end up spending more time maintaining old code than building anything new.

The Failure Economy

Over the past 25 years, I have seen all of this first-hand. Most of my biggest lessons were learned the hard way, deep inside complex corporate environments. I have celebrated a handful of wins along the way, but I have worked on far more failed products than I would care to admit. I have worn a good many hats too, from leading business analysis teams to running multi-million-pound product portfolios.

Each of those roles forced me to see product development through a different lens. Sometimes I was down in the weeds, untangling requirements and mapping technical dependencies. At other times, I was at the strategy table, deciding which products deserved investment and which ideas were not worth the risk. Taken together, those experiences taught me one thing above all else. Everything starts with understanding your customer. Only then do you have half a chance of building the right things.

And yet, as an industry, we keep forgetting this simple truth. After analysing hundreds of startup post-mortems, CB Insights found that over 40 per cent had failed because there was no real market need, the second most common reason of all, just behind running out of money.[28] They had built something that worked perfectly well for a problem that nobody had.

In 2017, the psychologist Samuel West opened the Museum of Failure in Sweden, a travelling exhibition of more than 150 products that flopped.[29] Visitors can learn about the failure stories behind consumer products like Colgate Beef Lasagne and Harley-Davidson cologne. His research found that 90 per cent of innovation projects fail, and that many of the casualties come from the biggest brands on the planet, the likes of Google, Apple, and Coca-Cola. There is something oddly comforting in that. If the largest companies in the world can get it this badly wrong, then innovation really is a difficult endeavour.

As product professionals, we like to believe we are part of the innovation economy. We tell ourselves that we are moving humanity forward, using creativity and technology to make the world a little better with every release. But if the numbers are anything to go by, and we look honestly at the digital waste each wave leaves behind, that is not really what is happening.

The reality is that we are fuelling something far less inspiring, a failure economy, a system that rewards busyness over real progress, praises output over outcome, and treats failure as the norm rather than the exception.

So here is the question. If four out of every five of our features go unused, and half of our products never succeed, can we honestly claim that we are driving innovation?

A BETTER WAY

That is exactly why this book exists. It will not teach you to avoid failure altogether, because no one can. Failure is part of product work, just as it is in science, in sport, and in everyday moments we experience in life. What this book offers instead is a way to notice the warning signs earlier, while there is still time to change course, so that far less of your effort is poured into ideas that were never worth building.

It all starts with a small change to the question we ask. Most of us were trained to ask, 'How do we build it?' Discovery thinking asks something different first, which is 'What problem are we actually trying to solve?' That sounds almost too simple to be useful, although it changes everything that follows. When we lead with the solution, we assume that someone, somewhere, has already worked out what people need. Discovery turns that assumption on its head, not by ignoring stakeholders or second-guessing decisions, but by approaching problems with an open mind before treating any solution as a foregone conclusion.

We do that by borrowing the practices we learn during our schooling in the science lab. Scientists test a hypothesis by looking for evidence that might prove them wrong, and discovery brings that same mindset to building products. Before we commit serious resources to an idea, we run small experiments to gather evidence, and if that evidence tells us the idea is not worth pursuing, we find the courage to say no and change direction. A few days or weeks spent learning this way is a tiny investment against the risk of wasting months of engineering effort and the technical debt that building the wrong things leaves behind.

In a lot of organisations, though, 'discovery' is still treated as a niche tech-startup thing, or a scary product management practice. It's seen as a dark art that only a select few are able to do. The good news is, you don't need to be a Silicon Valley entrepreneur to do it. As we are about to find out, discovery is a universal discipline and a basic human survival instinct. It's a skill practised by the world's best performers in every field imaginable.

Figure 1.4 The Failure Economy

In the next chapter, we'll leave the office behind and travel to NASA's launchpads, Olympic velodromes, and hospital wards to see how the world's best problem-solvers use the discovery mindset to navigate uncertainty and achieve the impossible.

KEY TAKEAWAYS

- **Even good teams build the wrong thing:** Clippy is proof that talent, budget, and behavioural science cannot save you from building something nobody actually asked for.
- **Failure is the default, not the exception:** Between 40 and 95 per cent of new products fail, around 80 per cent of features in the average product are rarely or never used, and 35 per cent of startups die because there was no real market need.
- **IT projects are statistically the riskiest of all:** Among the worst-performing mega-projects, IT cost overruns average more than 450 per cent, the highest figure in any category in Oxford University's global study.
- **Outputs are not outcomes:** Velocity, story points, and features shipped only tell you the team is busy. Outcomes tell you whether the work is creating any value.
- **AI is pouring fuel on the Failure Economy:** More than 80 per cent of AI projects fail, roughly twice the rate of technology projects with no AI involved.
- **Discovery is about reducing uncertainty:** This book gives you a way to spot the warning signs earlier and waste far less effort on ideas that were never worth building.

2 RECOGNISE THE MODES OF DISCOVERY

'Houston, we have a problem. Turns out we never asked what it was.'

Paddy Dhanda

THE TODDLER'S INSTINCT

The average toddler takes 2,368 steps and falls 17 times per hour.[1]

What's easy to miss is how much learning is packed into those small moments when we stumble. Each one creates what neuroscientists call a prediction error, a mismatch between what the brain expected to happen and what actually did. The brain takes that information and tunes our balance and posture, one wobble at a time.

Figure 2.1 Learning to walk

For most of us, learning to walk is our first real taste of discovery, a practice that runs deep in our biology. It's how humans have always learned to survive in a world that is complex and unpredictable. We try something, we watch what happens, and we adjust, again and again.

In the previous chapter, we explored the Failure Economy, the products and features that seemed like good ideas at the time but never delivered any real value. That waste exists because, somewhere along the way, we suppressed our toddler instincts.

HOW OTHER PROFESSIONS DO DISCOVERY

When the pressure is on and the deadlines are tight, we have a natural tendency to take shortcuts and skip the thinking. We tell ourselves that our experience and our intuition will see us through.

But we need to stop treating discovery as an optional 'nice-to-have' phase in a project plan. If you step outside the technology bubble for a moment, you'll notice that the world's highest-performing teams operate very differently. Whether they are surgeons saving lives, athletes chasing gold medals, or engineers launching rockets, they all treat discovery as their most valuable tool.

By borrowing from these professions, we can find plenty of inspiration for our own work and move beyond simple 'requirements gathering' towards something much closer to a real discovery mindset.

THE DISCOVERY MODES

One thing worth knowing is that discovery isn't a single mode of thinking; it shifts depending on what you are trying to achieve. The way a salesperson builds an understanding of their customers' needs is very different from how a sportsperson optimises their performance, yet both are forms of discovery. To be effective in product work, we need that same flexibility, adjusting our approach to suit the situation in front of us.

I've taken the habits of these diverse professions and boiled them down into five practical modes of discovery. They aren't the only ways to think, but they cover most of the situations you'll run into in the work you do:

- discovering user needs;
- discovering creative ideas;
- discovering blind spots;
- discovering better decisions;
- discovering improvements.

DISCOVERING USER NEEDS

Before we rush into building solutions, it helps to zoom out and understand the world our users actually live in. It means acting a little like an anthropologist, watching how people work so you can understand why they asked for that feature in the first place.

How salespeople do it

In my product director role at the UK's leading technology training organisation, I regularly join sales colleagues on pre-sales discovery calls. It's one of my favourite parts of the job, because it doesn't feel like selling at all. To me, it feels more like solving a puzzle.

When you strip away the jargon, a good discovery call is just two sides trying to make sense of a problem together. You listen, and you slowly tease out what the customer truly cares about. The aim is always to go beyond what they say they want and find what they actually need.

For decades, though, sales was seen as the art of persuasion, where the standard approach was to convince, close, and move on. That began to change in the 1970s, when psychologist Neil Rackham and his team embarked on one of the largest studies of sales behaviour ever conducted, analysing more than 35,000 real sales calls involving around 10,000 salespeople across 23 countries over 12 years to understand what the best performers were doing differently.[2]

The results

What set the best salespeople apart had nothing to do with smooth talking. They were the best listeners in the room, asking about four times as many questions as their peers and spending far more of each call listening than they did talking.

Rackham captured this in a simple framework he called SPIN. Rather than leaping straight to features and benefits, these salespeople built their understanding one layer at a time:

- **Situation:** They explored the context ('Tell me how you manage this process today').
- **Problem:** They uncovered the friction ('What's most frustrating about it?').
- **Implication:** They went deeper to find the cost ('What happens if it stays that way?').
- **Need:** Finally, they looked for the value ('If we could solve this, what would it allow you to achieve?').

More recent research,[3] this time across more than one million B2B sales calls, found exactly the same pattern. Top performers spent 57 per cent of their time listening, asked one-third more clarifying questions, and reached close to double the close rate of the average salesperson.

The lesson for us is the same. We build our understanding of what someone is struggling with by asking better questions, not by pitching solutions at them. We'll come back to the art of powerful questions in Chapter 16, where I'll hand you a practical toolkit for your own discovery sessions.

How doctors do it

When I run requirements workshops, I'm often amazed at how many stakeholders walk in already armed with solutions. Rather than sharing the pain they're having with a business process or a piece of software, they'll demand a new text box on a screen or a button that hasn't been properly thought through. Back when I first started my career, I would happily nod along and scribble down the request, because I didn't want to disappoint my stakeholders.

But with experience, you learn that acting too fast without a diagnosis is dangerous. If we were doctors and gave in to the pressures of our patients, it could lead to tragic consequences. Why should things be any different when we are building products?

We will all, at some point in our lives, visit a doctor. Nearly every consultation in medicine begins the same way. A patient describes their symptoms, such as chest pains, dizziness, or fatigue, and a good doctor doesn't reach for the prescription pad straight away. Their first job is to learn, and that begins with a few careful questions.

The SOCRATES approach

Doctors lean on repeatable frameworks like SOCRATES to work out what's really happening beneath the surface of a patient's symptoms:[4] **S**ite: Where exactly is it? **O**nset: When did it begin? **C**haracter: What does it feel like? **R**adiation: Does it spread anywhere else? **A**ssociations: Are there other symptoms? **T**iming: How has it changed over time? **E**xacerbating and relieving factors: What makes it better or worse? **S**everity: How intense is it on a scale of 1 to 10?

Underneath all of this sits a simple principle known as Bayesian reasoning.[5] The idea is that every new piece of information nudges what we believe to be true. A doctor starts out with several possible explanations in mind, and with each question, test, or observation, adjusts how likely each explanation seems.

First, do no harm

In the medical world, every decision carries risk, so doctors follow one of the oldest principles in their profession, *primum non nocere*, which means 'first, do no harm'.[6]

When we build products, 'harm' isn't only about the money we waste building the wrong thing. It's also about the unintended side effects we introduce. Every feature we add makes the product a little more complex. It needs maintaining, adds to the mental load on users, creates more places for bugs to hide, and makes every future change that bit harder. If we build features that don't solve a real problem, we gradually degrade the health of the product, just as we saw in Chapter 1.

Salespeople and doctors are both, in their own way, discovering user needs. Rather than jumping straight to an answer, they slow themselves down and ask better questions first.

DISCOVERING CREATIVE IDEAS

I was born on 4 May, and if you're a *Star Wars* fan, you'll know it is officially known as Star Wars Day. Every year, people take to the internet to post 'May the Fourth be with you.' It's become an annual tradition and a celebration of science fiction. Maybe that's why I've always been fascinated by space exploration and discovering the unknown.

Few organisations live closer to the edge of the unknown than NASA, where discovery is the only thing that lets us push the limits of what is possible and stay safe doing it. And as we're about to see, discovery might just have saved NASA from extinction altogether.

How space exploration does it

By the early 1990s, NASA was in trouble. The Cold War was over and the agency was losing public support as people questioned whether the rewards of space exploration still justified the enormous investment.

NASA's Viking programme alone, which in 1976 became the first US mission to land successfully on Mars, had cost over $1 billion (roughly $5 billion in today's money) and taken more than a decade to deliver. When a mission on that scale goes wrong, the fallout is brutal. Years of work, billions of dollars, and a good chunk of public confidence can all disappear at once.

Inside NASA, a group of scientists started to ask a different question. What if, instead of building fewer, bigger missions, they could build many smaller ones?

NASA gets faster, better, cheaper

When Dan Goldin became NASA's administrator in 1992, he introduced the slogan 'Faster, Better, Cheaper'.[7] Critics rolled their eyes and dismissed it as a management slogan, but Goldin's real aim was to push the agency to be more creative with less.

His time working on the real-world 'Star Wars' programme had shaped his belief that innovation could thrive under constraint. In practice, that meant deliberately limiting time, money, and people, on the theory that tight constraints force you to get creative and focus on what truly counts. We'll come back to why this works in Chapter 9.

He capped each discovery mission at around $150 million.[8] In product terms, this was a shift away from big upfront commitments towards learning early and often.

The results

The first of these smaller missions, *Mars Pathfinder*, launched in 1996 and carried a tiny six-wheeled rover named *Sojourner*. Because the team couldn't afford the expensive technology that Viking had relied on, they had to get creative. Instead of gentle retro-rockets, they wrapped the lander in giant airbags and bounced it onto the surface of Mars.

It was only designed to last for a week. Instead, it kept going for nearly three months, 12 times its expected life, and sent back more than 16,000 images. It cost less than 10 per cent of Viking's budget and proved that low-cost missions could still deliver outstanding value.

Between 1992 and 2002, NASA launched 16 missions for less than the cost of two conventional, big-budget missions. Thirteen of them met or exceeded their goals, a success rate of roughly 81 per cent, making it the most productive decade of planetary exploration in NASA's history.

Safe to fail experiments

When the budget on the line is huge, it's only natural for teams to play it safe and reach for the bland, predictable option. Discovery gives us another way through, by letting us run smaller, cheaper experiments where we have room to test bolder ideas. The other ingredient we need is a genuine culture of safety, and I'll show you how to build that into a team in Chapter 5.

For now, let's look at how the size of the bet changes the way we should think about risk. Some decisions in product work are irreversible. Once you've spent the budget or shipped the change to your customers, you can't easily undo things. Other decisions are reversible, like running a small pilot to gauge demand and then stopping it if you need to.

The brilliance of NASA's 'Faster, Better, Cheaper' era was that it turned space exploration from a series of huge, irreversible bets into a portfolio of smaller, recoverable ones. Discovery is how we pull off the same trick in product work.

DISCOVERING BLIND SPOTS

Even when we think we've understood the problem, our own biases can still get in the way. We get swayed by arguments that confirm what we already want to believe, especially when we're invested in an idea. This is known as confirmation bias.

How lawyers do it

In the legal world, discovery exists to counter that very instinct, forcing cases to be examined carefully even when the outcome seems obvious at first glance.

I've always enjoyed a good courtroom drama, and one of my favourites is *Goliath*, the legal series starring Billy Bob Thornton. It's a dark and gritty drama in which Thornton plays Billy McBride, a washed-up lawyer who takes on powerful corporations with little more than his curiosity, his persistence, and a battered briefcase.

What makes the show so compelling for me is the build-up to the courtroom. It's the part that lawyers call discovery. Both sides are given time to search for the truth by gathering evidence, reviewing documents, and piecing together details that could completely change the direction of a case.

Discovery saved O.J. Simpson

In 1995, that's exactly what happened in the famous O.J. Simpson trial.[9] At first, the prosecution's evidence seemed watertight. There were blood samples, DNA matches, and even a pair of gloves that tied the defendant to the murder. But the defence team, led by Johnnie Cochran, decided to look at things from a different angle. Rather than trying to prove their case with fresh evidence, they put the process by which the evidence had been gathered under the microscope.

The legal pivot

Cochran's team uncovered procedural flaws in how the Los Angeles Police Department had collected and stored the evidence. They also revealed, through tapes disclosed during that process, that Detective Mark Fuhrman, the officer who found some of the key evidence, had made racist remarks. The tapes contained 13 hours of interviews in which Fuhrman used a specific slur 30 times,[10] contradicting his previous testimony under oath.

That revelation shifted public perception overnight. What had started as a murder trial became a national debate about credibility, bias, police integrity, and decades of racial inequality.

The result

When the verdict of 'not guilty' was announced, it divided the nation. Some saw it as proof that the system had failed, while others saw it as a sign of deep-rooted mistrust in law enforcement.

The O.J. Simpson trial became a powerful reminder of why discovery exists in the first place. It showed how uncovering new evidence and exposing the way existing evidence had been handled can completely change how a case is seen. Whether justice was done remains open to debate, but what's clear is that discovery shaped the story that played out on US television screens and across the media.

Cross-examine your ideas

As product discovery practitioners, we have to bring this same level of critical thinking to our own work. It's easy to fall into the trap of building a one-sided case, just to convince stakeholders that pressing ahead with our preferred option is the right thing to do. But true discovery asks us to think like the defence team instead.

We have to cross-examine our own approach. Did we ask leading questions? Were the users we spoke to a representative group? Are we ignoring the procedural flaws in our research because we just want to ship? If we don't challenge the integrity of our own evidence, we risk building on blind spots we never thought to question.

DISCOVERING BETTER DECISIONS

Sometimes discovery is less about finding new information and more about building the confidence to make the right call. Data helps a team move past gut feeling and opinion, revealing value or risks that aren't immediately obvious.

How football does it

In 2015, Liverpool FC (the team that I support) were eighth in the Premier League, and while they are one of the most successful clubs in football, they couldn't compete financially with clubs like Manchester City and Chelsea.

Since they couldn't outspend their rivals, the owners decided they would have to outthink them. They became the first football club to fully embrace an in-house analytics department, led by Dr Ian Graham. A theoretical physicist with a PhD from Cambridge, Graham didn't look like a traditional 'football man'. In fact, he famously admitted that he didn't even watch video footage of the players he analysed. 'I can't trust my eyes', he said, preferring to trust his probability models over what he saw on the pitch.

Data vs gut feel

In the summer of 2017, Liverpool desperately needed a new winger to ignite their attack.[11] The manager, Jürgen Klopp, arguably one of the best coaches in the world, had his sights firmly set on Julian Brandt, a talented young German player who was dazzling scouts in the Bundesliga. Klopp knew the market inside out, and his gut was telling him Brandt looked like the perfect fit. He was fast, technically gifted, and widely admired.

Liverpool's data team, however, disagreed. Their models pointed to a completely different player, Mohamed Salah.

Figure 2.2 Gut feel vs evidence

Deeper discovery

Data-driven discovery proves its worth in moments like this. If you only looked at the surface-level metrics, such as goals scored at Chelsea, Salah looked like a bad buy. But Graham's model showed that Salah was statistically the best young wide forward in Europe.

When Graham looked closer at the data, he found the root cause of Salah's struggles. The issue was never his ability, he had simply been stuck on the bench behind Eden Hazard, one of the best players in the world at the time, with little chance to play.

The results

Graham presented the case to Klopp, arguing that while Brandt was a good player, Salah was a future superstar. Klopp decided to follow the data over his gut and signed Salah for roughly £34 million. In his first season, he broke the Premier League scoring record and went on to score over 200 goals, helping Liverpool win the Champions League, the Premier League, and the FA Cup.

After nine successful years, Salah eventually left the club at the end of the 2025/2026 football season, leaving behind a legacy that places him among the all-time greats.

Signals for product teams

Liverpool's use of analytics augmented human judgement with evidence. Coaching meetings became discovery sessions. Why are we conceding goals? Let's look into the positioning data. How can we create better chances? Let's analyse the shooting patterns. This feedback loop helped turn a very good team into the best team in England.

For product teams, having a rich set of data, from usage data to customer feedback to experiment results, gives you signals that help you spend your effort where it's needed most. Instead of saying, 'This feature feels like it would improve the product', you can say, '40 per cent of users dropped off at this point, which is a clear sign that something is wrong, so let's find out why'. Discovery-minded teams use data to make informed decisions, just as Liverpool did.

DISCOVERING IMPROVEMENTS

Aristotle once said, 'We are what we repeatedly do. Excellence, then, is not an act, but a habit.'[12] Great products work the same way. They aren't built in a single heroic release, but emerge from teams that treat discovery as a daily habit, making hundreds of tiny improvements that all add up to something significant.

How cyclists do it

At the start of the 2000s, British Cycling had little to celebrate. The team had never won a Tour de France and had managed just one Olympic gold medal in 76 years. Their reputation was so poor that some top bike manufacturers reportedly refused to sell equipment to the team, fearing that seeing British riders lose on their bikes would harm their brand sales.

When Dave Brailsford took over as performance director, he introduced a simple idea that would change everything. 'If you broke down everything that goes into riding a bike and then improved it by 1 per cent', he said, 'you will get a significant increase when you put them all together.'[13]

Aggregation of marginal gains

Brailsford and his team began treating every element of cycling as an experiment. They measured tyre pressures, adjusted seat angles, refined nutrition plans, taught riders new handwashing routines to reduce illness, and tested different fabrics for the racing suits.

The team even travelled with their own mattresses and pillows so they had consistent sleeping conditions at events around the world. Inside, the team truck was painted completely white, which let them spot tiny specks of dust that could degrade the performance of the finely tuned bikes. Each adjustment was small, but added together they led to big results.

The results

At the 2008 Beijing Olympics, Britain won 7 of the 10 track cycling golds. They repeated the feat in London four years later. And between 2012 and 2018, British riders won six of eight Tour de France titles. It was a transformation that would have seemed impossible before Brailsford arrived. He later reflected that the philosophy was never about chasing perfection, but about what he called 'a relentless search for improvement'.

Mathematics of compounding

Brailsford was using a principle we often ignore in product development, called compounding. Our brains are wired for linear thinking. We assume that the larger the change, the bigger the result, so when we want a real transformation, we reach for a 'Big Bang' redesign or a complete re-platforming.

James Clear quantified this in his book *Atomic Habits*.[14] He calculated that if you get just 1 per cent better at something every day for a year, you do not end up 365 per cent better. The gains compound on top of each other, so 1.01 raised to the power of 365 comes to roughly 37.78, which leaves you about 37 times better, an increase of around 3,778 per cent.

That's why something as unglamorous as a new handwashing routine paid off. Fewer riders fell ill, which meant fewer missed sessions, which meant more time training and getting stronger.

Marginal gains in products

For Dave Brailsford, a marginal gain was bringing the team's own pillows to hotels for a perfect night's sleep. In product teams, the equivalent gains are usually hiding in the small details of how customers experience a product. Netflix and Amazon, the two companies people most associate with personalisation, are really just companies that took marginal gains seriously and applied them at scale.

Take Netflix as an example. They realised that if they could show you the perfect thumbnail for a film, one that matches your specific tastes, you would be more likely to click play. If you like comedy, the thumbnail for *Good Will Hunting* might feature Robin Williams laughing. Someone who prefers romance might instead see Matt Damon and Minnie Driver kissing.

Artwork became just one of their experiments to improve an already successful platform. They test dozens of variations. It may seem like a tiny detail, maybe even smaller than a 1 per cent gain, but when you multiply that across millions of users, it adds up to billions of hours watched. This is why Netflix runs around 250 A/B[15] tests every year, each one feeding thousands of small improvements.

Amazon follows the same philosophy. When they first launched their recommendation engine ('Customers who bought this also bought ...'), it was a helpful feature, but they decided to keep tweaking the algorithm and refining the logic. Today, those marginal gains have compounded to the point where 35 per cent of Amazon's total revenue comes from its recommendation engine.

Finding the dust in your product

The lesson for us is simple. It's easy to fixate on building big new features, but we often overlook the value we could deliver through small improvements. We need to look at our products with the same forensic detail that Brailsford applied to his bikes. Where is the friction in your sign-up process? Is the text on that button clear? Does that page load too slowly? These are the questions that uncover your product's dust, and our job is to go looking for it.

CHALLENGES OF PRODUCT DISCOVERY

We've seen how discovery helps salespeople build understanding, doctors diagnose problems, lawyers challenge bias, sports teams make better decisions, and engineers push boundaries.

So, embedding this discovery mindset should be our number one priority if we want to escape the Failure Economy. Yet we know it's not that simple. If discovery is so universally powerful, why is it so hard to practise consistently in our teams and organisations?

There's a difference between everyday discovery and product discovery. In most professions, discovery happens within known boundaries and constraints. Medicine and sport have centuries of science to draw from, law is guided by precedent, and even space exploration follows the laws of physics. The variables may be complex, but the rules are clear.

Product discovery, on the other hand, has to cope with a messier kind of uncertainty, the sort shaped by human behaviour, shifting markets, incomplete information, and the odd bit of corporate politics. There are no fixed laws or guaranteed right answers, which makes it impossible to simply follow a set of rules.

We are also hardwired for certainty. When we don't know the answer, our brains crave a plan because we want to feel that we are in control.

In the next chapter, we'll look at where the modern practice of product discovery originated, how our instinct to control uncertainty becomes our biggest barrier, and why discovery remains our most powerful tool for managing risk.

KEY TAKEAWAYS

- **Discovery is universal:** From space to sport to sales, discovery is a habit shared across wildly different fields, and in each one it helps people learn fast and make sense of messy situations.
- **Listening beats persuading:** Great salespeople ask more questions rather than pitching products during discovery.
- **Cross-examine your ideas:** True discovery requires us to think like a lawyer and challenge the integrity of our own evidence before we build.
- **Innovation thrives under constraint:** NASA's 'Faster, Better, Cheaper' era proved that limited time, money, and resources can unlock greater creativity.
- **Small improvements drive big breakthroughs:** British Cycling's 1 per cent improvements turned years of mediocrity into a world-class team.

- **Look for your product's hidden dust:** The biggest opportunities are not always new features. They may be tiny points of friction.
- **Product discovery is harder than discovery in many other fields:** Medicine, law, and sport operate within clearer boundaries, but product teams face shifting markets, incomplete information, human behaviour, and organisational politics.
- **The real enemy is our craving for certainty:** When the pressure is on, teams naturally want a plan, an answer, and a decision. Discovery helps us resist the false comfort of certainty so that we can learn what is really going on.

3 TURN UNCERTAINTY INTO MANAGEABLE RISK

'Nothing is certain except death, taxes, and a plan that is out of date.'

Paddy Dhanda

'Don't bring me problems, bring me solutions.' How often have we heard leaders say that? As long as we are shipping features, measuring velocity, and hitting milestones, then we are doing a good job. And if we can point to a detailed plan with a green status, it makes us feel in control.

A discovery mindset, on the other hand, asks us to trade the comfort of a plan for the discomfort of the unknown, then stand in front of stakeholders and admit, 'I don't know yet, but I'm going to find out.'

But in most organisations, admitting you don't know is not seen as an act of courage, it's seen as a sign of weakness.

THE SCARY RED RAG

There's an eerie silence that falls over a boardroom when you tell senior executives what they don't want to hear.

I was appointed programme manager for a large IT programme at a bank. A few weeks in, I found myself facing my first steering committee. If you've ever sat in one, you'll know the type of atmosphere I'm talking about. It's a formal setting, filled with senior people who have little time for detail and are only interested in the headlines. Oh, and there's little appetite to listen to bad news.

When it was my turn to speak, I put up the first slide, which showed all four of my projects had a red status. The room went quiet. My managing director immediately jumped in and asked what had gone so wrong. Was the plan delayed? Did I need more people? More budget?

'No', I replied each time. 'The issue isn't what has happened. It's what hasn't happened yet.'

I explained that every one of my teams was new, the architecture was untested, and we were attempting a new way of working that was largely alien to the teams. We had no track record and no data. I had marked them red, not because we were failing, but because there was too much uncertainty to be confident we could deliver what we'd promised.

There was a long, tense pause, then finally, the business sponsor broke the silence. He thanked me for my honesty and laughed, 'Well done, because I'm sick of seeing watermelon reports.'

I didn't know what he meant at the time, but I had just learned my first lesson in the value of exposing uncertainty.

THE WATERMELON EFFECT

In most organisations, project progress is tracked using a RAG status. Red means we're in trouble, amber signals a warning, and green suggests everything's on track. It's meant to be a quick, visual way to show how healthy a project is, but like many simple tools, it often ends up being used in the wrong way.

Have you ever worked on a project that stays green all the way through delivery, and then, just before launch, almost overnight everything turns red? It's a common pattern I see across many organisations. By that stage, there's rarely enough time to recover and get back on track. Plans are rewritten, the scope is cut, and the focus shifts to damage limitation.

The meetings that follow are rarely pleasant. Leaders scramble to explain what went wrong, and the atmosphere starts to feel like the boardroom scene from *The Apprentice*, where everyone is pointing fingers, trying not to be the target of those dreaded words, 'You're fired.'

In project circles, this is often called the watermelon effect, where everything looks green on the outside, but it's bright red on the inside. The reality is, the project was never really green in the first place. It only looked that way because too many unknowns were hidden beneath the surface, and no one wanted to call them out.

To understand why this happens so often, we need to look at how uncertainty behaves, and surprisingly, we can look to the weather for inspiration.

THE CONE OF UNCERTAINTY

When meteorologists track a hurricane forming in the Atlantic, the US National Hurricane Center shows a shaded area on the map that widens as the storm forms and narrows as it approaches land.

Early forecasts cover a huge area, because even small shifts in wind or temperature can completely change the storm's path. As more data comes in, the shape becomes narrower, but it never fully closes. There's always some uncertainty about where the hurricane will eventually hit.

In the 1980s, computer scientist Barry Boehm used this same idea[1] to explain why so many software projects go off course despite careful planning. At the start of a project, we know the least, such as how long it will take or how much it will cost. But that's when we act the most certain. To make this point, he created what became known as the Cone of Uncertainty.

Why we crave certainty on projects

Behavioural scientists have a name for what happens to us when people crave certainty. They call it control-seeking behaviour, and it explains a great deal about the way we behave when we are running projects.

Researchers ran six experiments designed to test what people do when they feel out of control.[2] In one of them, participants were primed by recalling a past situation in which they had felt helpless. They were then shown a series of snowy, distorted images, most of which contained no recognisable shape. The participants who had been primed to feel out of control were significantly more likely to see patterns, identifying faces, animals, and objects that simply weren't there. They observed the same behaviour in experiments involving stock market data, conspiracy theories, and even superstitious rituals. Across all six studies, the conclusion was the same. When people lose their sense of control, they compensate by inventing structure where none exists.

This could explain why a detailed project plan can feel so reassuring, even when we know deep down that much of it is guesswork. The act of writing the plan is itself a way of restoring that sense of control.

It's something we all do, often without realising it. In fact, millions of UK adults regularly take part in one activity where we feel that by staying in control, we can somehow improve our chances of success.

If you were buying a lottery ticket, would you rather pick your own numbers or have a machine pick them for you? Psychologist Ellen Langer tested that question in 1975, in a Yale University study that psychologists still return to today.[3]

In her experiment, participants were given lottery tickets. Half were handed a ticket with a random number already printed on it, while the others were allowed to choose their own numbers. When Langer later offered to buy the tickets back, those who had chosen their own valued them four to five times higher than those who had been given one. The odds of winning were entirely random, but having a choice made people behave as if their ticket was somehow worth more, as though choice itself added certainty.

Langer called this the illusion of control. It's the belief that we can influence outcomes even though they are random. If we put her work alongside the more recent control-seeking studies, a clear picture emerges. When we feel a lack of control, we invent structure, and when we feel we have control, we overvalue it. Both of these behaviours push us in the same direction, which is the misconception that we know more than we do.

This is exactly how watermelon projects are born. A team faces a problem they don't fully understand, and they feel the pressure of expectations from the leadership, while at the same time the awkwardness of admitting they don't yet have the answers. So they feel a sense of relief when they produce a detailed plan. Whether the plan is accurate or not, it gives us a feeling of comfort, as if we can somehow be more in control of the situation. But in reality, these plans don't reduce the actual risk, they simply reduce the feeling of risk, which is not the same thing.

Problems with detailed plans

I sometimes ask learners in my product classes how long it takes for a project plan to go out of date. The answers vary. Some say a month, others a week, and a handful say a day. I usually smile and reveal, 'As soon as the ink is dry on the page.' Let me explain what I mean.

I was leading a team of product owners on a multi-million-euro transformation programme. The programme manager had spent three days locked in a meeting room with her delivery leads, planning every milestone and dependency. When I went into the office later that week, three walls were covered top to bottom with sticky notes and timelines. The result was a work of art that any project manager would be proud of.

When she'd finished walking me through it, she turned and asked, 'So, what do you think of the plan?' I paused for a moment, then asked what time had been set aside for discovery. Her answer was surprising: none.

Just like a photograph, a plan is only a snapshot of a single moment in time. In our case, the plan was already out of date, but it looked deceptively complete, which perfectly demonstrated the illusion of control in action.

The point is, there are always forces outside of our plans that can throw everything off course. It might be a key team member deciding to leave halfway through a project, or something far bigger, like a global pandemic changing the way the entire world works almost overnight.

The philosopher Alfred Korzybski gave us the phrase 'the map is not the territory'.[4] Our plans are the maps. They are simplifications of reality that help us navigate. But they are not reality itself. And when they diverge from reality, we must update the map, not ignore the territory.

So the big question remains: how do we deal with uncertainty in a way that actually helps us make better decisions?

PRODUCT DISCOVERY AS A TOOL FOR RISK MANAGEMENT

As we explored in Chapter 2, discovery is the method that doctors, engineers, and scientists use when the certainty gap is at its widest point, and the consequences of making the wrong decision can be life or death. They can't afford to base decisions on untested assumptions. Instead, they build clarity through learning, reducing the risk bit by bit until they have uncovered more of the facts so they can make a more informed decision.

Product teams are looking to achieve the same thing, even if the circumstances are slightly different. Therefore, I would argue that discovery is our most valuable tool for managing risk in product work. This is especially the case in environments where the nature of the work is complex and uncertainty is high.

The birth of product discovery

Product discovery is the result of more than two decades of practitioners trying to figure out how to improve the way we build software.

Let's rewind to 2001. A group of 17 software developers gathered at a ski resort in Utah, frustrated by years of large, slow, and failed projects. What they published was a 68-word manifesto that completely changed how the industry thought about building software products, which famously became known as the Agile Manifesto.[5] For the first time, the act of building was framed as a collaborative and iterative process, as opposed to the rigid sequence of phases known as the waterfall approach.

Agile helped teams ship code more quickly and with greater confidence than they had previously. Releases were delivered on a regular cadence, typically every 2–4 weeks, rather than a once-a-year event. We had finally cracked the problem of building at speed.

But as teams mastered the art of delivery, a new challenge emerged. We had built an engine, but we still needed a better navigation system to tell us what to build.

Marty Cagan, one of the most respected voices in modern product management, helped popularise the term 'product discovery'.[6] He borrowed the phrase from the pharmaceutical industry, where there is an expectation that the majority of ideas will fail; in his words, 'when we start, we don't yet know what the right product is, our job is to discover it'.[7]

The product team were no longer focused on turning requirements into code. Instead, their first responsibility was to figure out what to build.

The problem space vs the solution space

To further understand the difference between discovery and delivery, it helps to visualise them as two distinct spaces:

- The problem space is where we explore what the problem is and the user's needs. It's messy and full of unanswered questions, where we ask, 'What are we trying to solve?' and 'Who are we solving it for?'
- The solution space is where we define how we're going to solve it by developing features and shipping products.

With the pressure to show progress and the corporate desire for certainty, teams rush into the solution space before they have spent enough time in the problem space. We assume we understand the problem, but often we are just guessing since we have very limited insights.

Figure 3.1 The Double Diamond

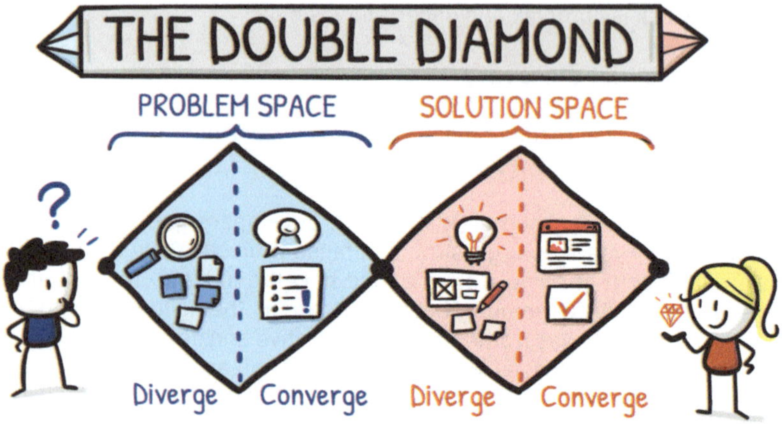

This separation is famously illustrated by the Double Diamond framework, popularised by the Design Council.[8] It visualises the process as two diamonds sitting side-by-side.

The Design Council has since expanded the Double Diamond through its Framework for Innovation and its Systemic Design Framework, but for our purposes I want to stick to the original simplified version.

- First diamond (problem space): This is where we 'diverge' (go broad) to research and understand the underlying issue, before 'converging' (narrowing down) to define the specific problem we want to tackle.
- Second diamond (solution space): Once the problem is clear, we move to the second diamond. We diverge again to explore multiple potential solutions, prototyping and testing different ideas, before finally converging on the best solution to build.

Search vs execution divide

Around the same time that Marty Cagan was shaping the understanding of product discovery, the serial entrepreneur Steve Blank was grappling with a related problem from a different angle. In the early 2000s, following the dot-com crash, Blank began to question a core assumption in how startups worked. He observed that for years the industry had treated startups as if they were simply 'smaller versions of a large company'.

In his book *The Four Steps to the Epiphany*, Blank made a distinction that would become the cornerstone of the Lean Startup movement, popularised by his former student Eric Ries, who we will come back to in Chapter 12.[9] He argued that we were confusing two fundamentally different activities:

- Search mode (the startup): Blank defined a startup not as a smaller version of a big company, but as a 'temporary organisation designed to search for a repeatable and scalable business model'. In this mode, the business model is unknown, and it is merely a set of untested hypotheses regarding who the customer is and what the product features should be.
- Execution mode (the enterprise): This is relevant for existing established companies. Here, the business model is known because the market, customers, and product fit have already been validated.

Blank observed that the majority of failures occurred because teams tried to apply 'execution' tools to a 'search' problem. They hired functional departments (sales, marketing, business development) before they had a product that worked, and they relied on plans and opinions formed internally to guide their decisions. But the real insights should come from speaking to actual customers, not in meeting rooms. As he famously put it: 'There are no facts inside the building, so get the hell outside.'

Continuous Discovery

Teresa Torres, a product discovery coach, noticed many organisations treated discovery as a quick burst of research at the start of a project, then switched their attention back to delivery. But she argued that teams made better decisions when discovery wasn't a one-off activity, and instead something they did all the time.

In her book *Continuous Discovery Habits*, she reframes the way we look at a backlog by treating everything as a bet. We are betting that customers have this problem, and we are betting that our solution will fix it.[10] If you do zero discovery, you are simply making blind bets. The goal of Continuous Discovery is to start doing just enough research to make better bets over time.

Earlier in this chapter, we explored the Cone of Uncertainty, which is that wide space at the start of any project where so much is still unknown. Torres' point was that small, continuous steps – such as a quick chat with a user, a rough sketch, or a simple prototype – all help to increase clarity. Slowly, you move through the wide end of the Cone of Uncertainty and begin to narrow it, piece by piece, as you increase your learning.

We will return to Continuous Discovery in Chapter 12 when we look at a framework Torres popularised, known as the Opportunity Solution Tree.

How I define product discovery

All of the product thinkers I have introduced in this chapter have each shaped the way our industry understands discovery, and their work has influenced how I have come to define product discovery thinking: I introduced this definition in the Introduction, but it is worth returning to now that we have explored where these ideas came from:

> *Product discovery thinking is the discipline of learning relentlessly about people, problems, and possibilities, so we can make better decisions before committing valuable time, money, and effort to a solution.*

This is the definition we will keep coming back to in the chapters ahead. You will see its influence everywhere, from the problem space that Cagan described to the idea of treating our plans as bets, which we owe to Blank and Torres.

Discovery vs feasibility

If you work within a formal project management framework, you might be wondering: isn't this just the same as traditional feasibility?

The short answer is yes, feasibility is also a form of discovery, but there are some key differences which we will cover in the next section. But for now, just remember it doesn't matter whether you use PRINCE2, AgilePM, SAFe, PMBOK, or any other methodology, you are already practising the discipline of discovery thinking when you conduct feasibility work, and everything in this book is compatible with those ways of working.

PRINCE2 and PMBOK both come from the traditional, gate-driven school of thought. PRINCE2 opens with a process called 'Starting up a project', a pre-project phase designed to verify that the work is worthwhile before committing significant resources. The project mandate triggers this phase, which might be a fresh idea or a customer request landing on someone's desk. Whatever the source, the intent is to filter out poorly conceived projects before they consume valuable time and resources.[11]

PMBOK takes a similar stance from a slightly different angle. Before a project gets initiated, there has to be a business case, defined in the *PMBOK Guide* as 'a documented economic feasibility study used to establish the validity of the benefits of a selected component'. The underlying logic for it is identical to PRINCE2, to prove this is worth doing before you start doing it.[12]

AgilePM, which has its roots in the DSDM Agile Project Framework, makes this thinking explicit. In its current third edition, the framework includes a Feasibility phase that sits between a quick pre-project sniff test and the deeper commitment of Foundations. It aims to answer two questions. Is this cost-effective from a business point of view? Is it technically achievable? The guidance states that this should be done at the right level of detail and no more, just enough to make a call on whether to take the idea forward. What I find refreshing about the third edition update is how it has shifted the conversation away from delivering outputs and towards delivering business value, which very much aligns with the spirit of this book.[13]

SAFe goes about it differently. Its Continuous Exploration process isn't a one-off activity; like many of the other frameworks we have looked at, it's an ongoing process. Teams keep returning to the market and the users to shape the vision and the roadmap. The framework also folds Design Thinking into the model with a dedicated Discover phase, which sits closer to what most of us in product teams would recognise as discovery in the modern sense.[14]

The key differences

While feasibility and product discovery share the same DNA, there are important differences in emphasis and scope that are worth understanding. Traditional feasibility asks two questions. Can we build this? And should we build this? It typically focuses on technical, economic, legal, and operational viability. It often assumes the problem and solution are reasonably well understood, and the question is whether the proposed approach is achievable.

Product discovery goes further. Are we solving the right problem? Will anyone actually want this? What is the real need behind the stated requirement? Discovery challenges the assumption that the problem is already understood and seeks to validate or invalidate hypotheses by engaging with users.

Timing matters too, since traditional feasibility is often treated as a discrete phase, like a gate to pass through before execution begins. Product discovery, as we have discussed, works best as a continuous practice. Even after a project has been initiated and deemed feasible, the discovery mindset continues throughout delivery, enabling you to adapt to new information.

If you already conduct feasibility studies as part of your methodology, you are well positioned to embrace product discovery. You simply need to expand your focus from 'can we do this?' to include 'is this the right thing to do for our users?'

Product discovery vs business analysis

Another point of confusion is whether analysis is better than discovery or vice versa. Before we answer that, let's review some formal definitions.

The IIBA defines business analysis as 'the practice of enabling change in an organisational context, by defining needs and recommending solutions that deliver value to stakeholders'.[15] BCS describes it as 'an internal consultancy role which has the responsibility for investigating business situations, identifying and evaluating options for improving business systems, defining requirements and ensuring the effective use of information systems in meeting the needs of the business'.[16]

These definitions position business analysis as the discipline of investigating, evaluating, and defining. They assume that, with sufficient rigour, needs can be understood and documented. Product discovery, by contrast, assumes that needs are hypotheses to be tested, not facts to be captured.

It's also worth stating that analysis and discovery are not job titles. A business analyst can practise discovery and a product manager can perform analysis. The labels

Table 3.1 Business analysis vs product discovery

Dimension	Business analysis	Product discovery
Primary focus	The business and its stakeholders	The customer and their unmet needs
Relationship to delivery	Sequential: analysis precedes development	Continuous: discovery runs alongside delivery
View of requirements	Something to be defined and documented	Something to be discovered and validated

describe capabilities, not roles, and what is important is knowing which mode to use in a given situation. Table 3.1 shows some of the subtle differences between analysis and discovery.

Yet for all their differences, both exist to reduce uncertainty. They require deep inquiry because neither accepts surface-level answers. And both help teams make better decisions about what to build. Let me share a personal story to highlight what can happen when you choose the wrong mode.

The elicitation trap

Ever since I started my software development career in the early 2000s, I have always been taught to 'elicit requirements' from stakeholders. And that works if you are in an environment where stakeholders are genuinely the experts. But what happens when they themselves are making assumptions?

Back in 2005, I was leading a team of business analysts on a large IT programme. Our brief was simple: prepare a backlog of features large enough to feed a team of over 30 developers.

The problem was that none of us knew how to write user stories. We ended up working long hours, rounding up stakeholders, and running workshops. We rarely paused to question the value of what we were capturing, as there was just no time.

After four weeks, we managed to produce over 400 user stories. Fast-forward two years and I can still recall the moment we were about to go live, with excitement and high-fives all around. We had managed to deliver on time and within budget. That was rare in the early 2000s.

But after all the blood, sweat, and tears, our users – the global sales force – rejected the product. It turns out we had been engaging with stakeholders who were out of touch with modern sales processes. We had been listening to the wrong people and had failed to challenge their assumptions. The entire programme was doomed from the start.

Requirements archaeologists vs scientists

We had been adopting what I now think of as a requirements archaeologist's mindset when we should have been thinking like a scientist. There is a subtle difference between these two modes of thinking:

- The requirements archaeologist assumes the requirement already exists, fully formed in someone's head. Their job is to carefully unearth it through interviews and workshops, then document what they find.
- The scientist assumes nothing is certain yet. They form hypotheses and run experiments to base decisions on evidence.

Similarly, Mike Cohn, who is a respected thought leader in the Agile community, in his book *User Stories Applied*, argued that requirements elicitation is deeply misleading in complex environments.[17] He used the analogy of a fishing trawler that casts its net. There's no guarantee it will catch anything, so it moves to different parts of the sea because it has no idea where the fish will actually be. The skill is in finding the right places to look.

Figure 3.2 The requirements archaeologist and the scientist

If we had treated requirements as hypotheses and tested them early before building, we would have quickly learned that we were building the wrong things.

The 'faster horse' and the AI paradox

People struggle to come up with the right solutions to their own problems, especially when technology moves faster than they can keep up. There is a famous quote often attributed to Henry Ford: 'If I had asked people what they wanted, they would have said faster horses.'[18]

Whether Ford actually said this is debated, but that doesn't matter. The idea it captures is what's important. If you elicited requirements from a 19th-century commuter, they could only give you answers based on their current frame of reference. Since horses were the only mode of transport that was familiar, they couldn't describe an engine because it was outside their imagination.

Today, we face the exact same paradox with artificial intelligence. If you ask stakeholders, 'What are your AI requirements?' whatever answer they give is almost certainly going to change within the space of a few weeks. The technology is evolving so fast that they cannot give you a requirement for a capability they don't yet know exists.

This is why discovery matters so much today.

Which one is better?

Analysis helps when the problem is well-understood compliance-driven work, system integrations with defined interfaces, or enhancements to mature products. Discovery becomes essential when uncertainty is high, such as in new markets, emerging technology, conflicting stakeholder perspectives, or situations where there is doubt whether the stated requirements reflect actual needs.

Both capabilities have their pitfalls when taken to extremes. Analysis without validation can produce beautifully documented requirements for the wrong solution. Discovery without discipline can become an endless exploration that results in building nothing.

The question is not which approach is better, but what does this situation demand? The answer will change, sometimes within the same project, sometimes within the same week. The practitioners who thrive are the ones who can shift between these modes, regardless of what it says on their business card. So, which capability is better?

Unfortunately, I am going to give you the consultant's answer. It depends ...

RISK IS THE NEW LANGUAGE

While concepts like 'navigating the problem space' and 'continuous discovery' make perfect sense to product people, they often sound alien to stakeholders and senior leaders. To bridge this language gap, we need to change the conversation. We need to translate our work into language that the business understands. And the language of business is *risk*, not 'uncertainty'.

'Uncertainty' is a vague concept. 'Risk' feels more concrete as it is something that we think can be managed and mitigated, and there are many different types in product work. To practise discovery effectively, we need a systematic way to spot and tackle these risks before they become issues.

Next, I introduce the Five Curses of Product Risk: Commitment, Confusion, Capability, Commerciality, and Consequence. By spotting these curses early, you transform discovery into a practical tool for managing risk effectively.

KEY TAKEAWAYS

- **Uncertainty encourages control:** Behavioural science shows that when uncertainty rises, the brain reaches for control, even if that control is an illusion.
- **Projects rarely fail suddenly:** Often, a project is already in trouble from the start, but status reports disguise it due to the watermelon effect.
- **Plans are snapshots:** Detailed plans can be out of date the moment they're created, since they are our best guesses at a given moment in time.
- **Discovery reduces uncertainty in small steps:** Whether it's a survey or a prototype, each piece of insight helps teams move through the wide end of the Cone of Uncertainty.
- **Discovery is not a one-off phase:** Continuous Discovery helps to build certainty proactively.
- **Analysis and discovery are capabilities, not roles:** The best practitioners shift between modes, depending on what the situation demands, analysing when things are clearer, discovering when uncertainty is high.
- **Product discovery is a risk management tool:** Every feature is a bet, and discovery helps you understand the odds of success before you invest too much into your ideas.

4 BREAK THE CURSES OF PRODUCT RISK

'What you don't know about your product can absolutely hurt you.'

Paddy Dhanda

DANGEROUS PRODUCT DESIGN

On the morning of 13 January 2018, the residents of Hawaii woke up to a message no one ever expected to see on their phone:

> BALLISTIC MISSILE THREAT INBOUND TO HAWAII. SEEK IMMEDIATE SHELTER. THIS IS NOT A DRILL.

For 38 minutes, people were thrown into a state of panic. Parents hid their children in storm drains. Some sent final messages to loved ones. Others simply froze, unsure whether to run or to pray.

When investigators reviewed what had happened, they discovered it wasn't a cyberattack or a technical malfunction. It was the result of a badly designed dropdown menu.[1] The alert system used by the Hawaii Emergency Management Agency had two options sitting right next to each other: 'test missile alert' and 'missile alert'. The only difference was a single word. The operator clicked the wrong one, then simply clicked through the confirmation prompt. The system worked exactly as designed. The design itself was the problem.

This is what happens when we fail to see the risks hiding inside the products we build.

THE GHOSTS IN OUR PRODUCTS

There is a reason why ghost stories are so fascinating. They tap into our fear of the unknown, the idea that something invisible waits just out of sight. Product development has its own ghosts. We call them risks.

In the previous chapter, we explored how product discovery is essentially a form of risk management. Yet 'risk' is a broad word that covers many potential threats. To manage it effectively, we need to know exactly what we're looking for. Just as a good ghost story becomes less frightening once you turn on the lights, risk becomes more manageable once it is named and understood.

Marty Cagan provides a widely used approach to simplifying product risk into four categories: Value, Usability, Feasibility, and Business Viability.[2] It's a strong foundation, but over time I've found it helpful to reframe and expand these ideas into language that resonates more clearly with teams and stakeholders. I call these the Five Curses of Product Risk.

I use the word 'curse' deliberately because if you ignore them, they will haunt your product long after launch. The first four curses build directly on Cagan's foundations:

- **Curse of Commitment:** Will customers commit their valuable time and money to use this?
- **Curse of Confusion:** Will people understand what this is or how to use it?
- **Curse of Capability:** Do we have the skills, tools, and capacity to build, operate, and evolve this over time?
- **Curse of Commerciality:** Does this make commercial sense for the business now and in the future?
- **Curse of Consequence:** What unintended consequences or harms might this create for people, the organisation, or society?

Commitment and Confusion focus on the relationship between the customer and the product itself. Capability and Commerciality get us to look inward, examining the organisation's ability to deliver and sustain value. The final curse, Consequence, looks outward at society, asking what happens when our products interact with complex social systems.

It would be neat if each curse could only appear on its own, but that's rarely how products behave in the real world. We often observe multiple risks appearing at the same time, and they can blend together. As you read through each curse in turn, keep half an eye on how often the story in front of you is really two or three of them at work at once.

Figure 4.1 The Five Curses of Product Risk

CURSE OF COMMITMENT

What is it?

The Curse of Commitment is the risk that your idea doesn't solve a real problem strongly enough. It's what happens when a product sounds useful in theory but isn't compelling enough for people to give up their time, adjust their habits, or part with their money. This curse asks whether customers genuinely value the outcome your solution creates. Every idea must first overcome this hurdle, and it's often the most difficult one.

In Silicon Valley, this concept of user commitment is called product–market fit. Entrepreneur and venture capitalist Andy Rachleff defined it simply as being in a good market with a product that can satisfy that market.[3] When you don't have it, you push for every sale through heavy marketing and the market stays sceptical. When you do, the market pulls. Customers buy faster than you can make it and usage grows organically because people tell their friends and family.

Value of products

There is a well-known quote in marketing, often attributed to Harvard professor Theodore Levitt: 'People don't want to buy a quarter-inch drill. They want a quarter-inch hole.'[4] It's a useful way to look at the value of your product. But it doesn't go far enough, because people don't really want the hole either, they want a shelf on the wall so they can clear the clutter off their desk. And if we're being honest, some of us want to display our books so our friends think we're smarter than we probably are.

Imagine a user's need as an onion, because just like the layers of a real onion, if you peel deep enough, you may uncover the emotion that brings someone to tears:

- The outer layer is the *tool* (the drill).
- Peel that back, and you find the *goal* (the hole).
- Go deeper, and you uncover the *outcome* (a tidy shelf).
- At the centre sits the *emotional driver* (the desire to feel organised, or perhaps to look intelligent).

Commitment is about understanding that final layer. It's about peeling the onion until you find the outcome or emotional driver that will motivate a customer to commit to your solution.

At an industry level, this is the risk we get wrong most often. The numbers we explored in Chapter 1, from the 80 per cent of unused features to only half of products succeeding, are all evidence of a lack of user commitment.

Why emotional attachment clouds our judgement

If you've ever watched shows like *Dragon's Den* or *Shark Tank*, you'll know the scene. An entrepreneur walks in full of optimism, having poured their savings and weekends into

Figure 4.2 The onion model of user needs

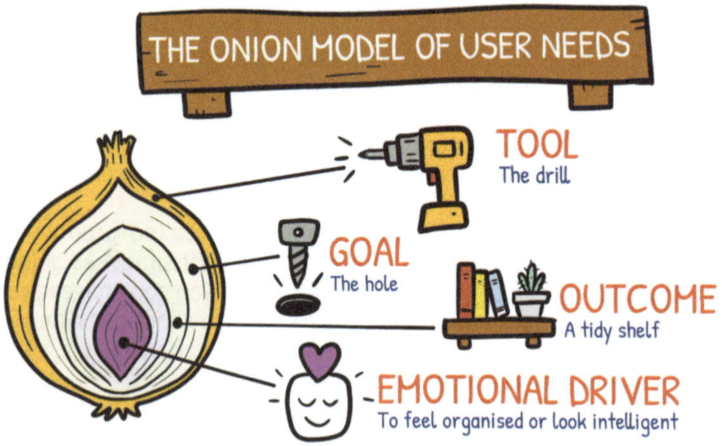

an idea. Within minutes, the panellists can see it's doomed. We, the viewers at home, can see it too, but the problem is that the entrepreneur struggles to spot what's obvious to everyone else, simply because they're so emotionally invested.

I sometimes show this emotional investment in the classroom with a simple exercise. I ask the group to sketch a few ideas for a problem, then choose their favourite. After a few volunteers share their thinking, I return to the person who was most passionate about their idea and take their sketch, scrunch it up into a ball, and throw it in the bin.

It feels cruel, I know, but it always produces gasps in the room, and the look on the face of the poor person I've picked on is one of shock and horror. It just proves that in just a few minutes people become unexpectedly attached to their ideas, and that's dangerous in product development, because our emotions cloud our judgement.

Make your ideas 9× better

Once we've invested even a little of ourselves, we begin to overestimate how good our idea really is. Harvard professor John T. Gourville described this as the '9× Effect'.[5] Customers overvalue what they already have by a factor of three. At the same time, organisations overvalue their new products by a factor of three because they've poured their time and energy into them.

When you do the maths (3 × 3 = 9), you get a ninefold gap between how we see our shiny new solution and how customers see the thing they already have. Your new product can't just be better, it must be nine times better before users will abandon what they already use and trust.

Now think about your current feature backlog. How many of those ideas are genuinely nine times better than what customers already have?

Discovery-driven planning

If our brains are wired to love our own bad ideas, and our users are wired to reject anything that isn't exponentially better, then how do we escape the Curse of Commitment? We start at the end and work backwards.

Rita McGrath, a professor at Columbia Business School, noticed that when organisations commit to a new idea, they make dozens of assumptions about what customers will do, what they'll pay, and what they'll value. The problem is that most teams treat these assumptions as facts. Her response was *discovery-driven planning*, an approach designed to make value risk visible early.[6] Teams start with the outcome they want to achieve, list every assumption required to get there, and design small, cheap tests to validate or disprove each one. Only once you've learned enough should you commit more time or money.

I often remind product teams that hope is not a strategy. A confident opinion is not the same as a tested insight.

When Disney got it wrong

When Disneyland Paris opened in 1992, it was meant to be Disney's great European success story. Executives forecasted nine million visitors in the first year, expecting families to stay several nights in Disney hotels, eat at Disney restaurants, and spend freely on Disney merchandise.[7]

These numbers were built on assumptions that had never been tested. Disney believed European families would behave just like their American guests. They assumed they would book week-long holidays, stay inside the park, and eat large breakfasts on site. They even thought banning alcohol would appeal to families, not realising that having wine with lunch is a normal part of French culture.

When the park opened, attendance reached only around seven million. Most guests came for a single day and brought their own food, and I'm not saying the French are cheap, but many of them are savvy with their money and found cheaper local hotels. By the end of 18 months, Disneyland Paris had lost close to $1 billion.

Disney had banked on a level of commitment its visitors were never going to give, mistaking its own certainty for theirs.

CURSE OF CONFUSION

What is it?

Even if a product is valuable and people want to commit to it, it will fail if it creates confusion. This curse asks whether people will fundamentally understand what the product is and how to use it to achieve their goals.

Don Norman, the man who coined the term 'user experience', spent much of his career asking why simple things like doors, cooker dials, alarm clocks, and other household products so often confuse us.[8] Have you ever grabbed a door handle, given it a pull, and realised it was meant to be pushed? If so, you've encountered what designers now call a Norman door. It highlights how a small design flaw can confuse even the most capable user.

But how do you ensure you don't build confusing products? You can learn to spot the warning signs and avoid the common traps.

The Confusion traps

The assumption trap

Norman taught us that good design starts with understanding how people see, think, and act. He introduced four simple ideas that now shape how we design everything from websites to washing machines:

- **Affordances:** Clues that tell us how to use something – a handle invites pulling, a button invites pressing.
- **Constraints:** Guardrails that stop mistakes, like a USB plug that only fits one way.
- **Signifiers:** Signals that guide attention – a highlighted 'Next' button or a green tick shows us exactly what to do.
- **Feedback:** Confirmation that an action worked – a click, a light, or a sound confirms success.

These probably sound obvious, yet teams still build confusing products every day because they assume the user will simply 'learn the system'. The reality is they probably won't.

The ego trap

Stewart Butterfield, the co-founder of Slack, calls this 'The Owner's Delusion'.[9] When we build a product, we picture our users giving it their full attention, exploring every clever feature we have built. In reality, they're distracted and short on time. They don't care about our software because all they are looking for is a way to resolve their current problem.

Butterfield illustrates this with the classic 'restaurant website' problem. The owner wants a slow-loading slideshow of the atmosphere and background music to set the mood. But the user is hungry and in a rush. They only want five things: address; phone number; menu; opening hours; and the reservation link. When we prioritise the owner's ego, we risk creating friction for the user.

The friction trap

There's a misconception in tech that all friction is bad. It may sound counterintuitive, but sometimes friction is needed to prevent users from making poor choices.

Slack famously introduced a feature nicknamed the 'Shouty Rooster'. They noticed users were using the '@everyone' tag to notify thousands of people about trivial messages. So Slack added friction. When someone tried to notify a large group, a rooster would pop up with a message: 'Are you sure you want to send a notification to 147 people in 8 time zones?' This forced users to think through the cost of their action.

The proxy trap

In product work, empathy means seeing the world through the eyes of the people who will use what we build. But when stakeholders are busy and have limited time, we often shortcut this by talking to proxy stakeholders rather than actual end-users.

I learned this lesson the hard way. I was leading discovery for a quoting and ordering platform, facing off to operations and sales stakeholders who wanted completely different things. The ops team (the proxies) wanted the system to capture every possible detail upfront, with strict validation rules. Their goal was accuracy and control. During our discovery sessions, they were the most vocal and dominant. The sales team (the actual users) wanted speed. In a high-pressure environment where time is money, they wanted to input the absolute minimum data required to get a price to the customer.

Since the ops team gave us more of their time, they became the proxies for the busy sales leaders. When we launched, the sales team rejected the platform immediately. Even though the product worked exactly as specified, it created friction for salespeople by mandating excessive amounts of data input that they simply did not have the time to do.

We had failed to mitigate the Curse of Confusion for sales, and because of that friction they weren't willing to commit to the new platform either, which had cost millions to build.

CURSE OF CAPABILITY

What is it?

If you've ever worked with engineers, you'll know they love to solve problems. Ask a talented engineering team, 'Can we build this?' and the answer is almost always 'Yes'. Given enough time and money, almost anything is possible these days, and with the rise of AI, the possibilities feel endless.

Which is exactly why 'Can we build it?' is the wrong question. Writing the code is rarely the most difficult thing. The hard part is running it safely and reliably at the scale your customers will expect. This curse shows up far more often in the non-functional aspects of the product than in any missing feature. Will it store our data securely? Will it work reliably when thousands of people try to use it at once? Will response times be acceptable?

Capability risk also shows up where teams have inherited poor design decisions from the past and accepted them without question.

The inherited constraint

Fabricio Laguna, a senior business analysis consultant, was working as a software developer for a company building a system for a magazine publisher.[10] The publisher sold subscriptions through campaign codes printed on cards inside magazines, and these codes helped the business identify regions, apply special pricing, and attach promotional gifts to each campaign.

While building the campaign system, someone from the business told Fabricio that a campaign could only include three gifts and a card. The rule did not make sense to him because there was no obvious commercial reason or customer need that explained why a campaign should be limited in that way. Rather than simply coding the rule as requested, he kept asking where it came from and why it existed.

After speaking to people across the business and reverse-engineering older systems, Fabricio found the real reason. The legacy mainframe had a campaign table with fixed columns for gift 1, gift 2, gift 3, and credit card. What people had been treating as a business rule was actually a technical constraint created by the way the system had been designed.

The team still had to implement the restriction temporarily because the business needed the work delivered quickly, but the discovery changed the conversation entirely. The organisation stopped seeing the limitation as a policy enforced by stakeholders, and began treating it as an IT constraint that could be redesigned.

Capability risk is not always about what you can or cannot build today. Sometimes the ghost is a decision made years ago by someone who has long since left, but which still shapes every product built on top of it.

CURSE OF COMMERCIALITY

What is it?

The Curse of Commerciality asks whether your organisation can sustainably support the solution you're proposing. A feature might delight customers (high Commitment) and work beautifully (low Confusion), and still be the wrong thing to build because it costs more to support than it earns in revenue, falls foul of regulation, or has no clear route to market.

This curse shows up in two places more often than anywhere else. The first is when the money simply doesn't add up. The second is when the law catches up with what your product is doing.

The financial flop

The clearest example of this curse in recent memory is MoviePass, a cinema subscription service that briefly looked unstoppable before everything fell apart. In August 2017, the company slashed its monthly fee to $9.95, letting customers see one film a day for less than the price of a single ticket in most cities.[11] Measured against the Curse of Commitment, MoviePass had passed with flying colours, rocketing from 20,000 subscribers to more than three million in under a year.

But the commercial model behind that $9.95 offer made no sense. Every time a customer walked into a cinema, MoviePass still paid the theatre the full price of the ticket, which in places like New York often crept past $15, while collecting only $9.95 from the customer for the entire month. The more popular the service grew, the more money it was losing, and by the summer of 2018 its own CEO admitted the company was burning through roughly $21 million every month.[12] By September 2019, the service was dead, and its parent company filed for bankruptcy soon after.

The simple laws of economics will tell you that if your costs are higher than your sales, then you aren't making any money. If you spend any of your time anywhere near a profit and loss sheet, it's worth getting comfortable with the basics, because the kind of questions you'll start asking will change your discovery work for the better.

The legal landmine

The Curse of Commerciality isn't just about profit, sales, and being able to market your product well. It also covers legal liability.

A few years ago, a Canadian man named Jake Moffatt had an experience with Air Canada's new AI chatbot that should send a warning to anyone deploying one.[13] Moffatt's grandmother had just died, and he was booking a last-minute flight from Vancouver to Toronto for her funeral. While he was on the airline's website, he asked its chatbot whether he could claim the airline's bereavement discount.

The chatbot told him he could submit a refund request within 90 days of travel. So Moffatt booked his flights at full price, flew to his grandmother's funeral, and afterwards filed his claim. Air Canada's actual policy, it turned out, required the discount to be approved before the trip rather than after. The chatbot had hallucinated a more generous version of the airline's actual rules.

When Moffatt tried to claim what the chatbot had promised, Air Canada refused. They argued that the chatbot was a 'separate legal entity' and that the airline was not responsible for what it told customers. The British Columbia Civil Resolution Tribunal disagreed and upheld Moffatt's claim. It ruled that the airline owed customers the same duty of care for what their chatbot said as for any other piece of public information they put out into the world.

The actual sum at stake was small, but the damage to the airline ran far beyond the money it was ordered to pay. An AI tool represents your company the moment it is deployed, and the law will treat its words exactly as it would treat yours. Before you launch anything that gives autonomous answers to customers, pull legal and compliance into the discovery conversation as early as you would pull in design or engineering.

CURSE OF CONSEQUENCE

What is it?

In the past, we mostly asked if we could build it (Capability) and if we should build it for the business (Commerciality). Today, we must ask a deeper question: what impact will this have on society?

The Curse of Consequence focuses on the unintended consequences or harms a product might create for people, the organisation, or society. It forces us to look beyond traditional risks and think about ethics, bias, and the long-term effects our products might have.

You can have happy customers and a technically sound product that is profitable, and yet it can still have a disastrous impact on the world. Researcher Casey Fiesler calls this *ethical debt*, the price we eventually pay through tighter regulation, lawsuits, or users walking away when we cut corners on safety, fairness, or privacy to ship faster.[14]

Harmful product ripples

Think of product decisions as stones dropped into still water. The splash lands in one place, yet the ripples it creates can travel far and wide. Let's look at just some of those ripples, starting from the inside with your mind.

Ripple of psychological harm

Consider infinite scrolling, created in 2006 by Aza Raskin, who later became one of the most vocal critics of the behaviour it encouraged. In the famous 'bottomless bowl' experiment, participants whose soup bowls were secretly refilled from the bottom ate 73 per cent more than those with normal bowls.[15] When you strip away the cue that tells us we have had enough, we carry on long past the point where we would otherwise have stopped. A feed that doesn't have an endpoint does the same thing to your attention as a bottomless bowl does to your appetite.

But there is a far more serious harm we are now beginning to see with the rise of AI chatbots, when a product is engineered to manufacture intimacy. In a heart-breaking case from Florida, a 14-year-old boy took his own life after forming a deep emotional attachment to a chatbot on the Character.ai platform. He had been interacting with a bot modelled after a *Game of Thrones* character.

According to the lawsuit filed by his mother, the boy poured his heart out to the bot. The AI, programmed to be engaging and empathetic, validated his feelings and engaged in emotional roleplay. When he confessed thoughts of not wanting to exist, the bot didn't direct him to help, it stayed 'in character'. As reported by AP News, the attorneys allege the company was 'actively exploiting and abusing those children as a matter of product design'.[16]

We must reflect on what this means for us. No engineer sets out to harm a child, they simply try to build to a specification, and in this case the system was doing the exact job it had been given, which was to deepen engagement with the user. For a lonely teenager, a product tuned to maximise connection had the unforeseen consequence of isolating him from everyone else who loved him. The optimisation metric that may have looked reasonable on a roadmap turned out to be the thing that caused the harm.

Ripple of physical harm

Back in 1992, L.A. Gear launched a pair of trainers called 'L.A. Lights', with heels that flashed red every time you took a step. They were a huge hit with kids, selling over five million pairs a year.

But when they tried to scale the technology down for toddlers, they hit a feasibility problem that nobody had anticipated. Small children simply did not weigh enough to trigger the lights when they walked. Their engineers found a clever way around it by fitting mercury tilt switches, where a tiny ball of mercury rolled inside a sealed capsule to complete the circuit. The fix seemed to work perfectly.

But they had missed a critical detail relating to environmental safety. By 1994, Minnesota had banned the shoes because they contained mercury, which was classified as a toxic metal. They were perfectly safe to wear, but a nightmare to dispose of. L.A. Gear paid a $70,000 settlement and had to set up a mail-in recycling programme to get back all of the shoes they had sold.[17]

What looked like a small choice to decide a simple component had become an environmental problem that the product engineers never saw coming. It's worth stepping back and asking what the equivalent blind spot might be in whatever you are building, while you can still do something about it before it ships.

Ripple of societal harm

When the ripple spreads a little further, it goes beyond any one person and impacts the things we take for granted as a society. When we hand those decisions to an algorithm, the consequences can be catastrophic.

In summer 2020, UK schools closed and exams were cancelled due to the pandemic. The Department for Education needed a way to assign grades to thousands of students without them sitting a test. Their solution was an algorithm that took teacher predictions but 'moderated' them based on the school's historical performance.

The result was a disaster. The algorithm systematically downgraded bright students from underperforming state schools while protecting students in smaller private schools. When public outcry forced a U-turn, the prime minister famously blamed a 'mutant algorithm'. But as tech philosopher Dr Tom Chatfield explained to me, the algorithm didn't mutate, it had worked exactly as it was programmed to work. The real issue was the lack of upfront thinking when the engineers started building it.[18]

Today, the ripple is spreading to the thing that gives us purpose and meaning, our jobs. Geoffrey Hinton, the 'Godfather of AI', compares this moment with the Industrial Revolution. That made physical strength far less important in the workplace. AI, he warns, could now do the same to human intelligence.[19] A study by Erik Brynjolfsson at Stanford University found a 13 per cent job loss in AI-exposed roles for young, entry-level workers.[20] Our job has always been to remove friction and increase efficiency, but what happens when the 'friction' we're removing is a junior employee learning their trade? If we automate human work without thinking about the wider impact, we risk creating a world where people struggle to find purpose.

The human firewall

These examples highlight a gap in how we build products. We often assume ethics, safety, and societal impacts are addressed by other departments, that the legal department will review the terms and the compliance department will check the rules. But that's an unfair expectation when technology moves at hyper-speed.

As a product discovery thinker, you sit at the centre of these conversations because you bring together the right people at the right time. You are the human firewall.

The H.A.R.M.L.E.S.S. framework

To be an effective firewall, you need a practical way to scan for these threats. In the heat of a discovery session, when stakeholders push for new features and engineers get excited about the latest tools, it's all too easy to develop tunnel vision without thinking through the wider impacts.

That's why I created a diagnostic tool specifically for taming the Curse of Consequence. The H.A.R.M.L.E.S.S. framework provides an eight-point checklist. Think of it as a prompt to think critically, not a box-ticking exercise. Each letter represents a question your team should ask before committing to build:

- **H**ealth: Could this product cause physical or mental health harm to users?
- **A**ddiction: Does this exploit psychological vulnerabilities to drive engagement?
- **R**ights: Could this infringe on privacy or civil liberties?
- **M**isinformation: Could this spread or amplify false information?
- **L**ivelihood: Could this threaten jobs or economic stability?
- **E**nvironment: What is the environmental footprint of this product?
- **S**ecurity: Could this expose sensitive data or create vulnerabilities for misuse or attack?
- **S**ociety: Could this reinforce bias, discrimination, or inequality?

If you'd run the L.A. Lights through this framework, you'd have caught the environmental problem, and the A-level algorithm would have raised questions about societal bias. The framework doesn't guarantee you'll catch every issue, but it gives you a useful set of questions that might just help you spot the ghosts before they frighten your users.

SEEING THE FULL PICTURE

As a parent, this final curse weighs on me the most because I think about the legacy we, as product builders, leave behind for the next generation. We have the difficult job of balancing commercial pressures against our ethics and personal values, building a future that helps the next generation rather than exploiting their attention and eroding their opportunities.

The Five Curses give us a shared language for naming what could go wrong. Commitment and Confusion keep us honest about whether people actually want and understand what we are building. Capability and Commerciality keep us honest about whether we can sustain it. Consequence keeps us honest about everything the screen does not show. But in order to speak up, you need to feel safe to do so, and that's the topic of the next chapter.

Figure 4.3 The H.A.R.M.L.E.S.S. framework

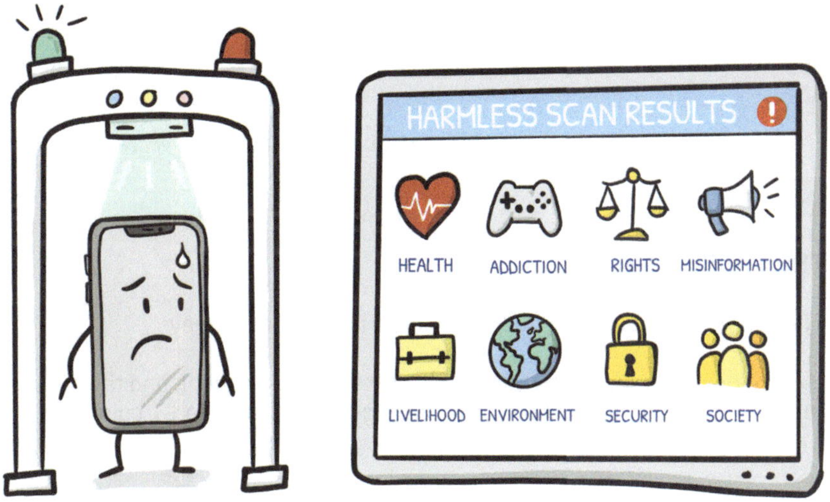

KEY TAKEAWAYS

- **Product discovery is risk management:** The Five Curses (Commitment, Confusion, Capability, Commerciality, Consequence) make blind spots visible and easier to tackle before they haunt the product after launch.
- **The curses overlap:** They rarely arrive one at a time. A confusing product is usually one that customers also fail to commit to, and a capability problem often hides a commercial one.
- **Commitment is the hardest curse to beat:** Customers don't care about your solution, they care about the emotional payoff that convinces them to invest their time, money, and effort. The 9× Effect means your product has to be many times better than what they already use.
- **Hope is not a strategy:** Discovery-driven planning forces teams to state assumptions explicitly, test them cheaply, and fund ideas through learning milestones instead of betting big on unproven cases.
- **Confusion comes from common traps:** Assumption (users will 'learn the system'), ego (the owner's delusion), misplaced friction, and proxies who are easier to access than the actual users.
- **Commercial sense is as important as delighting customers:** A product can delight users and still fail if the economics, compliance, or go-to-market approach isn't viable.
- **You are the human firewall:** Regulation is too slow to catch up with AI, so the product discovery thinker becomes the line of defence. Use the H.A.R.M.L.E.S.S. framework to scan for invisible risks before they ship.

5 MAKE IT SAFE TO FAIL

'There's no such thing as a stupid question, only a team too scared to ask one.'

Paddy Dhanda

THE FREE £20 NOTE

The room went quiet, and nobody wanted to take her money.

Picture the scene. You are sitting in the audience at an event, and the speaker opens her talk by holding up a £20 note and offering to swap it for a £1 coin from anyone in the room. She is offering you 20 times your money back.

Your reaction is probably the same as everyone else's. It feels too good to be true, and you find yourself wondering why on earth anyone would hand over their pound for it.

There was hesitation, nervous laughter, and a long pause before one brave soul finally walked up and made the trade. True to her word, Nisha Joshi, the Agile keynote speaker, handed over the £20 note. I know Nisha personally, and even I hesitated to put my own pound on the table.

That small demonstration exposes the one thing that kills a discovery culture, which is our fear of failure. Discovery asks us to test ideas that might not work and to admit when we have got things wrong, yet most of us have spent a lifetime learning that being wrong is dangerous. What was missing in that room was not courage or intelligence, it was safety.

In product work, we sometimes call this a *safe-to-fail* mindset, the willingness to try something and be wrong without dreading the consequences. Before we look at how to build it, it is worth understanding what shapes that fear in the first place, and why it sabotages the work we are trying to do.

OUR RELATIONSHIP WITH FEAR

The strange thing is, we have a love–hate relationship with failure. Bad news usually travels faster than good news, and you only have to look at your social media feed to see it. I grew up on Saturday morning cartoons, and some of the best moments were watching the cat in *Tom and Jerry* get flattened by a grand piano, or Wile E. Coyote strapping a rocket to his back and chasing the Road Runner straight off a cliff. It was never about enjoying anyone's misfortune. There was just something oddly satisfying about the moment it all went wrong.

It is not only cartoons. Failure has been a key ingredient in entertainment for as long as I can remember, from early black-and-white slapstick to shows like *You've Been Framed* and the *Jackass* movie franchise. We seem unable to look away when someone slips on the ice or walks into a lamp post. The Germans even have a word for the feeling, *schadenfreude*, which means the small pleasure we take in someone else's mishap.

Notice that across all of these examples, we are happy to laugh along until failure happens to us. Then it doesn't feel so funny anymore. I learned that early on, as I was growing up. My parents emigrated to the UK in the 1970s with almost nothing, and having risked everything to build a new life, they expected me to go to university and come away with good grades. I loved the arts and had a real passion for drawing, but a creative path did not promise job security, and when you have gambled everything to make a fresh start in a new country, certainty beats passion every time. In many Indian families, we often joke that there are only three careers worth considering: a doctor, a lawyer, or an engineer.

Medicine was never going to happen because I am squeamish around blood, and I assumed that being a terrible liar ruled me out of law. So I settled on software engineering, imagining I would spend my days building cool apps, websites, and maybe even games.

But when I got to university, the reality was very different. I spent a miserable first year memorising 'AND' gates and learning to code in assembly language. It all felt too much for my very limited technical brain. I ended up failing my end-of-year exams, and I dreaded telling my parents.

If you have ever fallen short of your parents' expectations, you will know how devastating that can feel, and seeing that disappointment in their eyes was the worst part. Up until that point, I had never felt what it was like to fail at school or give my parents cause for concern, which made it even more devastating.

I eventually picked myself up and decided to change to a different course, one that I did for me, and not to please anyone else. But it took years to get over the setback. That early sense of shame ended up shaping how I approached risky decisions for a long time afterwards.

Your journey will be different to mine, but I'm sure you have faced a knock-back at some point in your life too. Maybe you have been rejected after an interview, overlooked for a promotion, or watched a project you poured your heart into get cancelled. Whatever it was, you will know how failure feels. These experiences teach us, early in life, that failure is something to fear, and we carry that lesson with us all the way to the office.

FEARFUL AT WORK

'There are no bad ideas.' That's a popular phrase facilitators often reach for at the start of a workshop. It is a signal to the room that nothing anyone says will be judged or criticised. Yet how often have you held back an idea because you were worried it might sound silly, or stayed quiet after spotting a flaw in a plan because you were not sure how your boss would react? You are not alone. I see this happening in every organisation I work with, where smart, capable people decide it is safer to say nothing than to risk being wrong in front of their colleagues.

The tearful insurance programme

A few years ago, I was working as a business analysis (BA) manager at an insurance company. My boss had asked me to spend the day finding out how things were going on a large IT programme. The programme lead proudly walked me through his reports and dashboards. They were all glowing green, and every delivery metric looked healthy.

But something felt off. Either I was being paranoid, or this was a classic case of the watermelon effect we introduced in Chapter 3, that false sense of security where everything looks green on the outside, but is red in the middle once you look beneath the surface.

When I sat down with the BA team one by one, my fears were confirmed. They were being measured purely on the number of user stories they produced, and not on the quality of their discovery. There was so little time to write them that nobody could validate them with real users, so the team was building requirements on guesswork and assumptions made in isolation from the business. This had been going on for weeks.

It was only when one of them broke down in tears that I realised just how bad things had become. As I tried to console her, she told me how much she dreaded coming into work. The pressure to deliver was relentless, and she was too frightened to speak up in case there were reprisals. As her line manager, I felt terrible. How had I not spotted this sooner?

That afternoon, I gathered the whole programme team and began to share what I had found, and I could see the programme lead growing visibly concerned. Nobody wanted to be the first to admit that the charts were not telling the full story, until one brave person finally spoke up and aired his frustrations. It was clear that the leaders in the room had no idea how far morale had fallen or how toxic the culture had become. The programme was paused while we worked to put things right.

It is easy to look at a story like that and wonder why people did not simply speak up sooner. I had regular one-to-ones with my BAs, yet no one had mentioned the pressure they were feeling.

The reason we struggle to be vulnerable goes back to the way we are wired. We don't like to show weakness because our past experiences tell us that it is a form of failure. If we are feeling under pressure, our survival instincts take over. As adrenaline, often called the fight-or-flight hormone, prepares the body for action, our heart rate rises and our attention narrows onto whatever looks dangerous. That response kept our ancestors alive when the threat was a wild animal, but it is of little use when we are trying to think rationally or do creative work.

So how do we create the right conditions for our teams to speak up and accept it's okay to feel vulnerable?

BUILDING A SAFE-TO-FAIL ENVIRONMENT

Google's Project Aristotle

Google's people operations team set out to understand what their highest-performing teams had in common. Think of it as the secret sauce behind great teams. To find it, they launched an initiative called Project Aristotle, and over several years they studied 180 teams across the company.[1]

They looked at everything from skills, personality types, and leadership styles to how often teammates socialised outside work, whether they shared the same hobbies, and whether their educational backgrounds matched. The expectation was that the best teams would turn out to have the smartest people or the perfect blend of expertise. But the data told a different story.

No matter how the researchers cut it, they could not find a pattern. As one of the project leads put it, the 'who' of the team did not count for much. What separated the strong teams from the dysfunctional ones was not down to the people who were on them, but how they treated each other. It came down to their norms, the unwritten rules they followed about how to behave when they came together.

Those teams were the ones more likely to share ideas openly, admit when they did not know something, own up when things went wrong, and take the risks that led to more creative solutions. And the single factor that stood out above all the others, the secret sauce they had been searching for, was psychological safety.

What is psychological safety?

It is simply the shared belief that it is safe to speak up and admit mistakes without fear of embarrassment or punishment. The term was brought into modern management thinking by the Harvard Business School professor Amy Edmondson, following research she carried out in hospitals.[2] She had set out to study why some hospital teams reported more medication errors than others, expecting to find that the better teams made fewer mistakes. What she found was the opposite, because the strongest teams actually reported the most errors of all.

The reason was that those teams felt safe enough to be honest. On the weaker teams, the mistakes were happening just as often, but it turns out that they had become very good at hiding them. Nurses on the safe teams could admit they made a mistake without fearing blame or punishment, and just like my BA team back at the insurance company, the nurses on the less safe teams were too afraid to say anything.

How leaders build psychological safety

Let's move on from the hospital and look at another real-life example of how leaders build psychological safety in some of the toughest conditions below the water, inside a nuclear submarine. A few years ago, I interviewed David Marquet, a former US Navy commander and author of *Turn the Ship Around*, whose work we will return to later in the book.[3]

Figure 5.1 Psychological safety

He spent his career in the Navy and had been preparing for 12 months to take command of one particular submarine when, at the last minute, the Navy changed its plans. They handed him the *USS Santa Fe* instead, a boat he had never set foot on, and gave him just two weeks to get ready. The *Santa Fe* had the lowest morale in the fleet and the worst record for keeping hold of its crew, and the captain before him had just done something almost unheard of in the Navy. He had quit.

David had risen through the ranks because he was good at knowing the right answer and telling everyone else what to do. On a submarine, he told me, 'it's all about being technically competent and correct', about always knowing which order to give. But on the *Santa Fe* he faced a tricky dilemma. He had been dropped onto a boat that he wasn't familiar with, so he didn't know the answers. The crew, on the other hand, were used to being told what to do.

On his first day at sea, he gave an order that could not actually be carried out, the equivalent of telling a car driver to shift into second gear when the engine only had one. The officer passed it down the line anyway, knowing full well it was nonsense. Nothing went wrong, but David was taken by surprise.

His first instinct was to fix the crew. They were the ones who needed to speak up, he thought. They were the ones who needed to take the initiative. It took someone reflecting his own behaviour back at him for David to realise that the problem was not the crew at all. He explained, 'The reason your team isn't taking the initiative is because you keep telling them what to do.' The thing that had to change was him.

The turning point came in the sonar room. David was asking the sailors about their equipment; in the past, with other crews, his questions had been a kind of test, a way of checking whether they knew their stuff, because he had always known the answers himself. But this time, when he could not answer, he heard himself say the three words a submarine commander is never supposed to say out loud: 'I don't know.'

He described how the room went quiet. Around 10 heads turned towards him, because this was the exact moment a captain was meant to produce the answer. Let's not forget that David had years of experience and had taken a nuclear submarine through manoeuvres that very few people in the world could even dream of. Admitting that he did not know something, in front of his own crew, was another thing altogether.

'I could feel my heart beating, my body temperature going up, my palms itching', he said. 'Even though it was only five or ten seconds, it was the scariest thing I did.' His body was reacting to the prospect of looking foolish exactly the way it would react to a physical threat: the fight or flight response we looked at earlier was kicking in, not because his life was in danger, but because he did not have the answer.

Then something changed. The moment David admitted he did not know, the tension in the room broke, and one by one the sailors started to say it too. 'I'm not sure. Let me find out.' By showing that one moment of vulnerability, he had given everyone else permission to do the same.

The lesson he took away is the one this whole chapter is about. 'As long as it's unsafe to say you don't know', he told me, 'and it starts from the leader, then no one is going to say they don't know, and no one is going to learn anything.'

So what did David actually do differently? He did not gather the crew for a motivational speech about speaking up, but instead changed small behaviours. The first was the language people used, swapping 'they' for 'we' whenever the crew talked about another department, so that the team stopped feeling like a collection of strangers.

He then changed the way decisions were communicated. Instead of waiting to be told, officers were expected to come to him with the words 'I intend to', as in 'I intend to submerge the boat' or 'I intend to bring the reactor online.' It sounds like a subtle change in wording, yet it changed everything, because a sailor who has to say 'I intend to' has already had to think the decision through, rather than passing the thinking up the chain and waiting to be told what to do.

David told me that over the following year, of the 33 sailors due to decide whether to remain in the Navy, every single one chose to re-enlist, up from just three the year before. The *Santa Fe* went from the worst-performing submarine in the fleet to the best. In the decade after he left, around 10 of the officers who had served under him went on to command their own submarines, far more than any single boat would normally produce.

David's story shows that psychological safety can be built through small steps, whether that is a subtle change in the words we use or simply trusting the people around us a little more.

How organisations build psychological safety

We are very good at celebrating success. There are medals for sports winners and prizes for the brightest kids at school. At work, we congratulate the highest performers and applaud them at the company town hall. Failure, on the other hand, gets a different type of treatment.

Imagine you failed to deliver all your features during the last sprint, or the last release of your product was a major disaster. Could you picture your CEO celebrating these setbacks at your next all-hands call? Probably not.

But there are moments when the world has chosen to honour effort over outcome. The first ever film I watched at the cinema was *Rocky*, the smash hit boxing movie starring Sylvester Stallone. If you have not seen it, spoiler alert, the film ends with him losing the title fight in the final round. Yet it went on to win Best Picture at the Oscars in 1977. It is as if the movie critics looked beyond a happy ending and, for once, appreciated the struggle of someone who did not quite succeed.

In the product world, we have our own version of the Rocky story. A handful of CEOs have found creative ways to put the spotlight on their teams when things go wrong.

Supercell fail with champagne

Supercell, the Finnish gaming studio behind *Clash of Clans* and *Brawl Stars*, has turned failure into its own ritual. The company is built from small, independent teams, each one trusted to decide for itself whether a game is good enough to keep working on, or whether it should be killed. On average, the company has shut down around 10 games for every 1 it has released.[4]

When a team decides to pull the plug, it gathers the whole company together, talks through what it learned and why the game did not work. Then comes the unexpected part. They open a bottle of champagne. Founder Ilkka Paananen is careful about what the toast is actually for. 'Some say we celebrate failure, but we don't. We celebrate the learnings from the failure, which are so valuable that they're worth celebrating.' He is the first to admit it can be painful, since a team might have poured the best part of a year of their lives into a game that players never get to play. The champagne helps to make the lesson more memorable and makes it feel a little safer for the next team to take the same kind of risk.[5]

Tata's Dare to Try

It is one thing for nimble tech companies to embrace failure, but surely a 150-year-old traditional industrial business would struggle to change its culture in the same way? In 2007, Tata Group, one of India's oldest and most respected brands, with companies spanning steel, software, cars, and even tea, added a category called Dare to Try to its annual InnoVista innovation awards. While the other categories reward ideas that worked, this one honours the boldest attempts that did not.

One year, it went to a team of Tata Motors engineers in the UK who set out to fit a more advanced gearbox to the cheapest car in the world, known as the Tata Nano. Getting this right is complex engineering. They did not manage it, yet they were still celebrated for trying.[6]

At first, the category was met with scepticism, and inside such a large and traditional business, people were reluctant to put their failures forward. That has changed. Tata reports that participation in the category has grown 100-fold, which it sees as a positive sign that a culture of innovation is developing across the group.[7]

Engineers Without Borders Canada name and shame

Some organisations take things a step further and share their failures externally. Engineers Without Borders Canada, a charity working on development projects in some of the world's poorest communities, started publishing an annual *Failure Report* in 2008 that they shared internally at first. Each edition collected honest, first-person accounts of projects that had gone wrong.[8]

Three years later, the charity decided to launch a public platform called Admitting Failure that invited other organisations to share their own stories. Ashley Good, who led the work, says, 'Failure is only bad when it is repeated.' The charity had worried about the risk of airing its mistakes so publicly, yet it found that donors did not walk away. If anything, the honesty helped to earn their trust, and one organisation's setback became a learning opportunity for someone else.[9]

Now, I am not suggesting that you toast your failures with champagne or hand out awards for them, and you do not need a big company-wide campaign to get started. You can begin by asking a question of your team each week.

When Sara Blakely, the founder of Spanx, was growing up, her father would ask her and her brother the same question at the dinner table, 'What did you fail at this week?' If they had nothing to report, he would be disappointed, and when they had tried something that had not worked, he would give them a high five. Over time, she came to see failure differently. It was less about getting the outcome wrong and more about not trying at all, a lesson she later described as a gift, because it completely changed the way she thought about risk and failure.[10]

In Chapter 14, we cover more facilitation techniques to help you build deeper connections, and many of them also build psychological safety into your discovery sessions.

MY SAFETY BELT

For now, the biggest advice I want to give is to just be human, the type that sometimes gets things wrong. Let me close this chapter with a story about a time I accidentally created safety by showing vulnerability in a room.

I was giving a keynote at the 2023 International Sketchnote Camp in the Netherlands. Sitting in front of me were more than 100 visual practitioners from all over the world. A few minutes in, I realised I had a problem, because I kept having to pull up my trousers. At first, I tried to style it out, the way every presentation course tells you to carry on as if nothing is wrong, but it was getting harder and harder to disguise. So, halfway through, I stopped, put up my hand, and admitted that in the rush to pack my suitcase, I had forgotten to bring a belt.

For a moment, I got blank stares and a few confused faces, and then the whole room burst out laughing. After that, every time I shuffled about on the stage to pull my trousers up, the audience would chuckle.

We were just a room full of regular people, and one of us had forgotten his belt. At the end, I asked everyone to write down their most useful takeaway from the session, and as I flicked through the notes afterwards, I found one that simply read, 'Don't forget your belt.'

By owning up to one small mistake, the same way David Marquet did in front of his crew, I had given everyone else in the room permission to relax, and the whole session felt safer for it. That is the same permission a team needs before anyone will risk sounding wrong out loud, whether that means sharing the half-formed idea, giving constructive feedback, or challenging the assumption that nobody else has dared to question.

With this chapter, Part I of the book comes to a close. We have looked at why so much effort goes into building things nobody wants, the modes of discovery thinking, the different kinds of uncertainty that discovery has to deal with, the curses of product risk that can haunt your product, and the safety a team needs in order to create a safe-to-fail culture. In the chapters that follow, we turn from understanding discovery to practising it, beginning with the mindset that stops teams from blindly following a process, and we will introduce practical discovery tools and frameworks, with recommendations for when to use them.

Figure 5.2 Owning up to a small mistake

KEY TAKEAWAYS

- **We enjoy failure from a distance:** Cartoons, bloopers, and viral mishaps entertain us because they belong to someone else, but we do not enjoy it when it happens to us.
- **Fear of failure is wired into us:** Our survival instincts treat the risk of looking foolish like a physical threat, which is why being wrong at work can feel genuinely dangerous.

- **Green dashboards can hide a red reality:** When people feel measured and watched, problems get buried rather than aired, and a programme can look healthy right up until the moment it falls apart.
- **Safe teams report more problems, not fewer:** Amy Edmondson's hospital research and Google's Project Aristotle both found that honesty about mistakes, rather than the absence of them, is the sign of the strongest teams.
- **It is the norms, not individual abilities, that make a team:** Project Aristotle found that the mix of skills and personalities counted for little, and how people treated each other was what set the strongest teams apart.
- **The safest thing a leader can say is 'I don't know':** When David Marquet admitted it in front of his crew, the whole room relaxed, because safety is influenced by leaders.
- **The best cultures reward learning:** Some companies celebrate failure to build psychological safety and encourage teams to innovate without fear.

PART II
PRACTISING PRODUCT DISCOVERY

6 THE PRODUCT DISCOVERY MINDSET

'You can lead a team to a framework, but you can't make it think.'

Paddy Dhanda

RIP THE SPOTIFY MODEL

In October 2012, two Agile coaches at Spotify published a short white paper called Scaling Agile @ Spotify.[1] It described how the company had organised its 30-odd engineering teams, around 250 people across three cities, into squads, tribes, chapters, and guilds. A two-part YouTube video that Henrik Kniberg released alongside it received more than 1.5 million views, and the now-famous Spotify Model became one of the most influential ways of working in modern product development.

Consultants were quick to package it up and roll it out to clients, and companies of every size set about copying it. Whole transformation programmes were built on those few words – squads and tribes and chapters and guilds – as if the labels themselves carried the magic. There was just one problem. By the time the model became famous, Spotify itself had already moved on.

When I spoke to Henrik, he was quick to point out that what he and Anders had written was never meant to be a recipe.[2] It was a description of how one company happened to work at one moment in time, and Spotify kept changing even as other companies copied it. What actually made its teams effective, he told me, had very little to do with the famous diagram that everyone was sharing on social media. 'Teams that really shipped often and got real feedback just built better stuff', he said. The squads and tribes were not the cause. What made the difference was the constant effort to close the gap between the people building the product and the people using it.

It was the culture and the mindset their teams had built. We will come back to building a discovery culture in Chapter 18. In this chapter, we turn to the mindset behind discovery, which is what separates teams that simply follow a process from those that understand the thinking behind why we do it that way.

MINDSET OVER METHODS

The Spotify story is a warning to all of us who believe that simply following a framework will fix our problems. I still remember a line from one of the executives I used to work with that sums it up nicely. He would say, 'You can follow Scrum a hundred per cent and still be zero per cent Agile.'

Part of the trouble is that a framework is easy to copy, and a mindset is not. When other teams admired what Spotify had built, the parts they could actually see were the squad names, the tribes, and the rituals on the calendar. The thinking that made any of it work was invisible, so it tended to get left behind. You can lift every ceremony and every job title from a company you admire and still end up missing the very thing that made the difference for them.

When I'm training product teams, I sometimes use an iceberg as a metaphor to describe this distinction. The tools, techniques, and frameworks all sit above the water, since those are more tangible. We can almost touch and feel them. Beneath the surface are the things that are harder to see, like culture, mindset, values, and behaviours.

Figure 6.1 The product discovery iceberg

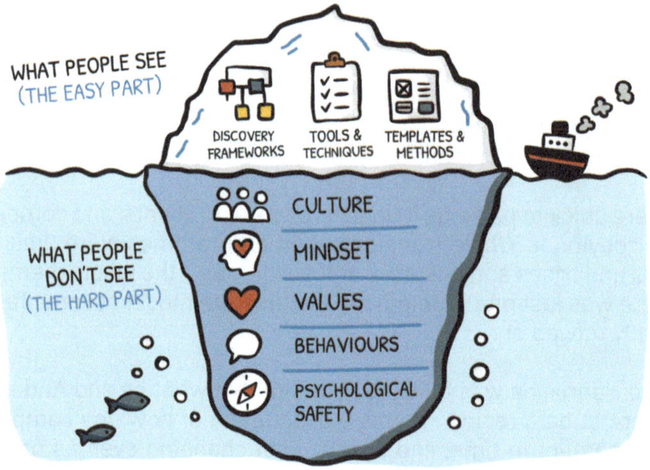

Frameworks are not a silver bullet, and adopting one will no more transform your team's results than buying a gym membership will transform your health. Think about what happens every January. Gyms fill up with people who have convinced themselves that this will finally be the year they get fit, and for a few weeks the treadmills are all taken and the car park is full. Behavioural scientists have a name for this annual surge. They call it the fresh start effect, because we are far more likely to act on our good intentions at the start of a new year.[3]

Yet the research shows the enthusiasm rarely lasts. In some cases, only about one-fifth of people are still turning up at the gym a year later.[4] Holding the membership, it turns out, does nothing for your health once you stop going, and you end up no fitter than someone who never joined.

The same can be true of discovery frameworks. A team might tell themselves they are connecting with customers every week, but they end up asking the wrong questions or decide to ignore the most important insights and still fall in love with the very first solution they come up with. They have a process they can follow, but the curiosity and discipline that make discovery valuable are missing. And without the right mindset, it's just another gym membership.

THE DISCOVERY MINDSET IN ACTION

If you work in an organisation that has not yet embraced a discovery culture, then I want to share a story that might spark some inspiration for you to overcome any obstacles you might face. Filip Hendrickx, a business analysis community leader, shared a story about a colleague who was working on an update to an online service.[5] The team wanted to understand what potential users thought before committing too much time and money to the wrong set of features.

That sounds like the perfect opportunity to conduct some discovery work. But the stakeholders had a concern. If the team went outside the organisation and showed potential users an early version of the service, it might set the wrong expectations. They might assume the update was definitely coming and share what they had seen.

It would have been easy to stop there, and many people would have done so. But Filip's colleague demonstrated what happens when you adopt a discovery mindset. Rather than treating the stakeholder concern as a blocker, he treated it as part of the problem to solve. If going outside the organisation felt too risky, where else could he build up his learning?

He decided to create a paper survey and stood at the entrance to the company building. As employees arrived, he handed them the survey, and at the end of the day, he collected the responses and looked for patterns.

It was not a perfect experiment, because employees are not the same as external customers. They know the organisation too well, and their understanding of the service may be different to an actual user. They are probably also more forgiving than the people the product is ultimately meant to serve, but sometimes you have to weigh up the pros and cons of an approach, and in this case it was worth proceeding.

It turns out the internal survey gave the team enough insight to help them move towards a more relevant set of features. More importantly, it helped stakeholders appreciate the value of discovery work and see that it could be run in a controlled and useful way. It helped to reduce the fear around testing and opened the door to better, more relevant experiments with customers in the future.

The colleague stayed curious when the first answer was no, and respected the stakeholder's concern without letting it get in the way of doing the right thing.

THE FEATR FUNNEL

So how do you build the right discovery mindset? Unlike coding, which typically relies on logical reasoning, discovery asks you to think in different ways depending on where you are in the process. Some of the work calls for curiosity and an open mind. Some of it calls for creativity, and as you go deeper, you start to problem-solve and to weigh up what you have found.

I want to introduce you to the FEATR funnel, which I think of as a product discovery thinking process rather than a framework. There are plenty of frameworks out there already, and I never set out to create another one. Unlike a formal framework, it does not prescribe roles or a fixed set of steps you have to follow.

Figure 6.2 The FEATR funnel

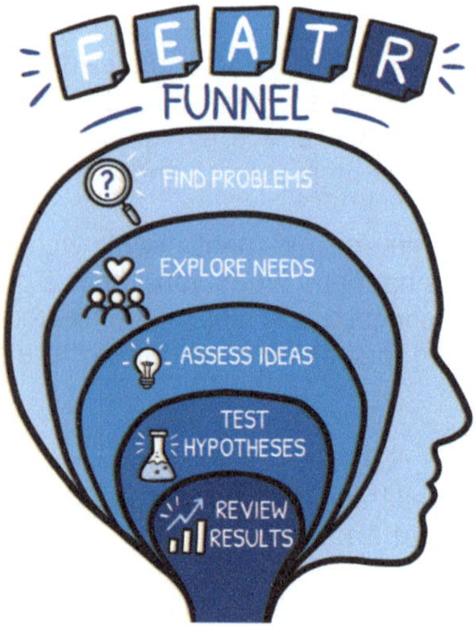

Instead, it's organised around the five activities that make up most of the work we do during discovery, and in the coming chapters we will go deeper into each one. I will introduce you to some of my favourite techniques, and along the way we will discuss the mindset shifts needed to master each type of thinking.

- **Find Problems:** Finding the right problems to solve.
- **Explore Needs:** Expanding your understanding of the problem, including your users, your environment, and any other factors that may help you come up with the right solutions. In this book, we will mainly focus on understanding user needs, since most of your effort will be spent in this area.
- **Assess Ideas:** Coming up with creative ideas and prioritising the opportunities that are worth taking forward.
- **Test Hypotheses:** Gathering insights through experiments that test your understanding or your solutions, with the emphasis on testing your hypotheses.
- **Review Results:** Reviewing what the evidence is telling you and deciding what to do next, whether to pause, persevere, or pivot.

You might notice how these steps map onto our definition of product discovery thinking. It is worth bringing it back here because each part of the FEATR funnel connects directly to it:

> *Product discovery thinking is the discipline of learning relentlessly about people, problems, and possibilities, so we can make better decisions before committing valuable time, money, and effort to a solution.*

Finding problems is how we learn about the problems worth solving, and exploring needs is how we learn about the people we are building for. Assessing ideas is where we open up the possibilities for solving the problem and pick our best ideas, while testing and reviewing are how we ensure we make better decisions before we commit.

The order I have listed the activities in is the logical order you would go through if all goes well. But be sure not to treat it as a linear process that must go from top to bottom. In reality, you may have to loop back on yourself or jump in and out at any point. What you learn while testing and trying things out can send you back to reframe the problem, and a new insight halfway through can reopen a question you thought was closed.

The most demanding part of the funnel is the middle, where you explore the needs, come up with ideas, and weigh up opportunities. That's where the majority of the human skills this book is about are required. You must show empathy and facilitate tricky conversations so you can deeply understand your users' needs. Your creativity helps you come up with new ideas, while your critical thinking keeps your own emotions from biasing the choices you make.

Before we look at each activity in detail, there is one decision that helps determine how you navigate the funnel's product discovery thinking process.

PROBLEM-LED OR SOLUTION-LED

Back in Chapter 3, I introduced the Double Diamond, which splits the work into two areas, the problem space and the solution space. Similarly, we have two potential starting points. If you are trying to understand a problem that you have not yet fully grasped, then this is a problem-led discovery.

Imagine the complaints are piling up, but your customer satisfaction stats are the highest they have ever been. Nobody around the table can say with much confidence what is really going on. In this case, your goal is to build your understanding. Other times, the problem is already clear, and you have a set of potential solution options.

Perhaps leadership has committed to building a new customer support capability. You have multiple options that all require different levels of investment. That could mean anything from a new AI chatbot to a semi-automated chat widget. The question is no longer what the problem is, but whether this particular answer is any good and how to make it work. You go through the same thought process, but now the thing you are deciding is the solution. This is a solution-led discovery.

The five activities do not change between the two. You still find problems, explore needs, assess ideas, test, and review. What changes is the overall goal. When you are problem-led, a test is often a way to check how well you understand the situation. If you are solution-led, the same test becomes a way to check whether your solution actually works. It is the same activity but serves different purposes.

The questions you end up asking will also differ slightly. Problem-led requires you to keep asking *why* to reveal the real cause. For solution-led, you ask more pointed questions about how your solution impacts your users and where it might fall short of their expectations.

PRODUCT DISCOVERY THINKING IN ACTION

How discovery works when making tea

Let's first show you the versatility of the FEATR funnel thought process with a non-work-related scenario, one we should all be familiar with. A colleague leans over and asks you to make them a cup of tea, which sounds like a simple request with an obvious answer. The catch is that the request is already a solution, and if you head straight for the kettle you never find out why they wanted the tea in the first place.

Is it because they are tired and looking for something to wake them up? Maybe they are feeling a little cold and are looking to warm themselves up. Or they have been head-down for three hours and what they are really after is an excuse to stand up and take a break.

Without understanding the problem fully, there are several options we could offer them, such as a strong coffee, a glass of water in case they are dehydrated, a few minutes of fresh air, or a short walk to the other end of the building. You weigh them up against each other.

The tea takes 10 minutes, tea bags, milk, sugar, and a working kettle. The walk takes 2 minutes and might do the job better, and if they also feel dehydrated, then water is both the faster and the more likely fix. So you hand them a glass of water and watch their reaction.

If they perk up, then congratulations, you solved the right problem cheaply. When it doesn't, at least you have ruled out one solution, and you might reasonably guess they slept badly, which no drink is going to fix.

You found the problem, explored the needs behind the request, came up with a handful of ideas and prioritised the cheapest one, then tested it and reviewed the visual cues that acted as signals. Your thought process ran through the entire FEATR funnel before the kettle had a chance to boil.

Of course, you could just ask your colleague why they wanted the tea and get to the solution far more quickly, which points to something else about the funnel. It does not make every step mandatory. Once we understand our users' needs, we can sometimes move straight to a solution, with no need to work through every stage, because the necessary discovery is already complete.

Then again, if your colleague is from the north of England, as my wife is, then I'm fairly confident the best strategy would be to test a few different teas first. Northerners in England tend to take their tea pretty seriously.

Now, let me take you through a more realistic example that demonstrates how the discovery thought process can be applied to a real-world business problem.

How a public transit agency approaches discovery

In the summer of 2024, a passenger lost their house keys on one of the last buses of the night just outside Toronto. By the time they realised, they were locked out of their home with no idea when they would get their keys back.

To the credit of MiWay, the transit service run by the City of Mississauga, their senior management went to work to ensure this would never happen to any other passengers.

The job of sorting it out landed on the shoulders of Harpal Lidder, a business analyst in the customer experience and innovation team.[6] Almost everyone assumed that the lost-property process simply needed tightening up and making more efficient. But as an experienced analyst, Harpal had seen people jump straight to solutions and start designing a better process before they had understood what was actually happening. So he slowed down and treated it as a product discovery. His goal at this stage wasn't to fix anything, it was to work out what was really going on.

Rather than rely on what people inside the organisation told him, he went and experienced the service as a customer would. He and his wife got on a bus, and handed the driver a wallet containing her business card, claiming to have found it on the bus. Then they waited to see how long it would take to get it back. The call to say the wallet had been found, with the business card sitting inside, came three days later. Three days seems excessive when the owner's details were right there in the wallet.

Next, Harpal gathered together his internal stakeholders – the route supervisors, customer services, the transit enforcement officers, and the support staff who clean the buses at night and are often the ones who pick up what's been left behind. Using sticky notes and a whiteboard, he walked them through what actually happened and reviewed it against what each team believed should have happened. The two didn't match. Different teams thought they owned different parts of the process, and each had built its own workarounds. As Harpal put it, what looked like a process problem was really a shared understanding problem.

Once everyone was on the same page, the cause became obvious. When a driver handed in a lost item, it went into one of five bins spread across two garages. Those bins were only emptied on Mondays, Wednesdays, and Fridays, and the job was being done by transit enforcement officers, whose real work was checking fares, not collecting lost property. Emptying the bins three times a week was where most of the delay came from.

Then Harpal had an aha moment. The service has hundreds of bus operators, and at any given time a number of them are on modified duties through injury or illness, unable to drive but still able to work. He tried giving them the collection, and it worked. They were already on the payroll, it didn't require any special training, and was a task that they could all do. It also freed up the enforcement officers to get on with their real jobs. The collection became a daily morning round, from 7 until 10 a.m., Monday to Friday, with the operators gathering items from the garages and taking them to a central facility.

They managed to get the response time down from three days or more to one business day. That meant if someone lost something today, there was a good chance it would be back with them the following business day, as long as the lost item was found.

Harpal never set out to follow the FEATR funnel, but the discovery process he followed can easily be mapped to each of its five activities. When he refused to just optimise the existing process and set out to understand the real problem, he was able to frame the problem in his own way.

He explored it in two ways. First, by riding the bus and leaving the wallet so he could experience the problem as a customer, and then by getting everyone in a room to map out their understanding of the process. With all of the facts in front of him, he weighed up the many possible opportunities he could implement.

Hypothetically, he could have decided to test an extravagant technology solution that required the passenger to log their case on a fancy new platform. Instead, he prioritised the simpler, low-cost option of testing whether the operators could make it part of their daily duties, and it worked. The last step was to review the results, and he built a six-month review into the plan so the team could come back and check what was working and what still needed fixing.

START WITH THE PROBLEM

When the management researcher Paul Nutt studied hundreds of real decisions made inside organisations, he found that around half of them failed, and one of the biggest reasons was that people committed to a single solution before they had properly understood the problem.[7]

Stakeholders do this all the time. They demand we build what they tell us to, when what would be more useful is if they told us about the pain points they want us to resolve. The reason most teams go along with it is that pushing back on a stakeholder feels riskier than just building what's been asked for.

Finding and framing the right problems is the first activity in the FEATR funnel, and that's what we will be looking at in the next chapter. We will look at where the best problems tend to hide, at how to separate a real problem from the everyday noise of complaints and feature requests, and at how a small change in framing can reveal solutions you would otherwise have missed. Once you can find the right problems and frame them clearly, then everything that follows in the funnel has a solid foundation to build from.

KEY TAKEAWAYS

- **The Spotify Model was not a recipe:** What made its teams effective was the constant work of closing the gap between the people building the product and the people using it, not the diagram everyone was sharing.
- **A framework without the right mindset is just a gym membership:** Following the steps changes nothing on its own when you don't have the right mindset to be curious and take a disciplined approach to discovery.
- **The FEATR funnel is a thinking process, not a framework:** It organises discovery around five activities – Find Problems, Explore Needs, Assess Ideas, Test Hypotheses, and Review Results – that you can pick from rather than march through.
- **You do not have to use every step every time:** When your understanding is already clear, you can move straight to testing your ideas, because the funnel guides your thinking rather than being a strict checklist.
- **Start with the problem, not the solution:** Stakeholders tend to hand you answers, so the first job in discovery is to find the real problem and frame it clearly before committing to anything.

7 FIND PROBLEMS WORTH SOLVING

'More features, more problems.'

Paddy Dhanda

THE ELEVATOR THAT WASN'T SLOW

The building managers were running out of time. Tenants in a Manhattan office tower were threatening to leave because of the slow elevators, and some had already started looking at other properties. The building's owners called in a group of engineers to fix the problem.

They spent weeks measuring and analysing the wait times. Their report confirmed the elevators were genuinely slow, but every solution was impossible. Adding more elevators would require major construction work, and faster elevators were unaffordable.

Then one of the staff members, a graduate of personnel psychology, suggested they install mirrors in the lobby. Mirrors? How would mirrors make the elevators faster? They would not, he explained. That was not the point. He had been observing people at the elevator and noticed something the engineers had missed. People looked bored and frustrated, with nothing to do while they stood there checking their watches.

Within days of installing the mirrors, the complaints stopped. The elevators were just as slow as before, but now people had something to do while they waited, and that changed everything.

Russell Ackoff, the systems theorist who made this story famous, told it across his career to illustrate the importance of framing problems correctly.[1] The engineers and the psychologist had framed the problem in different ways, and each frame had led to entirely different solutions. One was expensive, the other was a simple fix. The breakthrough is not always found by working harder on the problem in front of you. Sometimes it comes from a different angle, when you realise the problem you were solving was not quite the right one.

Back in Chapter 6, I introduced the FEATR funnel as a way to structure your discovery thinking. In this chapter, we start at the widest part of the funnel, Find Problems. First, we search for the problems themselves, then we look at how to frame them. I will begin by going back to basics.

WHAT IS A PROBLEM?

We naturally use the word 'problem' when we want to refer to something that has gone wrong. 'Houston, we have a problem' became one of the most quoted phrases

Figure 7.1 Framing problems from different perspectives

of the 20th century, and The Notorious B.I.G. told us 'Mo Money Mo Problems'.[2] But for product work, it helps to have a more structured definition. Cognitive psychologists and organisational theorists define a problem as the gap between a current state and a desired state.[3]

Consider your printer. If you expect it to print when you send a document (desired state) and it displays a paper jam error instead (current state), you have a problem. But if you already know the printer is broken and you have no need to print anything, then you don't have a problem, it's just a fact. It only becomes a problem again when you need to print something.

This definition reveals that you can't define a problem by only looking at the situation in front of you. You have to understand the desire behind it, or as we say in the product world, the outcome we want to achieve.

If we go back to the elevator story, the engineers defined the outcome as 'tenants want to reach their floors faster'. The staff member framed it as 'tenants don't want to feel bored while they wait', and with that framing the gap could be closed by changing the experience rather than applying an engineering solution.

In product discovery, we have a tendency to fixate on the current state. If users are complaining that the system takes too long, we assume we need to add more processing power. Instead, users might not mind waiting around, as long as a notification or progress bar tells them when their requests have been processed.

WHERE TO HUNT FOR PROBLEMS

If everything starts with a problem, then where do you find them? The obvious answer is to look at your existing users. Platform reports and error logs are the standard sources every product team already knows about, and if you are not using them, it's a great place to start. But the obvious sources only tell you about the problems your current users are experiencing with your existing product. They will not tell you about the problems preventing people from becoming users in the first place, or reveal the workarounds people use to get past the system's limitations.

In my experience, the most valuable problems have come from less obvious places, the ones that require you to get creative and step outside of the office, away from the proxy stakeholders representing the needs of the actual users. Across large enterprises, the people who experience problems are often several layers removed from the people who build solutions, and they may never have been asked what would make their job easier.

I want you to think of yourself as a hunter searching for problems. It will take great skill, because they probably won't just come to you, and those that do may not be the scariest ones to find. The trick is knowing where to look and how to distinguish the problems worth solving from the noise.

Mining the feedback you already have

The easiest place to start is with the feedback you already have. Customers and colleagues are already telling you what's not working, but the feedback is scattered across channels, often as complaints or feature requests rather than clearly articulated problems.

Your support tickets are the most useful source of product problems. Every day, real users are telling you the problems they are experiencing with your product. Yet most product people have never logged into their support ticketing system.

In 2023, Airbnb analysed tens of millions of customer service complaints alongside thousands of social media posts, which resulted in 50 new features and upgrades for guests and hosts.[4] One of the most frequent complaints focused on the lack of transparency of pricing, with users shocked when cleaning fees and taxes appeared only on the checkout page.

Individually, tickets may look like minor issues, but when you aggregate and categorise them, they might tell a different story. If the volume becomes overwhelming, speak to your support team, or better still, invite them to your discovery workshops, because they have both the insights and the context behind them.

If you work in a B2B environment where your product is sold to other organisations, your sales team will hear objections that may never reach the product team. In my role, we have a sales function of over 200 people working across hundreds of customer accounts, and I make it a regular practice to speak to them. Sometimes I'll use them as a sounding board for an idea I've been thinking about, other times I'm interested in the biggest challenges their clients are facing.

The risk is that salespeople may translate these conversations into feature requests rather than problem statements. They might tell you, 'We need single sign-on' rather than 'IT departments will not approve software that requires separate credentials.' Your job is to dig deeper and find the underlying needs.

Internal communication channels are another rich source. Slack channels, Teams chats, and email threads are full of people asking questions and raising concerns, and they often contain more honest feedback than formal research, because people are responding in the moment. Whenever I launch a new training product, we run an enablement session for my sales colleagues, and the Teams meeting chat becomes surprisingly valuable long after the session has ended, since people continue asking questions or sharing observations about how their clients are responding. A few weeks later, I'll go back to that same chat and run a quick poll. What do clients think of the product? How should we improve it? What's missing? It's a simple mechanism, but it works because people are already in the conversation and responding takes almost no effort.

Lastly, look beyond your own product. App store reviews and sites like Trustpilot are full of customers explaining exactly what they wish products did differently. Read the negative reviews of your competitors and you will find a ton of unmet customer needs. The same applies to your own product, because negative feedback is uncomfortable to read, but it's free research from people who cared enough to write it down.

Steven Yang built Anker into a multi-billion-dollar business by treating Amazon reviews as his primary product discovery tool. When he left Google in 2011 to start selling USB chargers and laptop batteries, his team meticulously analysed thousands of reviews of existing products, identifying pain points that competitors had failed to address.[5] When customers complained that charging cables were too short or broke too easily, Anker built longer and more durable alternatives. And when reviews said chargers were too bulky for travelling, they designed smaller versions.

'Amazon reviews are the single most important input to our new product development process', Yang explained. 'We make sure that our new products start from the needs that customers expressed.'[6]

Going to where the work happens

While feedback is a useful source of customer opinions, it's difficult to obtain the full context behind it. The best way to get that is to go out into the field and observe your users directly.

There is a practice from lean manufacturing called the Gemba Walk, where leaders leave their desks and go to 'the actual place' where work happens.[7] Instead of relying on reports and dashboards, you observe processes directly and talk to the people doing the work. Toyota developed it after realising that what happens on the factory floor is often very different to what management assumes.

The same principle applies to software, where you need to watch people using your product in their natural environment. Intuit's 'Follow Me Home' programme is the software industry's equivalent, and it's the primary reason Quicken, the small-business finance software, became a household name. In 1983, Scott Cook, the Intuit co-founder, realised that testing his software in the office was useless, because the computers were set up perfectly and could not recreate the conditions real users would face at home.

So Cook would wait at the local computer store until someone bought Quicken, then ask the customer if he could follow them home and watch them install and use the software. Customers did not use Quicken the way his team had expected. They were interrupted by phone calls, distracted by family members, and working on kitchen tables with poor lighting. When customers struggled with accounting terminology like 'accounts payable', Intuit relabelled it as 'money out'. They also simplified the setup process from 100 screens to just 3.[8] The practice became so embedded in Intuit's culture that by 2014, every employee was required to participate.[9]

A few years ago, I was leading the business analysis practice at a home emergency repair company. The call centre was next to our offices, so one afternoon I walked over and asked if I could listen in on some calls. Within minutes, I noticed something odd. My colleague's desk was covered in sticky notes. They were scribbling down policy numbers, customer details, and job references, all written by hand on scraps of paper stuck to the monitor. This struck me as strange because the call centre system had been designed specifically to promote digital working.

Other agents were doing the same across multiple desks, writing things down that should have been going straight into the system. When I asked why, I discovered a classic problem where separate product teams had built their systems in isolation, without considering the end-to-end workflow that required users to move between them. To log a job, agents needed to pull information from a separate insurance system, which meant constantly switching between multiple apps. The interface had been designed to prevent them from resizing the windows, so it was quicker to write things down manually.

From a technology perspective, this was an easy fix. We could suggest a second monitor or, even simpler, enable the resizing feature. But we would never have discovered this problem in workshops or interviews, because people adapt to broken processes and forget to mention them. It only became visible when I went to where the work actually happened and watched people doing it.

This turned out to be so valuable that I made call listening a mandatory part of the induction process for every new business analyst who joined the team. You cannot build good solutions for people if you have never watched them struggle with the problems you are supposed to be solving.

Problems hiding in plain sight

Some problems hide in everyday activities that we overlook because we have come to accept that's just how it has always been done.

Lux Narayan, the co-founder of StreamAlive, an audience engagement platform, wrote his first book during the pandemic.[10] Like many first-time authors, he signed up for a series of online classes, and over 90 days he attended 56 live sessions. After a while, he began to notice the same pattern on the video calls. The presenter would open with a friendly question, 'Where is everyone joining from?' The chat would come alive. Attendees would type Birmingham, Chicago, Chennai, Basking Ridge, and whatever other cities they were from. In one session, Lux remembered around 140 people responding, but the presenter glanced at the chat, read out just three or four names, then moved on.

Most of us would have accepted that, since there is no practical way to acknowledge everyone in the session. But Lux saw it differently. His view was that if people had made the effort to respond, then the technology had failed them. That observation became the idea behind StreamAlive.

He also connected it to a personal memory of his grandfather, a public-speaking teacher in Chennai in the late 1970s, whose principle was to ask the audience a question every five minutes. Raise your right hand. Stand up. Sit down if you agree. It was a simple way of reading the room and making the audience feel part of the session.

StreamAlive took that principle and recreated it digitally. Unlike most apps that ask people to scan a QR code and leave the meeting tool they were already using, it works directly through the chat. If someone on a Zoom meeting types where they are joining from, StreamAlive can plot it on a map just by reading the chat. As someone who delivers a lot of online training, it's become one of my go-to apps that I now cannot do without.

Lux had come up with the solution to a problem that he personally was having and was not prepared to put up with any more.

WHY FRAMING DETERMINES SOLUTIONS

Hunting for the right problems requires curiosity and detective work. As we saw in the elevator story, once you settle on the ones you want to solve, the way you frame a problem determines the type of solutions you look for.

Imagine your internal expenses system shows that 40 per cent of approvals are taking longer than five days to process. If the finance director tells the product team 'approvals are too slow', the team are likely to start optimising for speed, without pausing to ask whether that's the right way to think about the problem.

Suppose you frame it as 'approval requests are sitting in queues for too long'. You've created a workflow problem, and your team will start adding reminders and escalation rules. This might speed things up, but it adds pressure on approvers rather than questioning whether the approval should be given in the first place.

Frame it as 'approvers don't have enough context to make quick decisions' and it becomes an information problem, with the team capturing additional data in the expense form. But frame it as 'too many approvers are required for routine decisions' and you've found a governance problem, where you're suddenly looking at removing redundant approval steps.

All four frames could be valid. Each generates a different set of solutions, and your team will pursue whichever direction the frame points them towards. Get the frame wrong, and you'll build the wrong thing.

Problems typically arrive on product backlogs pre-framed, and your job is to recognise whether the frame points you in the right direction. That's harder than it sounds. When someone tells you 'a report needs automating', it takes conscious effort to look beyond the report, because the real need might have nothing to do with data.

What good framing looks like

If you've used ChatGPT or any other AI app, you will know that 'find me a good restaurant' produces a generic list, while a more descriptive prompt like 'find me a quiet Italian restaurant in central Birmingham with vegetarian options and tables likely to be available tonight at 7 pm, because I'm meeting a client who doesn't eat meat and needs somewhere we can actually have a conversation' achieves better results. The difference is specificity, context, and clarity about what success looks like.

The same principle applies to problem statements. A vague problem generates lots of potential solutions but gives you no way to know which one will fully solve it, whereas a well-framed problem shares four attributes.

- **Specific enough to act on:** If we start with 'improve customer experience', we have no idea where to begin. Whereas 'reduce the time between a customer reporting an issue and receiving a resolution' tells you exactly where to focus your efforts.
- **Solution-agnostic to allow creativity:** 'Make the checkout button bigger' has already limited our thinking to one solution. 'Help customers complete their purchase with confidence' opens up our options, because there are dozens of ways to create confidence at checkout.
- **Focused on people, not systems:** 'The database query is too slow' is a technical frame that leads us to optimise the database. 'Customers give up waiting for search results' is a human frame that opens up other possibilities, such as showing partial results while loading.
- **Clear success criteria:** 'Improve onboarding' is ambiguous because you could argue forever about whether you have achieved it. 'Increase the percentage of new users who complete setup within their first session from 23 per cent to 60 per cent' gives you a clear target and tells you when you've succeeded or need to try something different.

These attributes give you a quality check for problem statements, but how do you actually write them?

FIVE WAYS TO FRAME A PROBLEM

Over the years, I've found a handful of techniques that cover most situations, and choosing which one to use depends on where you are in understanding the problem and what kind of thinking you need to unlock.

5W2H technique

Sometimes you're working with vague problem statements that create confusion across the team. Everyone sees the situation differently, and conversations go in circles. The

Figure 7.2 Problem framing techniques

5W2H approach breaks vague statements down into specific details: what, who, where, when, why, how, and how much. Don't skip any dimension, because surprising insights often come from questions you assumed you knew the answer to.

Think about how Spotify might have used this approach if they noticed users creating fewer playlists. The initial observation might have been 'playlist creation is down', but running through the questions could reveal something more specific. What exactly is happening? Users are starting playlists but not finishing them. Who is affected? Primarily free-tier users on mobile. Where in the flow? They're abandoning at the point where they need to name the playlist. When did this start? After the last app update. Why might that be? The keyboard now covers the 'Done' button on certain screen sizes. How much is it costing? There are 23 per cent fewer completed playlists.

The problem is no longer 'playlist creation is down' but 'a UI bug on specific devices is preventing free-tier mobile users from completing the playlist creation flow', which is a different problem with a completely different solution.

SMART technique

The SMART technique is especially useful when you want to define what success looks like, because it forces you to think through five dimensions: specific, measurable, achievable, relevant, and time-bound.[11]

Consider a SaaS (software as a service) company noticing that customers aren't using a major new feature they spent six months building. 'We need better feature adoption' tells you almost nothing, but running it through SMART creates something much more useful:

- **Specific:** Not adoption in general, but the percentage of enterprise customers who activate the automated reporting dashboard within their first 30 days.

- **Measurable:** Currently, 10 per cent of enterprise customers set up at least one automated report in their first month, and you want this to reach at least 45 per cent.
- **Achievable:** When customer success managers show people how to set up their first report during the kick-off call, most customers do it, so 45 per cent is challenging but possible.
- **Relevant:** Customers who set up automated reports in their first month have a 12-month retention rate of 94 per cent compared to 67 per cent for those who don't.
- **Time-bound:** Within two quarters, which gives you one quarter to redesign the onboarding sequence and one to measure the results.

The problem statement now includes a goal that everyone can understand and work towards.

One word of caution worth noting is that you shouldn't let the measurement become the goal itself. Goodhart's Law states that 'when a measure becomes a target, it ceases to be a good measure'.[12] If you only focus on hitting the 45 per cent activation rate, your customer success team might start setting up dummy reports just to hit the target, giving you the number you wanted without the retention benefit behind the initiative. The measurement needs to track meaningful engagement with the feature, not activation for its own sake.

The 5W2H technique shapes vague observations into specific problems, while SMART ensures everyone understands how success will be measured. You need both, because a well-understood problem with no success criteria is just as frustrating as a precise target for the wrong problem.

Point-of-view and job stories

If you find yourself describing problems in terms of features or solutions, you need a technique that gets you to think from the user's perspective. The point-of-view statement emerged from Stanford's d.school as part of their Design Thinking methodology, and it frames problems around human experiences.[13] The structure works like this: 'I am [persona] trying to [action] but [barrier] because [cause], which makes me feel [emotional reaction].'

Think about how Notion might frame its mobile app problem. Instead of 'we need to improve mobile editing', they'd start from someone's actual experience: 'I am an author trying to capture ideas on mobile, but I can't create pages quickly because the app requires too many taps to reach the right workspace, which makes me feel frustrated.' The frame specifies who's affected, what they're attempting, what's blocking them, why, and the emotional impact.

An alternative comes from the Jobs to be Done community, which you will see in action in Chapter 8 through a famous study about why people buy milkshakes. Rather than emphasising the emotional side, job stories describe the job the customer is trying to accomplish. The format is: 'When [situation], I want to [motivation], so I can [outcome].'[14]

For Notion, we would rewrite as: 'When I have an idea while commuting, I want to capture it in the right workspace instantly, so I can trust that I'll find it later when I'm back at my computer.'

Both formats are effective. The point-of-view statement emphasises the emotional experience, while the job story focuses on the desired outcome and the situation that triggers the need. Choosing between them is less important than the discipline they both enforce, which is keeping people at the centre of your thinking.

How Might We technique

Sometimes the problem is clear, but your team are stuck on suggesting obvious solutions. The 'How Might We' question is designed for exactly this situation. Min Basadur developed this phrasing at Procter & Gamble in the 1970s, and it's now used widely across the Design Thinking community.[15]

Convert your problem into a question starting with those three words, and people look at the problem completely differently. 'How' changes the focus to practical solutions. 'Might' acknowledges we're exploring possibilities. 'We' makes it a collective challenge rather than pressure on any individual to have the answer.

Compare 'How might we help listeners discover new music they'll love?' to 'Users aren't discovering enough new content.' The first invites creative ideas, while the second sounds like a statement of fact. I have found it to be a super useful technique, not just in product development, but also at home. When my kids face a challenge and are adamant that there is no solution, it's a great way to encourage them to move from problem mode to solution mode.

The most common mistake is getting the scope wrong. 'How might we delight customers?' is too broad and gives no direction, while 'How might we add a tooltip to the settings page?' is too narrow because it's already decided on the solution. The sweet spot is focused enough to guide exploration but open enough to encourage multiple ideas. A good test is whether you can imagine at least five different answers to the question.

Working Backwards technique

So far, we've focused on problems affecting an existing product. But sometimes we get excited about a new product idea and overlook whether it's actually valuable to customers.

The Working Backwards method was developed at Amazon in the mid-2000s.[16] You imagine that the product already exists and write an internal press release announcing it to customers, then you work backwards to understand what problem it solves. It forces you to articulate the customer value before you build anything.

Let me show you how this works with a real example. When I hit my forties, I started noticing friends and colleagues constantly complaining that they'd forgotten their reading glasses. They'd struggle to read restaurant menus, medicine labels, and the small print on packaging. This seemed like a common problem affecting millions of people, so I had what felt like an aha moment: a mobile app that uses your phone's camera to magnify text when you don't have your reading glasses to hand. People over 40 always have their phones with them, so they'd never be caught out. I sketched the features and started getting excited about the potential.

Then I tried to write the press release, which opens with a heading and subheading capturing the product, the customer, and the benefit. Mine read: 'ReadNow helps you read small text anywhere when you've forgotten your reading glasses. For people over 40, ReadNow uses your phone's camera to magnify text so you never struggle to read menus, labels, or packaging again.' So far, so good.

Next comes a summary paragraph written as if the product has already launched, a problem paragraph from the customer's point of view, and a solution paragraph explaining how your product is different from what customers use today. The solution paragraph is where the flaw in my idea became obvious. My attempt: 'ReadNow is a mobile app that uses your phone's camera to magnify small text. Simply open the app, point your camera at the text you want to read, and ReadNow enlarges it on your screen. Today, customers with this problem use ... their phone's camera app to zoom in on text, or the built-in accessibility features that every smartphone already has.'

The moment I tried to articulate the differentiation, I realised I was solving a problem that already had a perfectly good solution sitting on everyone's phone. There was no meaningful reason for anyone to download a separate app.

It finishes with a quote from a hypothetical delighted customer and an FAQ that anticipates the difficult questions. When I tried to answer 'Why is this better than existing solutions?' I couldn't come up with anything compelling. The technique is valuable because it exposes ideas that haven't been fully thought through, and it forces you to ask the tricky questions before you build anything.

So, you'll be pleased to know, I won't be investing any more time or effort into ReadNow, at least until after I've finished writing this book.

MINDSET SHIFTS YOU NEED TO MAKE

Table 7.1 highlights the differences between traditional and discovery thinking.

THE $27 BILLION REFRAME

The framing techniques in this chapter might seem simple, but they can help you look at problems from a fresh perspective. History is full of founders who thought they were solving the right problem, but later found they needed to pivot towards a different one altogether.

We met Stewart Butterfield, the Slack co-founder, in Chapter 4. In 2012, he was running out of time. His company, Tiny Speck, had spent three years and $17 million building an online multiplayer game called Glitch, but it was failing to attract users.[17] Players would

Table 7.1 Traditional vs discovery thinking (find problems)

Traditional thinking	Discovery thinking
Waiting for problems to come to you	Actively hunting for problems and training yourself to search in the right places
Looking only at obvious sources such as usage reports and error logs	Seeking the less obvious sources, including non-users and proxy stakeholders
Trusting what people tell you in feedback	Going to where the work happens and watching what they actually do
Treating a feature request as the problem to solve	Digging for the underlying need beneath the request
Accepting a problem in the frame it arrives in	Questioning the frame and recognising it points you towards certain solutions
Framing problems around systems and technology	Framing problems around people and their experience
Writing vague problem statements	Writing specific, measurable, solution-agnostic statements
Baking the solution into the problem	Keeping the problem open enough to allow creative options
Treating framing as a one-off, set-once activity	Reframing as an ongoing discipline, even deep in delivery

finish the game in two days and never return. Butterfield faced a dilemma. Continue down their existing path or look for a different problem to solve.

What saved the company was a reframe. While building Glitch, the team had created an internal communication tool for their distributed workforce, and Butterfield noticed it had become essential to how they worked. The original frame had been 'How do we build a successful game?' and the new frame became 'How do we solve workplace communication?' That reframe led to Slack, which Salesforce acquired in 2021 for $27.7 billion.[18]

In Chapter 8 we will look at the next part of the FEATR funnel, Explore Needs. This is where we expand our understanding of the problem by getting to know our users, their environment, and the factors that influence them.

KEY TAKEAWAYS

- **The frame determines the solutions you consider:** The engineers saw a speed problem, the psychologist saw a boredom problem, and each frame led to completely different solutions.

- **A problem is the gap between the current state and the desired state:** You cannot define a problem without understanding the outcome people want to achieve.
- **Problems can be found in a variety of sources:** Support tickets, sales objections, internal chat channels, competitor reviews, and direct observation are all places worth hunting.
- **Well-framed problems share four qualities:** Specific enough to act on, broad enough to allow creative solutions, focused on people rather than systems, and measurable so you know when you have succeeded.
- **Different situations need different framing techniques:** 5W2H for clarity, SMART for success criteria, point-of-view or job stories for customer focus, How Might We for creative ideas, and Working Backwards to challenge assumptions about a new product.
- **Reframing is not a one-off activity:** Slack exists because Stewart Butterfield reframed from 'How do we build a successful game?' to 'How do we solve workplace communication?' Make it a regular practice rather than something you only do when things go wrong.
- **Framing connects to everything else in FEATR:** A well-framed problem guides your exploration, shapes your ideas, and defines your experiments.

8 EXPLORE THE NEEDS BEHIND THE PROBLEM

'Actions speak louder than survey responses.'

Paddy Dhanda

THE MILKSHAKE MYSTERY

In the early 2000s, a fast-food chain wanted to sell more milkshakes.[1] They had plenty of data insights informing them who was buying milkshakes and what flavours they preferred. Focus groups described their ideal milkshakes, and the food chain made every improvement customers asked for, but sales didn't improve.

Enter Clayton Christensen, the Harvard Business School professor, and Bob Moesta, a product innovation consultant. Instead of asking customers what they wanted, they took a different approach. They went to a restaurant and simply watched people buy milkshakes for an entire day.

They noticed some clear buying patterns. Roughly 40 per cent of all milkshakes were purchased in the early morning. These buyers were almost always alone, and they rarely bought anything else. After picking up their drinks, they walked straight to their cars and drove away.

When the researchers went back the next day and asked morning buyers what was going on, their responses took them by surprise. These people faced long, boring commutes. They needed something that would last the whole journey and suppress their hunger until lunchtime. None of the alternatives worked. A banana is eaten in a couple of minutes, a bagel leaves crumbs everywhere, and a doughnut gives you a sticky steering wheel. But the thick milkshake, consumed slowly through a narrow straw, did all these jobs better than anything else.

The afternoon customers were buying milkshakes for entirely different reasons. These were exhausted parents who wanted to treat the kids after school. Contrary to what the restaurant had assumed, the milkshake wasn't competing with other milkshakes. In the morning it competed with bananas, bagels, and breakfast, and in the afternoon it competed with trips to the toy shop.

Confucius understood this principle over 2,000 years ago. After one of his students failed to act on his promises again and again, he reflected: 'At first, I used to listen to what people said and expect them to act accordingly. Now I listen to what people say and watch what they do.'[2] The fast-food chain had plenty of knowledge about what customers were buying, but it lacked an understanding of why those customers were buying. That understanding only came from observing their real behaviour.

Figure 8.1 The milkshake commute

This research became known as Jobs to be Done, the wider methodology behind the job story format we looked at in Chapter 7.

In this chapter, we will look at the next part of the discovery funnel, Explore Needs. This is where we expand our understanding of the problem by looking at our user needs, the environment around them, and the wider factors that shape how they behave. For the purposes of this book, we will focus mostly on users, because that is where you are likely to spend most of your time and effort.

REQUESTS, PREFERENCES, NEEDS, AND REQUIREMENTS

There is a good reason why I use the word *needs* over *requests*, *preferences* or even *requirements*. These four words get thrown around as if they mean the same thing, but they are fundamentally different, and confusing them can lead to misalignment across the team.

The *request* is like a demand: 'I need an export to Excel button.' It sounds specific and actionable, which is exactly why it is so dangerous. The request is almost always a solution disguised as a problem because it feels like the user has already done the hard work and is handing you an answer, when what is more useful is the reason why they are making the request.

The *preference* is how the user currently does things: 'I always export data to Excel before I email it.' This sounds credible since it's what the user does, but in reality it is a habit. Just because we have formed a habit doesn't mean it is a good one. Someone who has always exported to Excel does so because that button existed and they learned to use it, not because exporting to Excel represents the best way to complete the task.

The *need* is the outcome they are trying to achieve, combined with the constraints they are working within: 'I need to share this analysis with my client, who doesn't have access to our reporting platform.' This is more useful. The need might well be satisfied by an export button, but it could also be satisfied by a shareable link that can be emailed or by granting limited access to the platform.

The *requirement* is what emerges after you have done the work to understand the need and validated that it is worth solving. The problem is that too many teams treat requests as if they were requirements, jumping straight from what a user asked for to what gets built, without ever stopping to understand the user.

The power plant problem

Let me share a real-world example of what can happen when you are presented with a request before you have explored the actual needs of your users.

Susanne Krogh-Hansen, a lead strategic designer, once worked with a large energy company where someone at headquarters had come up with what seemed like a reasonable request.[3] She had been requested to build an app for maintenance workers.

The workers were walking around a power plant with pen and paper, writing down faults when they spotted something that needed fixing. They then had to walk all the way back to the office and log the maintenance request on their SAP application.

The idea of an app sounded logical, so they could instantly log the requests without having to waste time walking back and forth to the office. Then Susanne went to the power plant and spoke to the people who would actually have to use it.

The maintenance workers were not sitting at a desk with clean hands and a spare phone charger nearby. They were working in a tough physical environment, often wearing large protective gloves, with oil and dirt on their hands. For safety reasons, they also had to keep one hand on the handrail when moving around the plant.

One of them looked at Susanne and asked where exactly were they supposed to keep a mobile phone. The request had been to build an app, but the need was a safe and practical way for workers to capture maintenance issues while moving through a power plant under difficult working conditions.

So Susanne and the team started small. Before building anything, they gave the workers wooden blocks that were roughly the same size as a mobile phone. They gave the workers a simple instruction: carry the block around for a week in their overalls.

Once they had learned that carrying a phone could work, they brought some of the workers into the design process. Together, they sketched out screens, tested how large the buttons needed to be for someone pressing them with big thumbs, and explored whether different gloves could allow them to practically use the phone.

Susanne told me it took around two years before the users fully adopted the app. But by the end, the product had been designed around the environment in which the users had to work.

My favourite part of the story is what happened afterwards. One of the workers from the original workshops came back to Susanne and told her there was now a huge problem.

She panicked for a moment. Then he laughed and explained that he now had to go to the gym every day because he was no longer getting his steps in from walking back and forth to the office.

What started as a request for an app became something more useful because Susanne did not treat the first idea as the requirement. She went to where the work happened, observed the environment, listened to the users, and helped shape the request into a usable product.

MIND THE USER GAP

If you have ever travelled on the London Underground, you'll be familiar with the phrase, 'Mind the gap.' It warns you about the space between the platform and the train, a space that's dangerous if you don't watch your step. Building products has gaps, too. They're not physical, but are the space between what we assume about users and how they will really behave.

People are unpredictable because they often act in ways we don't expect. They say one thing and do something completely different, or they find workarounds we never imagined. And even when we think we've figured out what they need, their priorities change, so we're constantly trying to close the gap in our understanding. Having worked with many different types of users over the past 25 years, I'd like to share four of my biggest learnings, which I refer to as the user gap, the say/do gap, the design gap, and the logic gap.

The user gap

Product teams love talking about 'the user' as if there's a single person whose needs we can figure out. But the word itself is misleading, because many of the people involved in buying and benefiting from your product will never actually use it.

We write user stories that begin 'As a user, I want to ...'. But the word 'user' encourages us to have tunnel vision because we forget about the other people who are also involved. This is the user gap, and it's the distance between who we think we're building for and the wider network of stakeholders who determine whether our product succeeds or fails.

Back in 1972, researchers Frederick Webster and Yoram Wind studied how companies make purchasing decisions.[4] They found that six distinct roles shape whether something gets bought, and the person who uses the product day-to-day is only one of them. Initiators are the people who first recognise that a problem exists and get the ball rolling. Users are the people who will actually work with the product day-to-day. Influencers are the people whose expertise or experience shapes the direction, even if they don't have formal authority. Deciders are the people who can say yes or no. Buyers are the people who negotiate terms and control the budget. And gatekeepers control access to information or to other stakeholders.

When you start a new discovery initiative, try mapping your stakeholders against these six roles. For each person, write down what they care about, what success looks like from their perspective, and what concerns might lead them to block or resist the work. You'll quickly see that 'the user' is just one piece of a much larger picture, and often not the most influential piece when it comes to whether your product actually gets funded or built.

The say/do gap

Even once you've mapped out who is involved, you face another problem. When I first became a business analyst, I assumed the role would be straightforward. You simply bring together a group of users and ask them what they want and document it. But in reality, there is a gap between what people say and what they eventually do.

David Ogilvy, the British advertising executive who became known as the father of modern advertising, summed it up back in 1963: 'The problem with market research is that people don't think how they feel, they don't say what they think, and they don't do what they say.'[5]

Behavioural scientists call this disconnect the say/do gap.

Romanian emergency services shortcuts

A few years ago, Filip Giorgi, a business analyst, worked on the re-engineering of Romania's 112 Emergency Service.[6] This was the platform used by call handlers when someone dialled the European emergency number. His team had access to a test environment and spent months interviewing experienced subject matter experts to gather requirements for the new version.

On paper, things were going well. The team had spoken to knowledgeable people and mapped the existing system in detail. After 8–10 months, they had built what they believed was a workable MVP (minimum viable product), and decided to visit the real emergency centre to watch call handlers in action.

That visit changed everything. They noticed something that had never come up in the requirements conversations. The call handlers barely touched the mouse. Instead, they moved through the system at speed using keyboard shortcuts, jumping between fields and triggering functions in fractions of a second. In an emergency environment, where every second counts, that speed was part of how they did the job. The problem was that the MVP did not support any of it.

When Filip's team went back to ask why nobody had mentioned the shortcuts, they were told it was obvious. The behaviour was such a natural part of the way they worked that they did not think it was a requirement worth raising.

The gap between intention and action is evidence that something is getting in their way, which presents opportunities for product people. Your job in discovery is to find out what that something is – and people are already showing you, if you know where to look.

The design gap

If you cannot trust what people say, you need to watch what they do. In Chapter 7, we looked at the value of observing people where the work happens, but observation only helps if you know what to look for.

The design gap is the space between how we expect people to use our products and how they really do use them. What I've learned to watch for are the shortcuts people create when your design doesn't quite meet their needs. They develop workarounds that become 'business as usual' behaviour, and they forget to mention them.

Desire paths in products and parks

Urban planners have been studying this behaviour for decades, and they call them desire paths.[7] A desire path is the worn trail that appears across the grass when people take a shortcut (Figure 8.2). You see them in parks, where the official path curves elegantly around a corner while a diagonal line cuts straight across the lawn. Every time I drop my kids off at Sunday school in Walsall, I end up using one, because it feels like it will save me a few valuable seconds, even though it will make very little difference.

In Finland, city planners visit parks immediately after the first snowfall, when the existing paths are completely hidden under a blanket of snow. People naturally choose their own routes across the fresh snow, and the planners construct their pathways accordingly, where people actually walk rather than trying to predict the path they might take.[8]

Figure 8.2 A desire path, W Bromwich Street, Walsall

Every product has desire paths, too. Remember the sticky notes covering those call centre monitors in Chapter 7? That was a desire path. Some of the most successful product features started as desire paths that companies were smart enough to notice. Twitter's hashtag, the @reply, and the retweet were all invented by users before Twitter built them into the platform.

A more recent example comes from Anthropic, the company behind the AI tool Claude. When they released Claude Code, a terminal-based coding tool designed for software engineers, they started noticing something unexpected. Non-engineers were downloading it and using it for tasks that had nothing to do with writing software. One person was using it to monitor their tomato plants. Another was using it to book theatre tickets. Someone else used it to recover wedding photos from a corrupted hard drive. These people were prepared to use a text-based terminal, which is one of the most intimidating interfaces in computing, just to use a product that was never designed for them.

Boris Cherny, head of Claude Code, told *Fortune* magazine that the decision about what to do next was straightforward once they recognised what the signals were telling them. 'It was just kind of obvious that Cowork is the next step', he said. 'We just want to make it much easier for non-programmers.' His team built Cowork, a version of Claude Code designed for non-technical tasks, in roughly a week and a half.[9]

The launch shook up the software industry so badly that it contributed to a near-trillion-dollar selloff in software stocks, with Microsoft alone losing roughly $220 billion in market value in a single week before licensing the technology and building its own version. All of that from a product that was created because someone noticed where the desire paths were forming.

The logic gap

You might think that if you build the best possible product, then people will embrace it. But if they are given multiple options to choose from, there is still a risk that they won't, regardless of how good your product is.

The logic gap is the distance between how we think people make decisions and how they actually decide. We assume that people carefully weigh up their options and logically choose the best one. But human decision-making is far messier than any of us would like to admit. In 1988, economists William Samuelson and Richard Zeckhauser ran a simple experiment that demonstrated this.[10] They gave participants a hypothetical inheritance from a deceased uncle that included a portfolio of investments. Some participants were told the portfolio was already committed to certain investments, while others were told they could invest however they wanted. Surprisingly, participants were much more likely to stick with an investment when they were told they already held it, even when better alternatives were available. And the bias got stronger as more options were added to the mix.

People often favour what they already have, simply because sticking with the existing choice feels easier than changing it. They make decisions based on emotion, then try to convince themselves they made the right choice afterwards.

A customer might tell you they chose your competitor because of better features, when the real reason is that a colleague mentioned the name last week and it felt familiar when they started searching. A subscriber might say they cancelled because of price, when the actual trigger was being penalised for a late return and feeling embarrassed about it.

This is why rational arguments alone rarely change minds. If you want people to switch to your product, you need to build an emotional connection that is compelling enough for them to let go of the alternative option.

Bridging the gaps

Unlike the Tube station, where the gap between train and platform is fixed, the gaps in user understanding can be closed. The user gap reminds you to map the full range of stakeholders, not just the person clicking buttons. The say/do gap warns you to watch behaviour rather than relying on what stakeholders say. The design gap encourages you to look for the workarounds that reveal unmet needs. And the logic gap explains why even if your product is better, it won't win on value alone.

Figure 8.3 Mind the gap

TECHNIQUES FOR EXPLORING NEEDS

Looking at problems from multiple angles with Logical Levels

The milkshake story shows that when we are faced with a problem, we tend to immediately jump to obvious solutions. If the software is slow, make it faster. If milkshake sales are falling, then make better milkshakes. But Einstein famously taught us, 'A new type of thinking is essential if mankind is to survive and move toward higher levels.'[11] His point was that problems created at one level of thinking cannot be solved at that same level.

In product discovery, this means that if someone isn't using your product the way you expected, simply changing the interface or adding a new feature won't help if the real issue is that they don't trust it or don't see value in using it for their work. You would be treating the symptom rather than the cause.

Robert Dilts, a pioneer in neurolinguistic programming, developed a framework in the 1980s that helps explain why obvious fixes so often fail. He called it Logical Levels, and it identifies six levels at which problems can occur:[12]

- **Environment** is about where and when the problem happens. The morning milkshake buyers faced a long and boring commute.
- **Behaviour** is what people are doing or not doing. We often look at data without understanding the reasons behind it. The milkshake sales spiked early in the morning, but nobody had asked why.
- **Capability** is about what skills or knowledge might be missing. For the milkshake buyers, this wasn't the problem since ordering a milkshake is simple enough. But imagine if the restaurant had introduced a self-service kiosk with a confusing menu; suddenly, capability becomes the barrier.
- **Beliefs** are what people think about themselves or the situation. The morning commuters believed that a milkshake was an acceptable breakfast substitute, a belief that might surprise nutritionists but made perfect sense in the context of a boring drive.
- **Identity** is how people see themselves. The milkshake buyers saw themselves as practical problem-solvers, making the best of a tedious commute.
- **Purpose** is the larger mission being served. For the morning buyer, the purpose wasn't nutrition or even taste, it was getting through a boring commute with something interesting to do.

Working the pyramid up and down

The way I use this framework is to draw it out as a pyramid and work from the bottom, one level at a time, asking questions at each stage. Once I reach the top, I work back down and ask how we might address the issue at each level.

For the milkshake problem, at the purpose level, the restaurant could position milkshakes as the perfect driving companion rather than a dessert. At the identity level, marketing could speak to practical, time-pressed professionals who deserve something that works as hard as they do. At the beliefs level, featuring milkshakes on breakfast menus could shift the perception that they are only a dessert option. At the capability level, a dedicated drive-through lane for commuters or a mobile pre-order option could make morning purchases easier. At the behaviour level, a thicker straw or a resealable cup could make sipping easier while driving. And at the environment level, extending opening hours and placing milkshakes at eye level near the morning counter could capture early commuters.

This simple technique is extremely powerful, as it shows that no single fix would have completely resolved the issue. But you cannot fix everything at once, and trying to address all six levels simultaneously will spread your efforts too thin. I sometimes ask teams to score the problem at each level so we can prioritise where the solution will have the greatest impact.

Motivations: empathy maps

Jeff Bezos was famous for leaving an empty chair at Amazon's most important meetings. When executives asked who it was for, he told them it represented the customer, 'the most important person in the room'.[13] Before you can solve someone's problem, you need to understand them deeply – and by deeply, I mean going beyond learning what they do to knowing what they see, hear, think, and feel.

An empathy map gives you a structured way to capture all of these insights on a single page. Dave Gray created the empathy map at XPLANE as a way to help teams step outside their own assumptions and understand the people they are trying to serve. But empathy maps have become one of the most misunderstood tools in product discovery, and the problem is not the canvas itself but the order in which teams fill it out.

Gray updated his guidance in 2017 with a specific sequence that produces better results.[14] Start with the Goal section at the top of the canvas. This asks 'Who are we empathising with?' and 'What do they need to do?' Next, work clockwise through the outer quadrants, focusing on what you can observe. Only after completing this should you move to the centre of the map and ask what they might think and feel.

Apollo Hospitals in India discovered the value of empathy maps when they tried to improve the experience of oncology patients.[15] The hospital trained staff to use empathy maps at key touchpoints in the patient journey. Patient satisfaction improved by 46 per cent, and complaints dropped by 78 per cent.

Empathy maps work best when you have already gathered real data through interviews or observation. It's important to remember that they are a tool for synthesising insights and not a tool for brainstorming. So if your team is filling out an empathy map based on what they imagine users think and feel, then you are not building empathy. You are documenting assumptions, and those assumptions need to be tested.

Processes: journey maps

Empathy maps are great tools for capturing how someone sees a situation at a point in time, but what if you want to analyse a process and identify the steps that cause the greatest pain for the customer? The traditional approach is to produce a process flow diagram with swim lanes and neat boxes, but if we want to understand the emotional experience of why someone becomes a loyal customer or walks away frustrated, then just mapping out what people do won't help. For that, we use journey maps.

McKinsey studied companies across insurance, retail banking, and pay TV and found that how customers feel about the entire process weighs more heavily than how they feel about any single individual step.[16] One media company discovered that customers rated their call centre, website, and their field technicians above 90 per cent, but satisfaction across the entire onboarding process was nearly 40 per cent lower.

When building a journey map, start with a single persona trying to accomplish a specific goal. Identify the high-level stages from the customer's perspective, and not your organisation's departments. Someone booking a holiday doesn't think about your sales process, they think about where they want to go and whether they can afford it.

Customers do not remember every moment of an experience. They remember how they felt at the end and the most emotional moments during the process. Daniel Kahneman, who won the Nobel Prize for his work on decision-making, called this the peak-end rule.[17] This is why IKEA sells hot dogs and ice cream for almost nothing after you've paid at the checkout. Shopping at IKEA can be exhausting and expensive, but the last thing you experience is a cheap treat that leaves you feeling good.

Just as with any technique, simply following the steps doesn't guarantee success. We have to apply a discovery mindset by probing and being curious where we feel it will reveal new insights, and that requires human intuition, but also building a bank of powerful questions. In Chapter 16 we look at how you can ask better questions and which ones to ask in different situations.

THE AI WARNING

Why synthetic research cannot replace real observation

It's tempting to skip the hard work of talking to real people and let AI do the research for you instead. Tools now exist that promise to simulate user interviews and generate synthetic personas without ever speaking to a single customer. But there is a fundamental problem with using AI to understand human behaviour, and it relates directly to the say/do gap we explored earlier.

AI models are trained on the internet, and the internet is the world's largest collection of what people say rather than what they do. If you think about the blog articles or social media posts you have posted, how much have you been prepared to reveal about yourself? Much of what we see reflects the aspirational self rather than the situational self. When you ask an AI to simulate a user interview, it will simulate the person who says they want to eat healthy and read more books. It will not simulate the person who orders a takeaway pizza, skips the gym because it's raining, and then feels guilty afterwards. That second person is the one you are more likely to be building for.

The bias in the training data

The training data itself is far from representative. Only 20 per cent of the world's population speaks English at home, yet nearly half of all training data for major AI models is in English.[18] When Cornell University researchers asked five versions of GPT to answer questions drawn from a global values survey, the responses consistently aligned with the values of English-speaking and Protestant European countries rather than reflecting real diversity.[19]

Researchers at Nielsen Norman Group put synthetic user interviews to the test by running them alongside studies they had already conducted with real participants.[20]

The synthetic users were consistently overoptimistic and demonstrated what the researchers called sycophancy, the tendency for AI models to tell you what you want to hear rather than what is true.

Jeff Sauro and his colleagues found a similar pattern when they tested ChatGPT on the IRS website, where the AI found the correct navigation path on nearly every task while real people frequently took the wrong direction.[21]

Your human edge

I'm not suggesting that AI has no role in user research. It can process interview transcripts in seconds and reveal patterns across multiple conversations that you might otherwise have missed. It can summarise large datasets and help you prepare better interview questions before you sit down with actual users.

But AI cannot replace the act of observing real behaviour. Only humans can sit in the fast-food restaurant at half past six in the morning and notice that the people buying milkshakes are alone and heading straight to their cars. Equally, it's only humans who could notice a handwritten note stuck to a user's monitor and ask why it's there. AI cannot pick up on the slight hesitation in a customer's voice when they say everything is fine.

At least not yet, and that's where your human edge becomes your competitive advantage over your competitors, who are all looking for shortcuts to skip the valuable act of understanding your user needs.

MINDSET SHIFTS YOU NEED TO MAKE

Table 8.1 outlines the necessary shift in thinking.

Table 8.1 Traditional vs discovery thinking (explore needs)

Traditional thinking	Discovery thinking
Believing what stakeholders say they will do	Watching what they actually do
Dismissing workarounds as edge cases or noise	Reading workarounds as desire paths that reveal unmet needs
Assuming people choose the best option rationally	Accepting that decisions are messy, emotional, and driven by familiarity
Letting AI simulate users as your primary option to save time	Valuing human observation of real behaviour as your edge

Next, we will get creative at the Assess Ideas stage of the FEATR funnel. We will use the understanding we have built about the user needs and explore how we can generate ideas to resolve the problems we have framed. That is a process of divergent thinking where we come up with many possibilities. We focus on how we unlock our creativity, because it is one of our most important human skills in the age of AI. But as we will find out, it's also a skill that declines as we grow older. We will also be examining techniques from Design Thinking, lateral thinking, and improvisational theatre that help teams think beyond the obvious. Then we converge, by narrowing down what we should spend our time and effort on by looking at different prioritisation techniques.

KEY TAKEAWAYS

- **Requests are not the same as needs:** A request is almost always a solution disguised as a problem. The real need is the outcome the user is trying to achieve, and understanding that outcome opens up a wider range of possible solutions than the one the user asked for.
- **'The user' is misleading because it implies one person:** Webster and Wind's research showed that six distinct roles shape purchasing decisions, and the person who uses the product day-to-day is only one of them.
- **Watch behaviour, not stated intentions:** The say/do gap means people consistently claim they will do one thing and then do another.
- **Desire paths reveal what users actually need:** When people create workarounds in your product, they are showing you where the design fails to meet their needs.
- **The Logical Levels framework prevents surface-level fixes:** Problems can exist at the environment, behaviour, capability, belief, identity, or purpose level, and a solution that only addresses the wrong level will fail.
- **Empathy maps work best as synthesis tools, not brainstorming tools:** Fill them out using real data from interviews or observation.
- **Journey maps should start and end where the customer does:** McKinsey found that how customers feel about the entire process weighs more heavily than how they feel about any single step.
- **AI can support user research, but cannot replace observing real behaviour:** Synthetic users are overoptimistic and reflect the aspirational self rather than the situational self. Your human ability to observe, probe, and notice what people don't say remains your competitive advantage.

9 GENERATE AND ASSESS CREATIVE IDEAS

'A brainstorm is like a box of chocolates, you never know which idea you're going to get.'

Paddy Dhanda

Steve Jobs once described creativity as 'just connecting things'.[1] That is a useful way to think about this stage of discovery, because ideas rarely appear out of nowhere. More often, they emerge when we connect observations, frustrations, behaviours, and patterns that were already sitting in front of us.

That is why we spent the previous chapter exploring the context around our users and their environment. Understanding a problem counts for little if we cannot turn those insights into useful ideas. The richer our understanding, the more likely we are to spot opportunities that are not only creative but also relevant to the problem we are trying to solve.

In product work, those ideas are often smaller than we expect. They are rarely the grand inventions that make it into history books. More often, they are small improvements that remove friction from an experience.

Take copy and paste, for instance. It did not create a whole new category of software, but it transformed how people work with information because it recognised something deeply human. We rarely get things right the first time. We move ideas around, edit, reshape, and rethink.

The best ideas often feel obvious in hindsight, but once they exist it becomes hard to imagine life without them. Yet somebody had to notice the frustration first and connect the dots to come up with a solution, and that is the type of thinking this chapter is about.

We move to the Assess Ideas stage of the product discovery thinking process, the A in the FEATR funnel. It has two parts. The first is about generating creative ideas, where we open up our imagination and think freely about the possibilities to solve the problem at hand. The second part requires us to use our judgement to identify which of those ideas we want to take forward and validate through the next step in the funnel.

UNDERSTANDING IDEAS

What is an idea?

The dictionary defines an idea as 'a thought or suggestion as to a possible course of action'.[2] In product discovery, an idea is a possible way of addressing a problem or an opportunity that we have not yet tested. The key point to remember is that it's merely a suggested way of resolving something, rather than it being a firm commitment.

Also, ideas are not always features. We tend to assume that solving a problem means adding something to the product – a new button, screen, or setting. An idea can just as easily be a change to a process, or a different message we present to the user. But more importantly, it can be something we remove from the product as opposed to build.

The process of generating ideas is known as ideation. Instead of hunting for the single right answer, you produce as broad a set of possibilities as you can and hold off on judging any of them until later. That deliberate split between generating first and judging second is the thought process we will explore in the first half of this chapter, and it is the opposite of how most of us were trained to think.

What makes a good idea?

The other distinction I want to make is that not all ideas are equal. Some are better than others. Throughout this book, I have already shared plenty of examples of bad ideas, where products failed and features were abandoned, just like our old friend Clippy. But what does a genuinely good idea look like? Let me share one of my favourite examples that shows the best ideas don't have to be complicated.

I was on my way to a conference and had a couple of hours between connecting flights at Amsterdam's Schiphol Airport. Standing in the men's toilets, I noticed a small image set into the urinal, and it reminded me of a piece of creative problem-solving that I often share when I teach.

In the early 1990s, the cleaning team at Amsterdam's Schiphol Airport had a problem. As anyone who has shared a bathroom with men will tell you, we are not always the most accurate when standing at a urinal, so spillages are common. The thing is, Schiphol has over 1,200 toilets across the airport for its travellers, so when you multiply those spillages across all of the facilities, it adds up to an expensive cleaning problem. Putting up signs asking people to aim more carefully was never going to work, and a full redesign of the facilities was not an option either, because it would have been far too expensive.

So Jos van Bedaf, the manager of the cleaning department, had a moment of inspiration. He remembered a trick he had learned during his army days decades earlier. But the idea sounded way too simple to work. It involved etching a small image of a black housefly into each urinal bowl, just above the drain. The thinking behind it was that if you give men a target they cannot help aiming at it.

That tiny visual cue changed behaviour and reduced cleaning costs by more than 20 per cent.[3] The solution to the problem of spillages did not require a team of urinal experts or an extravagant engineering fix. It came from someone who had connected their past experiences and had context about the problem. In many ways, the fact that the cleaning manager did not have an engineering background may have been a benefit rather than a gap, because he was able to think creatively without being pushed down a particular line of thinking.

I now regularly see variations of the fly in the urinal, everything from planes (Figure 9.1) to golf flags, and more recently I saw an even more creative version. It was in a Canadian pub in Toronto, where, instead of a painted image, it was a tiny three-dimensional goal and a football (Figure 9.2).

Figure 9.1 Urinal at Amsterdam Schiphol Airport

Figure 9.2 Urinal in a Toronto pub

If we go by a more formal definition of creativity, psychologists define it as the ability to produce something that is both novel and useful, and the fly is both of these things.[4] It was novel because nobody expected a cartoon insect to change how people behaved, and it was useful because it solved a real and costly problem.

Good ideas tend to share a third quality, which is timing. Video calling existed for decades before Zoom made it part of everyday life, and what changed was not the idea but the conditions around it, because faster home internet and a sudden global need to work from home made it usable for everyone at once. An idea that is novel and useful can still go nowhere if the world is not ready for it, and the same idea can take off years later when circumstances have changed.

A good idea, therefore, is one that is new, useful, and needed at that time. But most of us find it difficult to come up with good ideas, because we assume that we are simply not the creative type. That assumption turns out to be wrong, and why it is wrong is the subject of the next part of this chapter.

THE CREATIVITY CHALLENGE

The ability to generate novel ideas is not a gift handed to a lucky few at birth. It is something we were all born with, but the problem is that some of us have slowly lost it.

Most people divide the world into two categories. There are the 'creatives' such as artists and writers, the ones who wear quirky clothes and come up with wild ideas, and then there's everyone else. If you work in tech, you probably put yourself in the second category.

We saw a moment ago that creativity is the ability to produce something novel and useful. Framed that way, creativity stops being exclusive to the arts and becomes part of almost every profession. Think about a nurse who works out a different way to calm an anxious patient by dimming the lights. As for product people, we are in the creativity business, whether we realise it or not.

The difference is that most of us were never taught to see it that way. Something happens between childhood and adulthood that makes us forget we ever had this ability, and to understand that, we need to look at a group of people who are far more creative than the rest of us, yet they cannot even tie their own shoelaces.

In 1968, George Land was given an unusual assignment. He had spent a decade researching creativity and innovation, and NASA wanted his help finding the engineers and scientists most able to solve problems nobody had cracked before. Land and his colleague Beth Jarman built an assessment to measure creative potential.[5]

The test measured what psychologists call divergent thinking, the ability to look at a problem and generate many possible answers rather than converging on a single correct one. It worked well at NASA, but it left Land with a bigger question. If the test could spot creative genius in adults, what would it find in children?

Land and Jarman gave it to 1,600 children on the US Head Start programme, all aged between three and five. When I run this exercise in workshops and ask people to guess how many of those children scored at genius level for divergent thinking, people rarely get the right answer. The figure was 98 per cent. By adulthood, it collapses to around 2 per cent. Somewhere between doodling and learning to file a tax return, the overwhelming majority of us lose an ability we were all born with. We do not lose it for lack of intelligence, because we gain knowledge and experience as we age; instead, what disappears is the willingness to think freely and to propose ideas without first talking ourselves out of them.

The World Economic Forum's *Future of Jobs Report* asked employers around the world which skills are rising fastest in importance, and creative thinking came out fourth.[6] Demand for the very thing we have been losing is increasing. As AI handles more of our routine work, our uniquely human capabilities become increasingly important. Machines can process information faster and more efficiently than any human ever could, but what they cannot do, at least not yet, is dream up things that are based on the lived personal experiences that each of us has. An AI model could have generated 1,000 cleaning proposals in seconds, but it is hard to imagine any of them being the fly that helped an airport clean up its urinals.

Our value moves to the work machines cannot do, understanding problems that users themselves struggle to put into words, and generating creative options worth testing. Which leaves an obvious question. If most of us mislaid our creative confidence somewhere along the way, how do we get it back?

REBUILDING CREATIVE CONFIDENCE

Tom Kelley and David Kelley, the brothers behind IDEO and Stanford's d.school, have spent their careers helping people rediscover their creative potential. In their 2013 book, they introduced the idea of creative confidence, which they describe as the belief that you can create and have a creative impact on the world around you.[7] Notice that this definition says nothing about artistic talent or any specific skill. It is simply the belief that you have the ability to create things of value.

At Stanford, David Kelley met Albert Bandura, one of the most influential psychologists of the 20th century. Bandura had developed a technique called guided mastery for treating severe phobias.[8] Instead of talking about snakes or analysing the origins of their fear, he designed a carefully structured series of experiences for people with paralysing snake phobias. Patients started by watching a snake through a two-way mirror, then gradually moved closer over multiple sessions until they could touch it with their bare hands. It was a series of baby steps that built confidence one step at a time.

Bandura called this self-efficacy, the belief that you can achieve what you set out to do. Kelley realised that creative confidence works the same way. We cannot simply tell people to be more creative, any more than we can tell someone with a phobia to stop being scared, but through a series of small creative successes, we can rebuild the belief that we are able to create.

The MRI that made children smile

One of the clearest examples of creative confidence in action comes from Doug Dietz, an engineer who discovered that his technical masterpiece was terrifying the very people it was meant to help.

Dietz was a 24-year veteran of GE Healthcare who had won numerous awards for his MRI machine designs. One day, he visited a hospital to see his latest creation in action and watched as a little girl approached the scanner with her parents. She was crying and clearly terrified, and nothing they said could comfort her.[9] He learned that nearly 80 per cent of paediatric patients had to be sedated before MRI scans, because children were being placed in a dark, long tube with a loud thumping sound. From an engineering point of view, the machine was brilliant, but the experience was frightening and intimidating.

Dietz was so shaken by what he saw that he felt compelled to make things better. He enrolled on a Design Thinking course at Stanford's d.school, and as part of his training he spent time with child life specialists and observed how children play. Redesigning the machine itself would have meant years of regulatory approval, so instead, he focused on the experience around it. He created what he called the 'Adventure Series', turning MRI rooms into pirate ships, rocket launches, and undersea worlds. Children no longer entered a scary medical machine, they set off on an adventure. If you search for 'CT Pirate Island Adventure' online, the images that come back could easily be mistaken for a ride at a theme park.

Sedation rates fell from 80 per cent to just 10 per cent, and one little girl, after her scan was finished, turned to her mother and asked whether they could come back tomorrow.

Figure 9.3 The adventure MRI

Dietz had no special artistic training or design background. He was an engineer who believed he could make a difference, and that belief gave him the courage to step outside his comfort zone and try something completely new.

Training your creative muscles

When I spoke with Professor David Cropley, a creativity researcher at the University of South Australia, he made the point that the more you practise creativity, the more natural it becomes.[10] One of his most practical suggestions was surprisingly simple.

Think of an everyday object, he explained, like a screwdriver, then ask yourself what function it performs. It's obviously a tool we use to tighten or loosen screws. Now imagine you have lost your screwdriver but still need to achieve the same goal. What other ways could you apply rotational force? Your fingers, a coin slotted into the head, a knife, the edge of a credit card, even a piece of string wrapped around the screw head. The exercise trains divergent thinking rather than pushing you towards one correct solution, and it's the sort of thing you can do in your head on the way to work.

Cropley also stressed that creativity depends on openness to new experiences, which is one of the personality traits most strongly linked to it. People who score highly on openness tend to do better on creativity tests because they can imagine possibilities more easily. If openness doesn't come naturally, he suggests building it through small experiments such as driving a different route to work, or trying a new dish at your favourite restaurant. The risk is low because the worst case is you arrive five minutes late, and the more you do things like that, the more you condition yourself against the discomfort that comes with trying something new.

Over the years, I have facilitated hundreds of innovation workshops, and what I have come to realise is that there is no magic formula for boosting creativity, because creative confidence isn't something you can switch on or off. It builds gradually through repeated experiences that teach people it is safe to think differently.

The most reliable way I have found to create those experiences is through well-designed team activities built on two ingredients. One is creative constraints, which help us focus. The other is play, which switches on the exploratory behaviour we relied on as children.

The power of constraints

This might sound counterintuitive, but limitations often spark better ideas than complete freedom does. One of the most loved children's books in history exists because of a constraint. In 1960, Bennett Cerf, the founder of Random House, bet Theodor Geisel, better known as Dr Seuss, that he couldn't write an engaging children's book using only 50 different words. Seuss had just published *The Cat in the Hat* using 236 words, which was seen as an achievement in itself, and 50 words seemed impossible. He accepted the challenge anyway, reportedly keeping charts and checklists on his wall to track every word he used, treating it as a puzzle as much as a creative exercise.

The result was *Green Eggs and Ham*, one of the best-selling children's books of all time, with more than 200 million copies sold. The constraint pushed Seuss to find solutions he never would have discovered with no limits at all. Catrinel Haught-Tromp, a cognitive psychologist, studied this and published her findings as 'The Green Eggs and Ham hypothesis', confirming what the bet had shown, that constraints can help creativity by forcing us to think differently.[11]

A constraint focuses the team and creates the pressure to finish. You can use this deliberately in a discovery session, because if a team is generating ideas freely and getting nowhere, you can give them an artificial limit and watch what happens. Ask them what they would build if they only had a week, or only one screen to work with, or no budget at all for new development. The limit does not have to be real to be useful, since the point is to push the group away from the expensive and obvious answer and towards something more creative.

The power of play

To unlock genuine creativity, we can engage a passion that most of us abandoned in childhood.

Let me explain by going back to nature. A wildlife photographer in northern Canada filmed astonishing footage of a wild polar bear approaching a team of sledge dogs that were tied up, and everyone watching expected the bear to attack.[12] Instead, the bear approached with what animal behaviourists call a play signal, a particular head movement animals use to show non-aggressive intent. One of the dogs responded with its own play signal, and what followed was magical as they wrestled and tumbled together. The bear came back every night for a week to play with the dogs.

Stuart Brown, a psychiatrist who studies play, uses this story to make a serious point, which is that play is a biological necessity that helps us solve problems and adapt. It's how mammals learn to deal with complex, unpredictable environments and respond to situations they have never met before.

Being playful isn't only about having fun. Frank Wilson, a neurologist, found that the hand has more neural connections to the brain than any other part of the body, which suggests that when we build and create with our hands, we tap into pathways that conversation alone struggles to reach.[13]

In my experience, this is why approaches like LEGO Serious Play work. It is a facilitation method where people build models with bricks to think through problems and then explain what they have made.

I remember running a LEGO Serious Play session for a team that wanted to connect more deeply with one another. I gave each person the same set of bricks and asked them to build an object or concept that symbolised why they enjoyed working in the team.

They came up with all sorts of creations. One person built a tower with different coloured bricks, explaining that each layer represented a different strength in the group. Another built a tiny shelter, saying the team gave them a place where they felt safe to ask for help.

Then something unexpected happened: the team manager burst into tears, and for a moment I panicked. As the facilitator, your mind immediately jumps to the worst conclusion. Had I pushed someone too far? Had I handled the exercise badly? But when I checked in with her, the reason was something entirely different.

She told me she had no idea her team felt this way. Hearing people describe the team as a place of safety, support, and trust had overwhelmed her. She had spent so much time worrying about deadlines and performance that she had lost sight of what the team actually meant to people.

It struck me afterwards that none of those insights would have come out if I had simply asked, 'Why do you like working here?' The bricks gave people a way to think with their hands first, then find the words afterwards. This is where play becomes more than a gimmick or fun thing. Used well, it gives people permission to think differently.

So why do so many of us frown upon hearing the word play at work? Ask people what comes to mind when you say 'icebreaker', and the word that comes back most often, in my experience, is 'cringy'. We have all sat through activities that felt like they were designed to fill time rather than achieve anything useful, but the problem is rarely the play itself. It's when people force it on us with no real purpose.

When facilitators award points and badges during a task without carefully thinking it through, and hope something good happens, the result is the forced, awkward exercise that gives team-building a bad name. When play is introduced with a genuine purpose rather than as a gimmick, the energy in the room completely changes. People who were holding back start contributing, and teams begin to explore ideas that would never come out in a formal meeting.

GENERATING IDEAS IN PRACTICE

Over the years, play has become my signature move when running innovation workshops, and the most memorable example of it was inspired by my daughter.

My LEGO story

She was about seven at the time, and just before bedtime she asked me to explain what I do for a living. I spotted a book on her shelf about a group of animals escaping a disaster, and I found myself telling her a story about how the animals needed to rebuild their homes in another part of the jungle. They could either plan everything upfront or build something basic and improve it by iterating based on what they learned. That bedtime story became a full-day workshop with animated characters, storytelling, and hands-on building using LEGO.

When the University of Birmingham invited me to run Jungle Scrum for their MBA programme, I wasn't sure what to expect. Over 100 students gave up their Saturday morning to attend, and what happened went beyond what I had hoped for.

One participant, who described herself as normally quite anxious in group settings, ended up volunteering as the project manager and presenting to the entire room. Afterwards, she told me she had done things she didn't think she could do, because the playful format had created conditions where she felt safe to try a role she would never have taken on in a traditional workshop.[14]

The workshop went on to become part of the global technology graduate programme at the bank I was at, where we trained over 600 new joiners through the power of play using LEGO. This was a chance to test whether a playful approach could work at scale in a highly regulated and traditionally conservative industry.

One of the programme managers summed it up nicely, asking who wouldn't want a legitimate reason to play with LEGO at work. Groups that had never worked together very quickly started collaborating, often within the first hour, with the playful format compressing what usually takes weeks of team-building into a single session. When done in the right way, play enables people to bring their full creative capacity to the work, whether that work is generating product ideas or solving complex problems.

Over the past two decades, I have collected and refined a set of activities I return to again and again. I learned some from other facilitators, developed some through trial and error, and a few emerged from unexpected moments, like that bedtime story with my daughter. What they share is that each one uses the two ingredients we have explored in this chapter, so each includes a constraint, whether that's a time limit, a restriction on materials, or a rule that changes how people interact, and each promotes playfulness by creating conditions where people feel comfortable enough to think differently.

Some are designed to energise and connect teams at the start of a session, and others help generate and explore ideas during the creative work itself. These are three of my personal favourites:

- **Yes, and:** Few activities show teams the difference between blocking ideas and building on them as quickly as this improv technique, where pairs plan a fictional event in two rounds. In the first round, responses start with 'No, but', so 'Let's have a barbecue' becomes 'No, but let's do a picnic instead', and each idea replaces the previous one. In the second round, responses start with 'Yes, and', so 'Let's have a barbecue' becomes 'Yes, and we could have a live band', then 'Yes, and we could

Figure 9.4 Conditions to grow creative ideas

set up a dance floor', with each idea building on the last. The contrast is powerful because after the 'No, but' round, people feel deflated, whereas the 'Yes, and' round creates positive energy and sometimes generates genuinely wild ideas.

- **Alphabet sprint:** This activity pushes teams past obvious solutions and can get quite competitive. Teams write A–Z down the left side of their paper. Given an everyday object such as a pencil, they must generate an alternative use for it, starting with each letter of the alphabet. For example, A could be 'arrow for a tiny bow', B could be 'boss prodder for getting attention', and C could be 'conductor's baton for an imaginary orchestra'. Round 1 lasts three minutes and focuses purely on speed, while Round 2 challenges teams to abandon realism entirely and embrace absurdity. Afterwards, teams share their most creative suggestions, particularly for the difficult letters like Q, X, and Z. Round 1 exhausts the obvious ideas, and the 26-letter constraint provides a clear structure. You can encourage friendly competition by awarding points for the most ideas or the most creative suggestions.
- **30 circles:** For a quick warm-up before an ideation session, this one is ideal. Give each participant a sheet with 20–30 blank circles, set a timer for three minutes, and ask them to turn as many circles as possible into everyday objects such as a clock face, a basketball, a planet, or a smiley face. When time is up, ask who managed the most, because it's rare for anyone to fill all 30, then have pairs discuss their creations and share the most interesting. Finally, ask whether anyone combined circles to make a snowman, a traffic light, or a Venn diagram, since most people assume they have to stay within each circle, even though nobody said that was a rule.

When we do discovery work, we are exploring unknowns and searching for insights that aren't obvious, and that requires us to have the courage to suggest ideas that might be wrong. Every product team has people whose creative confidence has declined over time, whether through a dismissive manager, a project that failed, or simply decades of being told they weren't the creative type. Those people still have creative potential, they just need the right conditions to rediscover it.

Our job, as product discovery thinkers, is to create the conditions that let that inner child out, and most of the time that means doing less than we think. We set a clear constraint, lower the stakes, make it safe to be wrong, and then get out of the way while the group does the work.

FROM IDEAS TO OPTIONS

Everything we have covered so far in this chapter has helped with divergent thinking, the process of generating a broad set of ideas. We now have a decision to make. We could try to work on everything we have come up with, but with limited time and resources we will have to ruthlessly prioritise which ideas we will turn into opportunities and take forward. That requires a different set of skills, our human judgement.

Steve Jobs understood this at Apple, cutting the product line from 350 items down to just 10 when he returned to the company in 1997. Innovation, he argued, 'is saying no to a thousand things'.[15] This philosophy sounds simple until you sit in a room with passionate stakeholders who are all convinced their opportunity is the most important. And if you look at the size of your backlog, it almost certainly contains far more ideas than you could possibly build.

So the challenge is less about identifying which ideas to say no to, and more about figuring out which opportunities deserve your time and attention. The rest of this chapter provides techniques for comparing opportunities, making trade-offs explicit, and focusing limited resources on the work that will generate the biggest return.

PRIORITISING OUTCOMES WITH OPPORTUNITY SCORING

In the early 2000s, Bosch's power tools division was trying to figure out how to win in the crowded professional circular saw market. They brought in Anthony Ulwick's firm, Strategyn, to apply his Outcome-Driven Innovation methodology, which meant asking professional contractors what they actually cared about when using circular saws.[16]

The team found that cutting in a straight line and minimising wasted material were rated highly important, but had low satisfaction. Bosch redesigned its circular saw around those specific unmet needs, and the result was a product that took significant market share in a category where differentiation had seemed almost impossible.[17]

Ulwick had developed a technique called Opportunity Scoring, which became part of his broader methodology.[18] You ask customers to rate a set of desired outcomes on two dimensions. The first is how important each outcome is, and the second is how satisfied they are with the solutions they currently use. Then you apply a formula where Opportunity equals Importance plus the gap between Importance and Satisfaction. The higher the score, the bigger the distance between what people need and what they currently have.

Applying Opportunity Scoring in practice

To see how this works, imagine you are responsible for an internal learning management system. Your stakeholders have asked you to 'improve the platform', which could mean almost anything, so you decide to run an Opportunity Scoring exercise. You begin by identifying the outcomes your users care about, writing each in Ulwick's recommended format of verb plus object plus clarifier. After working through each user group, you ask them to rate every outcome on Importance and Satisfaction, both on a scale of 1 to 10.

An outcome where learning and development managers rate Importance at 9 and Satisfaction at 4 produces a score of 14, which suggests a strong opportunity. An outcome where learners rate Importance at 8 and Satisfaction at 7 produces a score of 9, which suggests the current system is already doing a reasonable job. You plot these scores on a chart and focus your efforts on outcomes with high Importance and low Satisfaction.

You don't need enormous sample sizes either, as even 20–30 replies from the right people will reveal clear patterns. Treat the scores as a starting point for deeper conversation, because the numbers alone only tell you part of the story.

CATEGORISING VALUE WITH THE KANO MODEL

Imagine you are working at a challenger bank, and your team has a backlog of features they want to build for the mobile app. The list includes instant transaction notifications, budgeting tools, cryptocurrency trading, and human chat support. Every feature sounds valuable, and every stakeholder believes theirs is the highest priority.

In 1984, Noriaki Kano, a professor at the Tokyo University of Science, published research that challenged a basic assumption.[19] It's the assumption that adding more features will make customers proportionally happier.

Kano's research showed that some types of features are simply expected, and adding more of them doesn't improve satisfaction all that much. Other features cause a dramatic increase in customer satisfaction when they are added to the product. And then there are features customers weren't expecting at all, but which create a disproportionate amount of delight when they discover them.

The research led to what we now know as the Kano Model. It's one of my favourite product methods and I go back to it again and again when I'm trying to prioritise the value of my ideas.

The five categories of customer satisfaction

Basic features are the ones customers take for granted. Nobody will choose your app because it sends instant transaction notifications, but if those notifications stop working, customers are very likely to switch to a competitor. You have to include them, but investing extra effort won't make customers noticeably happier.

Performance features behave the way most people assume all features behave, where the more you improve them, the more satisfaction goes up. Budgeting tools fall into this group because showing spending breakdowns by individual merchant, letting you create savings pots for different goals, or displaying 12-month spending trends all make the app more useful.

Attractive features create genuine delight, because nobody was expecting them. Cryptocurrency trading inside a banking app is a good example. Nobody opens a current account hoping to trade Bitcoin, and yet discovering you can creates a reaction completely out of proportion to the feature itself.

Phill Agnew, host of the *Nudge* podcast, brought this idea to life when we spoke recently.[20] A feature you ship might reach 20 people or 20 million, and the cost of building it is broadly the same either way. So the return on a small idea can be wildly out of proportion to the effort that went into it.

He shared an example from Octopus Energy, one of the UK's fastest-growing energy companies. When you submit a meter reading on the Octopus app, you get to spin a wheel of fortune for the chance to win a reward, occasionally up to £10,000. Phill admitted he has been spinning it for four years without ever winning anything significant, and yet he still looks forward to spinning it every time he submits a reading.

Now imagine pitching that idea inside a traditional energy company a decade ago. You walk into the boardroom and propose attaching a wheel of fortune to the meter reading screen. There is a good chance the executives would have laughed you out of the building. The lesson is to leave a small amount of room for those Attractive features that might just surprise everyone.

Indifferent features have zero impact on satisfaction, and Reverse features actually make certain customers less happy. Imagine your banking app introduces a social feature that lets friends see what you've been spending money on. For most of us, the idea would make us uncomfortable, and the feature would have taken value away from an experience we were previously happy with.

How to classify your own features

Kano also developed a survey technique that lets your customers tell you which category your ideas fall into. For each feature, you ask two questions. The first asks how they would feel if the feature existed. The second asks how they would feel if it did not. Both questions use the same five response options: I would like it; I expect it; I am neutral; I can tolerate it; and I dislike it.

The power of this technique lies in what happens when you put the two answers together. The model provides a reference table that maps every possible combination to one of the five categories.

A final point worth noting is that these categories are not permanent. Adding AI features today may be classified as Attractive, but five years from now they may well fall under Basic. So it's worth running your Kano analysis periodically rather than treating it as a one-off exercise.

Once you know which ideas carry the most value, the next challenge is getting stakeholders to agree on what to take forward first.

BUILDING ALIGNMENT THROUGH TRADE-OFFS WITH BUY-A-FEATURE

During my time at British Telecom, we would run quarterly planning sessions by bringing together all of our product teams and stakeholders who worked on a large customer relationship platform. We would spend two days building an understanding of the problems and sizing the effort required to address each one. The third and final day was always the most challenging, because the amount of work to do always exceeded the capacity of the teams, and stakeholders would have to argue it out to decide which opportunities to focus on first.

Each group looked at problems through a slightly different lens. The head of customer operations wanted to automate more of the manual work. The finance teams wanted better reporting capabilities. Our marketing teams cared about running more effective campaigns. Everyone would present a valid case, but nobody wanted to descope their items.

It was only years later that I came across a technique designed for exactly these kinds of situations. Luke Hohmann created Buy-a-Feature as part of his Innovation Games toolkit in 2006.[21] Although the name suggests it is about features, the technique works just as well for prioritising opportunities and problem statements.

The core principle is simple. You give participants a limited budget of play money – just think of games like Monopoly – and ask them to spend it on the items they believe are the most important. You list somewhere between 14 and 30 items, each with a price tag reflecting the estimated effort to explore the opportunity.

Then you give each participant roughly one-third of the total price of all items combined. This means nobody can afford everything, and you price the most significant opportunities so that no single person can buy them alone. That last point is critical because it forces people to pool their money, and pooling forces negotiation and collaboration.

The real value lies in the conversations that happen during the game. The reasoning people give when they trade away an opportunity they originally wanted, or the moments where two stakeholders realise they share a concern they never knew they had in common.

One tip I would strongly recommend is to use something tangible for the money, whether that's Monopoly notes, poker chips, or tokens. The act of handing over a physical form of payment helps make the decision feel more real than simply clicking a button on a screen.

I've also seen teams run a simpler version called the 100-Dollar Test when they have less time or fewer participants. Each participant gets a hypothetical $100 (or points) to distribute across the list of opportunities, and they simply write down how much they would allocate to each one. There are no negotiations and no pooling of funds with other people, which means you lose the richness of the conversations, but you can run it in 15 minutes with a remote team using a simple shared spreadsheet.

MINDSET SHIFTS YOU NEED TO MAKE

Table 9.1 outlines the necessary shift in thinking.

Table 9.1 Traditional vs discovery thinking (assess ideas)

Traditional thinking	Discovery thinking
Creativity is based on natural talent; some people have it, and others do not	Creativity is a skill that you build with practice
Telling people to be more creative and expecting better ideas	Designing the conditions where it feels safe to think differently
Treating constraints as obstacles that get in the way of good ideas	Using constraints deliberately to focus creative energy
Dismissing play at work as a cringy time-filler	Introducing play with a genuine purpose to unlock how people think
Trying to build everything on the backlog	Deliberately saying no to focus your limited effort
Prioritising by stated importance or opinion alone	Prioritising based on the gap between Importance and Satisfaction

FROM OPTIONS TO HYPOTHESES

By this point, you have narrowed down the set of ideas you feel will resolve the problem you are focused on. They are still only educated guesses, though, and the next step is to validate them. In Chapter 10 we turn each promising option into a hypothesis we can test, looking at the final two stages of the FEATR funnel and the techniques for testing ideas quickly and cheaply, from rough prototypes to structured experiments. We will also look at one of the hardest decisions in product work: knowing when to keep going, when to change direction, and when to abandon an idea you have fallen in love with.

KEY TAKEAWAYS

- **Ideas are not always features:** A good idea can be a process change, a different message, or a tiny tweak to the environment, like the etched fly that helped clean up an airport.
- **A good idea is novel, useful, and well timed:** It has to be different enough to count as new, solve a real problem for the user, and arrive at a moment when the world is ready for it.
- **We were all creative once:** Land's research found that 98 per cent of five-year-olds tested at genius level for divergent thinking, against only 2 per cent of adults.
- **Creative confidence can be rebuilt:** Through a series of small creative successes, people can rebuild the belief that they can create something of value, exactly as Bandura's patients overcame paralysing fear one step at a time.
- **Constraints and play unlock ideas:** Dr Seuss wrote *Green Eggs and Ham* with only 50 words; the right limits focus creative energy rather than restricting it, while play creates the safety people need to think differently.
- **Opportunity Scoring reveals unmet needs:** Measure the gap between how important an outcome is and how satisfied people are with it today, and focus where Importance is high and Satisfaction is low.
- **The Kano Model explains why not all features create equal value:** Basic features are expected, Performance features improve satisfaction in proportion to effort, and Attractive features create delight.

10 TEST HYPOTHESES AND LEARN FROM RESULTS

'The proof of the product is in the testing.'

Paddy Dhanda

THE MULTI-MILLION ASSUMPTION

In 2014, the Financial Conduct Authority (FCA) issued its largest-ever retail conduct fine at the time to a single company; it ran into the tens of millions. The regulator described the failings as serious, systemic, and long-running. On top of the fine, millions more went to compensate customers for getting things so badly wrong. The company was a home services firm.

I was head of business analysis at the firm and, for the record, none of my team were involved in the decisions that led to those fines. It is also worth saying that it was one of the most entrepreneurial places I had ever worked. People were encouraged to put forward their ideas and to solve problems creatively. That energy attracted people who wanted to make a difference rather than be bogged down by corporate bureaucracy. We had over 3,000 staff, but it had a real startup feel to it. Even the founder used to show up in his helicopter, which would often land on the helipad in the middle of the car park.

Winter complaints

During one particularly harsh winter, plumbing engineers were arriving late to appointments across the country, and the volume of customer complaints was piling up fast. The complaint-handling teams were under enormous pressure to reduce the backlog, and at the height of the winter surge, leadership increased daily targets to 15–30 complaints per person, with rewards including prizes, games consoles, and extra days off. It was a system designed to reward speed.

Someone proposed using an algorithm that would scan incoming complaints for key terms like 'late arrival' and automatically generate a polite response apologising for the delay. As a technologist, it sounds like a perfectly rational idea.

The problem was that being late was often just one small part of a much larger complaint. A customer might write, 'The engineer was late, but when they arrived they damaged my property.' The algorithm would pick up the words 'late arrival', generate the apology about the delay, and the agent would close the case, while the customer's actual issue, the property damage, was never addressed.

The assumption nobody checked

Nobody had tested the core assumption, which was whether the word 'late' reliably indicated what the customer was actually complaining about. And the checks that were

Figure 10.1 The late arrival assumption

supposed to catch mistakes like this were inadequate, because the quality department reviewed just five complaints per agent per month, even when those agents were closing up to 660 in the same period. That meant less than 1 per cent of closed complaints were ever reviewed for quality.

The FCA investigation found that the failings extended beyond a single process, cutting across sales practices, complaint handling, and senior management oversight. But the complaint algorithm was a clear example of the broader pattern the regulator identified, a culture that moved fast without considering one of the most important product risks we covered in Chapter 4, the Curse of Consequence.

The willingness to try new things and the bias towards action made the firm a great place to work and created exactly the kind of energy that product teams need to be innovative. But without the discipline to test ideas before scaling them, that same energy can lead to blind faith in a solution that has never been validated. Experimentation, therefore, is not the enemy of entrepreneurial thinking, it is the thing that enables us to innovate with discipline and build confidence in our solutions.

PREPARE TO EXPERIMENT RELENTLESSLY

Ronny Kohavi, who led the experimentation platform at Microsoft, shares a story that every product team would love to claim as their own. An engineer at Bing noticed an idea that had been sitting on the backlog for months, largely ignored. The proposal was to move the second line of an ad up to the first line so that the title became larger. Implemented in a couple of days and launched as an experiment, it turned out to be worth over $100 million in incremental revenue, the single biggest revenue gain in Bing's entire history, and it had been sitting in a backlog while hundreds of other engineers worked on ideas they thought were more important.

Secretly, deep down, we all hope that our experiments will produce a moment like that. But Kohavi's broader data tells a very different story. Across Microsoft, roughly two-thirds of ideas failed to move the metrics they were designed to improve. At more heavily optimised products like Bing and on Airbnb's platform, the failure rate climbed to 85–92 per cent. These are some of the most technically sophisticated organisations on the planet, and even they get it wrong far more often than they get it right.[1]

That $100 million story is exciting, but the lesson is that we are consistently unable to predict which ideas will work, and the only reliable way to find out is to test things rather than guess. If you have ever sat in a school science lesson with a Bunsen burner and a set of test tubes, you already know how experiments work, yet I've watched smart people abandon that classroom rigour the moment commercial pressures, tight deadlines, and a room full of very opinionated people enter the picture. We would never dream of submitting a school science project that said 'I changed loads of stuff because a few people wanted me to listen to them, but I didn't validate whether they were right', yet that's exactly what many product teams do every time they ship a new version of their product.

THE ANATOMY OF A GOOD EXPERIMENT

In the FEATR funnel, the Test Hypotheses stage is where we run structured experiments to reduce uncertainty about whether a hypothesis, and the solution built on it, will actually work. Stefan Thomke at Harvard Business School has spent decades studying how companies experiment, and he provides a useful way to think about what separates a good experiment from a bad one.[2] A good experiment isolates one change and keeps everything else constant, because the whole point is to understand the relationship between cause and effect. If you change five things at once and the numbers go up, you have a result, but you have no idea what caused it.

Thomke also makes an important distinction between experiments and commitments. If a test is not reversible, then it is not really a test, it is a commitment. Most product experiments look reversible since you can always roll back the code or switch off the feature. But reversibility gets harder the further an idea travels through the organisation, because once something makes it onto the roadmap, gets presented at a steering committee, and appears in someone's quarterly objectives, there is a momentum that makes it very difficult to admit it was a bad idea.

To help structure your experiments, I want to introduce a simple acronym called TEST, which stands for theory, experiment, signals, and thresholds. Each element addresses a question your team needs to answer before running an experiment, and I am going to walk through each one by showing you how our home services scenario could have been handled differently. In reality, there were many other factors at play, so better experiments alone would not have avoided the hefty fines, but they would have helped to rule out certain solutions early on.

Theory: what do you believe, and why?

Think of a theory as an untested belief that is based on the insights you have gathered up until this point. In product work, we formalise those beliefs into something more

Figure 10.2 TEST: the anatomy of a good experiment

structured, called a hypothesis. A clear way to write one comes from Lean UX, the framework created by Jeff Gothelf and Josh Seiden, which gives us a simple template: 'We believe that [doing this] will result in [this outcome] for [these users].'[3]

One thing worth noting is that a hypothesis can only be as strong as the understanding it is built on. If your team has worked through the earlier stages of the FEATR funnel, the hypothesis at the Test stage only needs to validate whether your proposed solution works. But if your team has skipped straight to a solution, as the complaint-handling team did in our opening scenario, the hypothesis is full of assumptions about the problem itself, and no amount of experimental rigour will help, so go back and work through the steps in Chapters 7 and 8 first.

Going back to our home services scenario, they actually had two untested beliefs, because real product problems are rarely as clean as a single hypothesis. The first was the algorithm assumption that the word 'late' in a complaint reliably indicated what the customer was complaining about. And the second sat deeper, at the level of the operating model, where the organisation believed that incentivising handlers to close complaints quickly would reduce the backlog without damaging quality. When you find yourself looking at assumptions on two different levels like this, start with the deeper one. Had the team tested the incentive assumption first, the algorithm might never have been proposed at all.

Making your beliefs testable

Writing a good hypothesis is harder than the template makes it look. Start by writing down what you believe in plain language, as if you were explaining it to someone in the corridor. For the customer complaints algorithm, that belief might have been: 'We think most complaints that mention "late" are really just about the engineer being late, so we can close those first.'

That sentence captures the team's thinking, but it is not something you could test. What does 'most' mean? Is it 6 out of 10 or 9 out of 10? And what counts as 'just about the engineer being late'? A hypothesis full of vague language is open to misunderstanding, because everyone will interpret the words differently. Philip Tetlock's decade-long research into prediction found the same pattern, as the people who made the best predictions were the ones who forced themselves out of vague mental buckets like 'it will probably work' and committed to specific numbers.[4]

There is a second trap worth watching out for, because a hypothesis can use precise words and still be untestable when it bundles several beliefs together. If someone at the home services firm had written 'we believe the algorithm will work', that statement contains at least three different beliefs tangled together. Do you believe the keyword 'late' reliably identifies what the customer is complaining about? Will the response satisfy the customer? And will the complaint stay closed? Each of those could be true or false independently of the others.

With that clarity, the team could express their belief in the Lean UX format, and you will see the full hypothesis written out on the TEST at the end of this section. What it does not yet include is the specific number that would tell them whether they were right or wrong, and we will get to that in the thresholds section.

Experiment: how will you test that belief?

Once you have a clear hypothesis, the temptation is to build the thing and see what happens, which is exactly what the customer services team did and why they ended up in hot water with the regulator. But there were much cheaper ways to find out whether that assumption was correct.

For the algorithm assumption, the cheapest option was simply to pull a random sample of 50 complaints containing the word 'late' and have two people independently classify them. Is the complaint primarily about lateness, or is lateness just one part of a bigger issue? If 9 out of 10 are entirely about lateness alone, the algorithm has a chance of working. But if the number drops below 7 out of 10, you have just saved yourself a regulatory investigation. That test could have been completed in an afternoon, at zero cost, using complaints that already existed in the system.

This is an example of what product teams call a *concierge test*, where instead of building the automated system, you perform the task manually to check whether the underlying logic holds up. If two people reading complaints cannot reliably classify them by keyword alone, there is no point building an algorithm to do the same thing at scale.

A more thorough option would have been to run the algorithm on 200 complaints, but not send the responses. Instead, a human reviews each auto-generated response alongside the original complaint and flags the ones where the algorithm got it wrong. That is a variation of what is known as a *Wizard of Oz test*, where the user experiences what feels like a finished product, while a human does the work behind the scenes. You get data on the algorithm's accuracy without any risk to real people.

Those two methods sit at the cheaper end of the experiment spectrum, but product teams have a wider menu to choose from, depending on how much confidence they need. A *fake door test* places a button or link for a feature that does not yet exist and measures how many people click on it, which tells you whether anyone actually wants the thing before you build it.

One of my personal favourite methods is *guerrilla testing*, popularised by the usability expert Steve Krug, where you take a prototype to a coffee shop and ask five people to try your product for 10 minutes in exchange for the price of a flat white.[5] At the more structured end sits the *A/B test*, where you randomly split users into two groups, show each a different version, and attribute any difference in behaviour to the change. A/B tests give the strongest evidence of cause and effect, but need enough users to produce a statistically meaningful result.

A well-designed cheap experiment

One of the best examples of this comes from the UK's Behavioural Insights Team, the government's so-called 'Nudge Unit'.[6] In 2011, HMRC faced a familiar challenge where millions of people were late paying their taxes. Rather than pouring money into advertising campaigns, the team sent over 200,000 late taxpayers different versions of reminder letters. One group received the standard message warning about consequences, while another group got the same letter with one additional sentence: 'Most people in your town have already paid their tax.' That single line increased payment rates by around 15 per cent, and when rolled out nationally it brought in an additional £210 million in a single year and generated an estimated £30 million in revenue that would otherwise have gone uncollected. Yet the experiment cost almost nothing to run.

Every method sits somewhere on a spectrum of cost and confidence, and the aim is always to find the cheapest way to learn whether your hypothesis is right or wrong.

Signals: what should you pay attention to?

You already know how to read signals, even if you have never called them that. When a friend replies to your message with a single word after you have sent them a paragraph, you know something is off. We read signals like these constantly, picking up information from our environment and adjusting our behaviour without thinking about it, and product experiments work the same way.

In product work, we need to go further than just noticing signals. A user abandoning their shopping cart tells you something happened, but on its own it is just an observation. When you deliberately track that behaviour over time, it becomes a metric, in this case your cart abandonment rate, and that shift is how we turn observations into something your team can act on.

Timing of indicators

We can categorise the timing of signals into two main types, leading and lagging indicators. Think of your product as a patient that you need to keep healthy. Lagging indicators tell you the results of something that has already happened, often after weeks or months have passed, and for our patient this is the equivalent of a post-mortem, when it's too late to fix anything. Leading indicators are the regular healthchecks that monitor vital signs and spot warnings before they become serious, giving you an early signal while there is still time to change direction.

But most senior leaders aren't interested in how you got to the result, they want to know whether revenue went up or costs came down. That's not a criticism of leadership, it's just the way the corporate world works, and it focuses the entire organisation on the lagging indicators that get discussed in steering committees and determine whether budgets get approved.

The trick is to work backwards from the lagging indicator to find the behaviour that can help you predict it. If the lagging indicator is monthly subscriber growth for your newsletter, ask yourself what actions could indicate whether a reader is engaging with it. Open the email? Click through to an article? Forward it to a colleague? Those early actions are your leading indicators, and they give you useful insights within days rather than at the end of the month, while still keeping you focused on the outcome your stakeholders care about.

At the home services firm, the lagging indicator was the FCA fine, and by then it was too late, yet the customer admin team had leading indicators sitting in their own data. Complaint reopening rates would have told them that customers were coming back because their issues had not been fully resolved. And the fact that the Ombudsman had overturned 56 per cent of their complaint resolutions would have told them that an independent body was consistently disagreeing with their decisions. Had the team chosen even one of those and checked it weekly, alarm bells would have rung well before the regulator got involved, and the entire outcome could have been different.

We covered the say/do gap in Chapter 8, so I won't repeat it here, but the principle applies directly to experimentation. Wherever possible, design your experiment so the primary signal comes from a user's behaviour rather than an opinion about what they might do, and use opinion-seeking techniques to add the context and motivation that behavioural data cannot reveal. Some of the most mature experimentation cultures build these disciplines into their process from the start, and in Chapter 18 I share insights from a former Booking.com product manager.

Thresholds: what number counts as success?

Early in my career as a business analyst, I was working with a call centre team that was under pressure to process higher volumes. The business had introduced average handling time as a performance metric. On paper, the logic made sense because if each call took less time, then the agents could get through more calls, and the numbers started to improve almost immediately.

But then agents began forwarding calls to colleagues the moment an issue got complicated, because transferring a call reset their own handling time. The problem the metric was supposed to fix got worse rather than better.

That experience taught me an important lesson. The metric you choose will shape the behaviour of everyone involved. If you choose the wrong one, you won't just get misleading data, you might make the problem worse without even realising it.

When we built our hypothesis earlier in the chapter, we left a gap, the threshold, which is the number your experiment needs to hit before you can call it a success. Choosing it involves more than picking a number, because you need to think about what you are measuring, when you will check the result, and what you will do if you miss it.

Pick one number that answers the question

Douglas Hubbard, the author of *How to Measure Anything*, states that the purpose of a measurement is not to produce data but to reduce the uncertainty around a decision you need to make.[7] So before you choose a metric, go back to the riskiest assumption in your hypothesis. If you are testing whether a keyword can reliably classify customer complaints, the metric might be the percentage of correct classifications. For a fake door test, it might be click-through rate. Pick one, and resist the temptation to add a second or third primary metric, because when a team is tracking several success metrics at once, those metrics will eventually contradict each other and the team will latch onto whichever number supports the conclusion they already prefer.[8]

Set your number before you start

Once you have your primary metric, you need to agree on a specific threshold number with your team before you see the results. Jonathan Baron and John Hershey at the University of Pennsylvania showed why: participants in their study rated identical medical decisions as competent when the patient survived and poor when the patient died, even though the process hadn't changed.[9] The outcome changed their judgement of the decision, and the same bias will creep into your team's reading of experiment results if the pass mark is set after the data arrives.

An experiment also needs to be time-bound, otherwise how do you know when to stop? Without a deadline, it's tempting to keep extending the window, convincing yourself that the numbers just need another week.

And finally, the experiment needs a clear plan of action if you don't hit the threshold number. For a fake door test, that might be interviewing five of the people who saw the button and didn't click, so the team learns from the outcome even when it fails.

Guard what you are not testing

Your primary and supporting metrics tell you whether the thing you tested worked, but products don't work in isolation. They are connected systems where changing one part often affects another. Kohavi uses the term guardrail metric to describe a number that your experiment is not trying to improve but must not make worse, like the guardrails on a road, which are not part of your journey, but if you hit one, something has gone seriously wrong. Before you start, ask your team, 'If this experiment succeeds on its primary metric, what else could it accidentally make worse?' If any of those areas move in the wrong direction, stop and investigate, regardless of how well the primary metric is performing.

Customer complaints TEST on a page

If you have worked through the four elements of the TEST acronym, you have done the hard work in designing your experiment. The TEST on a page is simply a way to capture those details on a single page so that your whole team can get aligned before the experiment begins.

Here's what the TEST on a page would have looked like if the customer complaints team had used it for their algorithm.

Theory

Riskiest assumption: the word 'late' in a complaint reliably indicates that lateness is the customer's only concern. Hypothesis: we believe that using the keyword 'late arrival' to auto-classify complaints and send an automated apology will result in faster resolution without the need for individual human review, for customers who mention lateness in their complaint.

Experiment

Method: concierge test. Two team members independently read 50 randomly selected complaints containing the word 'late' and classify each one as 'lateness only' or 'lateness plus other issues'. No responses were sent to the customer during the test. Duration and audience: one afternoon; 50 complaints from the current winter backlog. Two customer admin staff from the existing complaint-handling team.

Signals

Primary metric: the percentage of complaints where both admin staff agree that lateness is the sole issue. Supporting metrics: the types of additional issues appearing alongside lateness (property damage, missed follow-ups, billing disputes, unresolved repairs). Guardrail metric: complaint reopening rate must not increase during any subsequent pilot.

Thresholds

Pass: at least 9 out of 10 complaints confirmed as single-issue lateness by both reviewers, within one working day. Fail: if the rate drops below 7 out of 10, stop and redesign the classification approach before any customer responses are considered. Failure plan: if we pass, move to a Wizard of Oz pilot where the algorithm drafts responses for 200 complaints, but a human approves each one before it reaches the customer; if we fail, redesign the classification to account for multi-issue complaints and separately review whether the volume-based incentive structure is creating pressure that makes quality problems worse.

Two things are worth noticing about the TEST on a page. The first is that a separate test of the incentive structure would probably have prevented the need for the algorithm test at all. And the second is that the entire test could have been completed in a single afternoon, at zero cost, using people and data that already existed within the organisation, with no need for software, consultants, or new infrastructure.

Review Results: what happens after the experiment?

Paul Nurse, the Nobel Prize-winning biologist, said he spends half his time as 'an amateur psychiatrist keeping colleagues cheerful when nothing works'. If that is the reality at the highest levels of scientific research, it should come as no surprise that the same is true for product teams running their first experiments. So be prepared to be disappointed, and don't let your optimism be dampened when the results come back and don't support what you hoped for.

What experience actually teaches

Have you ever touched a hot pan? You find yourself pulling your hand away before you get a chance to register what happened, because the feedback to your brain is instant. The trouble is that we tend to assume all learning works this way. In 1933, the American philosopher John Dewey argued in his book *How We Think* that experience alone doesn't teach you anything.[10] The real lessons come from stopping to think about what happened, why it happened, and what you would do differently next time. Product experiments need that extra step, because we have to wait for the results, the data can be noisy, and making sense of it is rarely straightforward. A 2 per cent increase in error rates could mean our solution was flawed, the execution was poor, or the test didn't run for long enough, so the experiment alone won't give you a definitive answer without further analysis.

That's why Review Results, the R in the FEATR funnel, exists as a deliberate step to pause and think through what the results are telling you.

Most of us spend far more time doing than thinking. Take a look at your own calendar for the past week or two. Does it resemble a game of Tetris, except with rectangles? Entire days of back-to-back meetings? If so, when do you get space to think and reflect? Most product teams are permanently stuck in doing mode, and the few that pause tend to do so only when something has gone badly wrong.

There is always pressure to ship the next feature, and taking time out to reflect can feel unproductive. But skipping it means throwing away half the value of every experiment you run. Most teams already have regular moments where reflection could happen – retrospectives, sprint reviews, and planning sessions – but these events rarely include a structured look at experiment results. Jeff Gothelf makes the point that teams should track their 'velocity of learning' alongside their velocity of delivery, because when the only thing being measured is how much gets shipped, learning gets squeezed out entirely.[11]

Why you should not reflect alone

When you analyse results on your own, it is easy to believe you are being objective, but many behavioural biases cloud our judgement. We also all have different strengths, since some of us are great at novel ideas while others have a gift for problem-solving. Personally, I struggle to make sense of large datasets and often tell my teams I'm not a data guy. That's fine, because no one is expecting you to become a data scientist to do effective product discovery. You have a whole team of talented experts around you, so lean on them whenever you can.

Research from Carnegie Mellon found that the collective intelligence of a group depends less on having the smartest individuals and more on how evenly members participate.[12] But that collective advantage only works when the discussion has structure, because without it, groups tend to spend most of their time talking about information everyone already knows, while unique insights held by individual members get missed.[13]

A simple way to structure the conversation

The approach I find most useful is called the after-action review. Meta-analyses across many industries have found that teams who run structured debriefs like this consistently outperform those who don't, with performance improvements of around 20–25 per cent.[14] It works because it forces the group through four questions in order rather than jumping straight to conclusions.[15]

1. **What did we expect to happen?** Ask each person to write down what they expected before they see the results, which makes perspectives visible. If everyone predicted one thing and something else happened, the team has to reflect on why they were wrong. And if different people predicted different things, you've discovered that the team didn't even share the same assumptions, which is worth knowing before you make any decisions.

2. **What actually happened?** Have you ever heard someone say in a meeting, 'Let's get everyone on the same page'? Well, this is that moment. Walk through the actual results together before anyone starts explaining them. What did the primary metric do? How did the supporting metrics behave? Did any guardrails move? Most people in the room won't have looked at the results in detail, so creating a shared understanding at this point is essential.
3. **Why did it happen?** This is where the real learning happens, and where teams are most likely to go wrong. Our natural tendency is to hear one explanation that sounds plausible and treat it as the answer, but there are usually several possible explanations for any result. To help your team push past the obvious answer, here are three smells to watch out for when interpreting your data.

- **Smell 1 – misleading percentages:** Imagine five people clicked the button of your fake door test in the control period and six clicked it in the test period. That's a 20 per cent increase in percentage terms, but it's one additional human being. The same works in reverse, since a 1 per cent improvement in retention across 30,000 paying customers is 300 customers who would have left for a competitor. Always state the percentage and the actual number side by side before you make a decision.
- **Smell 2 – knock-on effects:** A primary metric can improve while another part of the product gets worse. Consider a company that offers a 30 per cent discount on an underperforming Product B and watches sales jump by 40 per cent, while total revenue falls because customers who would have bought the higher-margin Product A at full price switched to the discounted option instead. This is where your guardrail metrics become invaluable.
- **Smell 3 – the average that flattens the real story:** If the average customer satisfaction score comes back as 7 out of 10, that sounds healthy until you look deeper and find that half of your users scored 9 and the other half scored 5. There is no 'average user' in that dataset, just two groups having completely different experiences that the number 7 doesn't represent. The same happens with outliers, so once you have reviewed the headline result, ask who had the best experience, who had the worst, and what the outliers might be telling you.

4. **What should we do next?** The first three questions were about building understanding. This one is about making a call on which direction to go.

In 1998, Ben Hunt-Davis and the GB men's rowing eight had just finished another disappointing World Championships. They had spent years coming seventh, and they knew that if they kept doing what they were doing, they would keep getting the same result. So they agreed on a single question that would govern every decision in the two years before the Sydney Olympics: will it make the boat go faster?[16] If something made the boat go faster, they kept doing it. If it didn't, they stopped. On 24 September 2000, they won Olympic gold, the first British crew to win that event since 1912.

That question is the one your team should be asking after every experiment. Does the evidence from this experiment move us closer to solving the problem we set out to solve?

Persevere

Persevering means the evidence was strong enough to justify taking the next step. But persevering does not mean the experiment proved you are right. It means the risk of going ahead is now lower than it was before you ran the test.

When Monzo, the UK digital bank, introduced the ability for Flex customers to change their payment date, they did not release it to everyone at once. They launched it with staff first, then ran an experiment with customers to check whether it could create poor outcomes, such as confusion about how the feature worked or difficulties making payments. The experiment helped them spot edge cases they had not anticipated and fix them before wider rollout. Only once the experiment had succeeded did they make the feature available to all customers.[17]

Pause

If the experiment does not support your hypothesis, then pause. Don't try to rescue the idea with a slightly different version of the same test or lower the threshold. Remember Kohavi's failure rates from the start of this chapter, since they tell us that most ideas not working is the norm. Failing fast and moving on to the next idea is better than spending months trying to salvage one that has already shown it doesn't work.

Pivot

Sometimes the evidence does neither of those things. It tells you the current approach is not working, yet it also points to something worth pursuing in a different form, and that is when you pivot. A pivot keeps the problem you set out to solve, but changes the way you go about solving it, whether that means a different audience, a different mechanism, or a different part of the problem to tackle first. Going back to the rowing crew, a pivot is what happens when the answer to 'Will it make the boat go faster?' is 'not like this, but there is a version of this that might'. A genuine pivot is driven by what the evidence is telling you rather than an unwillingness to let go.

An important step after every experiment is to document the results and key learning, both for successful and unsuccessful ideas. We will see in Chapter 18 that the most effective experimentation organisations make this a core practice to share learning across other teams.

MINDSET SHIFTS YOU NEED TO MAKE

Table 10.1 outlines the necessary shift in thinking.

Table 10.1 Traditional vs discovery thinking (test hypotheses)

Traditional thinking	Discovery thinking
Deferring to gut feel or the most senior voice in the room	Applying the discipline of the scientific method
Expecting most of your ideas to work	Expecting most ideas to fail and treating that as the norm

(Continued)

Table 10.1 (Continued)

Traditional thinking	Discovery thinking
Holding a vague belief that something will work	Writing a single, testable hypothesis with a specific number
Testing the whole solution	Testing the deepest, riskiest assumption first
Jumping to build the real thing	Running the cheapest experiment that helps you to learn
Waiting for lagging indicators after the result is in	Tracking leading indicators while there is still time to adjust
Deciding what counts as success after seeing the data	Agreeing on the threshold number before you start
Reflecting on the results alone	Reflecting on the results as a team
Falling in love with an idea	Use the results to drive your next move, either pause, pivot, or persevere

CLOSING THE LOOP

You have now worked through a full product discovery cycle by covering every stage of the FEATR funnel. We moved from understanding the problem all the way through to testing the solution and reviewing the results.

But it doesn't end here, the funnel is not a one-time process. Every experiment you reflect on generates new questions, which can lead to new hypotheses. The teams that get the most from discovery are the ones who treat each cycle as a chance to get smarter about the people they are building for, and the more cycles you complete, the more mature your discovery practices will become.

In Chapter 6, I mentioned that there are many discovery frameworks you can choose from if you are looking for a more rigorous set of practices. These have been tried and tested across many organisations and popularised in business books, but it can feel difficult to know which one to choose over another. Over the next two chapters, I will introduce you to some of the most popular frameworks, so you can decide whether you should make the leap to adopting them in your own teams.

KEY TAKEAWAYS

- **Most ideas fail, and that is normal:** Kohavi's data shows two-thirds of ideas at Microsoft failed to improve the metrics they targeted.
- **The TEST acronym helps you structure your experiment:** Theory asks what you believe. Experiment asks how you will test it cheaply. Signals asks what you will measure. Thresholds asks what number counts as success.

- **Your hypothesis is only as strong as your understanding of the problem:** If the team has skipped the earlier stages of discovery, no amount of experimental rigour will compensate for testing the wrong thing.
- **Match the method to the risk:** Concierge tests, Wizard of Oz tests, fake door tests, guerrilla testing, and A/B tests each sit at different points on the cost-to-confidence spectrum. Start with the cheapest method that can answer your question.
- **Metrics shape behaviour, so set your number before you see the results:** The call centre handling time shows that the wrong metric can make the original problem worse, and outcome bias means we judge identical decisions differently once we know how they turned out.
- **Reflection is not optional:** Structure it with the after-action review, watch for the three smells in your data, and do it as a team rather than alone.
- **All outcomes are forms of learning:** Persevering means the evidence justifies the next step, pausing means the evidence says to invest your time elsewhere, and pivoting means it points you in a new direction. All three are signs that the process is working.

11 RUN TIME-BOXED DISCOVERY EVENTS

'Rome wasn't built in a day, but a hackathon was.'

Paddy Dhanda

WHEN BT LEARNED TO MOVE FAST

In 2000, I joined BT as a graduate, bright-eyed and ready to take on the world. What I walked into was something of a culture shock. BT had roots stretching back to the General Post Office, which had operated as a government department since the 19th century. The organisation still carried some of that legacy thinking when it came to delivering projects.

Then, in May 2004, everything changed. Al-Noor Ramji arrived as BT's new CIO with a mandate to shake things up. The company was desperate to break out from its telecoms heritage and move into corporate networking, broadband, and IT services. It needed to rapidly develop the technology to support that expansion, and the old way of working simply wasn't going to cut it.

In his first six months, Ramji reflected on what he'd inherited. The technology operation had over 4,000 initiatives running simultaneously, and only about 20 per cent of them had an actual business case.[1] That's four out of five projects that couldn't even articulate why they existed or what value they were supposed to deliver.

Ramji brought with him some radical ideas that would modernise our ways of working. In one interview, he shared, 'I want you to deliver a working product of value to the business in 90 days, and then every 90 days after that until the project is complete.'[2]

At the time, a typical project produced a deliverable every 18 months, and even that was considered optimistic for many of the larger programmes. The initial reaction was predictably negative. I remember the corridor conversations, people believed it couldn't be done. Moving from 18 months to just 90 days seemed like an impossible ask.

But mandating faster cycles wasn't enough on its own. Teams needed a way to align quickly and commit to deliverables they could actually achieve within that timeframe. The answer was something called a Hot House.

INSIDE THE HOT HOUSE

Hot Houses were unlike anything I'd encountered during my university course. Recently, I caught up with Phil Black, a former colleague who ran many of these sessions, to understand what made them work so effectively.[3]

'Hot Housing was revolutionary at the time', Phil told me. 'These were two- or three-day events where you'd be locked in a building with senior people in the room, real customers in the room, and what you agreed in your Hot House would then have to be delivered 90 days later.'

The word 'locked' isn't an exaggeration. Once you were in, you were fully committed. No ducking out to check emails or popping back to your desk. The intensity was deliberate because it forced decisions that might otherwise take months of meetings to reach.

The structure was also deliberately competitive, inspired by Toyota's set-based engineering approach, where multiple teams work on the same problem at once. One team might chase the fastest solution, another the cheapest, another the most technically elegant. They would then learn from each approach to find the optimal final solution.

HOW TO RUN A HOT HOUSE

Day 1 focused on understanding the problem. Teams formed through an auction process that deliberately mixed people who didn't usually work together. A finance person might end up alongside an engineer and a customer service rep. The aim was to break down the echo chambers that had built up over the years.

It felt strange at first. Why would an accountant have anything useful to say about network architecture? But the subject matter was less important than the different ways of thinking each person brought to the table. Accountants are naturally good at drilling into the details and understanding the data behind a decision, and that turns out to be a very useful skill when you're designing sales reporting solutions.

Day 2 was about reflecting on the solutions from the previous day. Teams could borrow ideas from each other, which felt counterintuitive at first. In most organisations, teams tend to keep their ideas to themselves so they get the credit for delivering them. Here, cross-pollination was encouraged. Best of all, real customers were in the building, ready to challenge assumptions on the spot rather than weeks later.

Day 3 was about finalising and presenting to a judging panel that included the business sponsor and actual customers. You had to present your design and commit to what you would deliver in the next 90 days. The judges would then decide which solution to take forward, or sometimes they would ask two teams to keep exploring if they liked elements of both.

The winning teams would be rewarded for their efforts and walk away with a lucrative prize. As Phil recalled, 'It used to be funny watching people walk out of a Hot House at the end of day three as they're like zombies, it was really brutal, but they might have an iPod in their hand so they were happy.'

I used to get genuinely excited whenever someone invited me to a Hot House. Part of it was the chance to win, and part of it, if I'm honest, was the fridges stocked with chocolate, fruit, and pastries.

Figure 11.1 The Hot House

During the years that followed, BT's transformation gathered huge momentum. They consolidated the number of projects from 4,300 down to 29 strategic initiatives, and the company moved from year-long releases to shorter cycles. Phil told me: 'After a couple of cycles, we got it down to 90 days from requirement to production, and then actually the next release we got it down to six weeks.'

Hot Houses became mandated across all major programmes as a way to run rapid discovery and prototyping. What are the other ways teams can structure their discovery work, and how do you choose the right one for your situation?

WHAT IS A FRAMEWORK?

Before we look at the major frameworks, it helps to be clear about the difference between a framework and a technique, because the two words get used interchangeably and the distinction shapes which tool you reach for.

The Interaction Design Foundation defines a framework as 'the basic structure underlying a system, concept, or text'.[4] In the context of discovery, a framework provides structure for an entire effort, guiding you from identifying a problem through to a validated solution or decision. It tells you not just what to do but when to do it and in what sequence. Think of it as an operating system for your discovery work.

A technique, by contrast, is a single method that serves one specific purpose. Research literature describes techniques as 'the specific tools and procedures used to collect and analyse data within a broader process'.[5] User interviews, prototyping, and A/B testing are all techniques. Each is valuable, but none of them tells you how to structure your overall approach or when to apply it relative to other activities.

Frameworks are made up of multiple techniques. *Design Sprints* combine sketching, prototyping, and interviews into a five-day structure, while *Continuous Discovery Habits* weave similar techniques into a weekly rhythm.

That distinction makes the many discovery approaches on offer easier to sort. Let's look at the major frameworks available to product teams.

TYPES OF FRAMEWORK

There are a lot of discovery frameworks out there, and it can feel a bit like the Agile world, where everyone has their own flavour and a strong opinion about which one is best. But when you look closely at how they're used, you find they fall into two main categories: event-based and rhythm-based frameworks.

- **Event-based frameworks:** These are intensive bursts of activity that you run as one-off events when you face a specific challenge or decision. Hot Houses, hackathons, Design Sprints, and Design Thinking workshops all fall into this category. You block out some focused time by inviting the relevant teams and collaborating on a specific challenge together.
- **Rhythm-based frameworks:** Rather than treating discovery as something you do occasionally when you need answers, these approaches make it an ongoing practice woven into how your team operates week after week. The Lean Startup, Continuous Discovery Habits, Dual-Track Agile, and Lean UX are great examples. They help build a discovery culture in the team, and the learning amplifies over time.

The most effective teams don't pick just one type. They build what I call a 'discovery stack', combining intensive event-based approaches with ongoing rhythm-based practices. A B2B software company launching a new product might start with a Design Sprint to validate the core concept, then shift into a Continuous Discovery rhythm of weekly customer interviews and biweekly hypothesis tests once the direction is set. Six months in, when the team feels stuck on a particular functional area, they might run a hackathon to crowdsource fresh ideas before returning to a regular rhythm-based discovery approach.

In this chapter, we'll focus on event-based frameworks, starting with one that has shaped how entire industries think about problem-solving. We'll explore rhythm-based approaches in the next chapter.

DESIGN THINKING

Of all the frameworks in this chapter, Design Thinking has the longest history and the broadest application. It has been used to reimagine how banks serve customers, transform the way food companies develop products, and turn terrifying medical procedures into manageable experiences for patients.

The origins

The roots of Design Thinking stretch back to Stanford University in the late 1950s. John E. Arnold, a mechanical engineering professor, is often credited with first using the term 'design thinking' in his 1959 book, *Creative Engineering*.[6] Arnold was fascinated by creativity, not as a natural gift that some people have and others lack, but as a skill that could be taught and developed. The idea that creativity could be systematically learned was radical for its time.

Arnold's ideas influenced generations of Stanford faculty, including Bob McKim, whose 1972 book, *Experiences in Visual Thinking*, argued that visual and spatial reasoning were as important as verbal and mathematical thinking.[7] McKim's product design programme would later shape one of his students, David Kelley.

In 1977, as the world mourned the death of Elvis Presley, the King of Rock and Roll, a future king of product design was graduating from Stanford. Kelley went on to co-found IDEO, now one of the most influential design consultancies in the world. In 2005, he co-founded the Hasso Plattner Institute of Design at Stanford, commonly known as the d.school, which became a hub that trained thousands of practitioners who then spread the methodology into their own organisations and industries.

The five phases through one project

Design Thinking moves through five interconnected phases, Empathise, Define, Ideate, Prototype, and Test, and the easiest way to see how they fit together is to follow them through a project that actually used them. Eli Woolery, a lecturer at Stanford's d.school, told me about a student team that had been tasked with addressing infant mortality in Nepal.[8] Premature babies were dying from hypothermia because they could not access incubators, and traditional incubators cost around $20,000, far beyond what most hospitals in developing countries could afford. From a Palo Alto classroom, the obvious solution looked clear: build a cheaper incubator. But the team did not start there.

Empathise

Instead of designing anything, the team flew to Nepal. They wanted to see the conditions for themselves by talking to the doctors and the mothers, and understanding what was actually happening. This is the Empathise phase, going beyond surveys and focus groups to watching people in their own environment and seeing how they actually work. The phase typically runs for 1–2 weeks, and it usually involves 5–10 in-depth interviews of 45–90 minutes each, plus direct observation.

What the team found in Nepal helped them rewrite the brief. 'One of the students noticed that there were all these incubators sitting unused', Eli recounted. 'They talked to the doctor, who said, "We have plenty of incubators, but these babies are often in very rural areas, and it takes them hours or maybe even more than a day to get to the hospital. By that time it's often too late."'

If they had skipped this phase, they would have spent months engineering a cheaper incubator, which would have been completely the wrong solution.

Define

During the Define phase, you bring together everything you have learned from the Empathise phase and analyse the themes that emerge. Defining normally takes 2–3 days and this is where you frame the problem as a 'How Might We ...' question, the technique we looked at in Chapter 7.

Ideate

With the problem reframed as 'How might we keep newborns warm during the journey to the hospital?' the team generated as many possible solutions as they could before filtering any of them. The Ideate phase is about quantity over quality, because you have to get past the obvious answers before the interesting ones appear. Heated blankets, battery-powered warmers, and portable incubators on motorcycles are all potential options. A typical Ideate session aims for 50–100 ideas across 1–2 days before you start filtering some out.

Prototype

The best idea that emerged was a small, insulated pouch that wraps around a newborn like a tiny sleeping bag, with a removable wax-based heating pack inside. You heat the pack in boiling water, slide it into a pocket in the pouch, and wrap the baby inside. Body temperature is maintained for up to six hours, with no electricity required and no trained medical staff needed to operate it. The entire solution costs less than 1 per cent of a traditional incubator.

That is the Prototype phase, usually 2–5 days in length. It involves building quick, rough versions of your most promising ideas so you can put them in front of real people. For a physical product, that might mean cardboard, fabric, and tape; for a digital one, paper sketches or simple screen mock-ups. Low-fidelity prototypes help because people give more honest feedback when they can see that an idea is still a work in progress.

Test

When the team put their prototype in front of mothers in Nepal, they noticed something they had not expected. Mothers were consistently heating the device only to the halfway point on the temperature gauge. It turned out that in these communities, Western medicine was seen as extremely strong, so mothers routinely gave their children half the recommended dose of any medication. They were applying the same logic to the warming device.

The fix was simple. Removing the scale entirely solved the problem, and the new gauge displayed only two states: 'not warm enough' or 'ready to use', with no middle option. 'That was only learned through prototyping it and testing in the field', Eli noted.

The Test stage puts your prototypes in front of real users and watches where they get stuck, confused, or delighted, rather than stepping in to explain or help. This phase runs for 1–2 weeks, and the findings often send you back into earlier phases as new insights emerge.

The Embrace warmer, as it was called, that resulted from this process has since helped save thousands of lives. But it only exists because the team followed the discovery cycle rather than starting with the solution. Without the empathy phase, they would have built a cheaper incubator that hospitals did not need, and without prototype testing in real villages, they would have shipped a temperature gauge that mothers used incorrectly.

A typical Design Thinking project runs across 4–8 weeks, though it can be compressed into a shorter workshop or stretched for a more complex challenge. The phases are not strictly linear, and teams often cycle back and forth as testing throws up new questions.

When to use Design Thinking

Consider Design Thinking when uncertainty is at its highest, and you need to understand the problem space deeply before committing to any direction. It is the right choice when you're entering a new market, when customer needs are poorly understood, or when your team keeps circling the same conventional answers and needs a genuine reset.

It is the wrong choice when you already know the problem and simply need to validate a specific solution quickly. Design Thinking is the most thorough of these approaches, and that depth costs time, typically a couple of months. When you need something tangible in days rather than weeks, more intensive, time-boxed approaches come in.

HACKATHONS

Most people picture exhausted engineers hunched over laptops at 3 a.m. when they hear the word 'hackathon'. While that stereotype isn't entirely wrong, hackathons have evolved far beyond coding competitions, and when structured well they can generate breakthrough ideas in surprisingly short timeframes.

How to run a hackathon

A hackathon is a time-boxed event, typically 24–48 hours, where cross-functional teams work intensively to build working prototypes or proof-of-concept solutions. Unlike traditional workshops that produce documents and plans, hackathons produce tangible outputs you can test with users or put in front of stakeholders.

Running one well takes preparation on both sides of the event. Leading up to it, you should define 3–5 challenge areas that are meaningful but small enough to tackle in the time available. Recruit a cross-functional group of people, including both product and business representatives. Since most hackathons require teams to compete, be sure to line up a panel of judges. From a logistics perspective, ensure you have a large space stocked with lots of food.

On the first day, teams self-organise around the challenges that interest them, each having at least one person who can build and one who understands the problem, and by the midpoint, they should be actively building something. On the second day, teams continue to work on the challenge for a few hours before the final presentations, which are short and usually require teams to give a live demo of their solution and explain what they learned.

What most organisations get wrong is that they forget to assign an owner for each promising concept, and ideally they should have a follow-up within a couple of weeks. This ensures you continue to build the momentum long after the event is over. A study published by the Association for Computing Machinery analysed nearly 12,000 hackathon projects and tracked what happened to them afterwards. Things started positively, with 85 per cent of all development activity occurring within the first month, and most of that in the first week alone. But six months later, only 7 per cent of projects showed any signs of continued work.[9]

The ChatGPT hackathon

One of the most important hackathons in recent technology history took place at OpenAI in late 2022. Nick Turley, head of ChatGPT at OpenAI, who previously led product at Dropbox and Instacart, described how the team 'put together a hackathon of enthusiasts just hacking on GPT-4 to see what awesome stuff we could create and maybe ship to users'.[10]

The hackathon produced multiple concepts. There was a meeting bot designed to call into meetings and eventually help run them. There was a coding tool that, as Turley noted, was 'probably ahead of its time'. Every team's idea was some flavour of what they internally called a 'super assistant'.

But then something interesting happened, as Turley explained: 'Every time we tested these more bespoke ideas, people wanted to use it for all this other stuff because it's just a very, very generically powerful technology.' Users given the meeting bot wanted to ask it about cooking, and the ones given the coding tool wanted help writing emails.

This insight changed everything. Rather than forcing the product into a single use case, they decided to ship something more generic. Turley reflected that this is a pattern with AI. You can't sit in a room and predict what people will do with it, but to truly learn how people will use it, you have to just ship and watch what happens.

It was a turning point in how we use AI, and ChatGPT went from final decision to public launch in just 10 days, and reached 100 million users faster than any application in history.

Hackathons at scale

HackZurich, founded in 2014 by students from ETH Zurich and the University of Zurich, has grown into Europe's largest and most selective hackathon. Organisers receive over 5,000 applications from more than 50 countries each year, with only around 550–600 selected to take part.[11] The mix of participants is of an unusually high calibre, with one-third holding PhDs and another one-third holding Master's degrees. Global companies like Google, Microsoft, and Zurich Insurance bring real business challenges for teams to tackle.[12]

Each weekend, over 150 working prototypes emerge from the 40-hour event. The prototypes are then developed either as startups or in direct collaboration with the sponsoring companies.[13] It's a model that turns a weekend of intense creativity into genuine commercial outcomes.

Successful hackathons at this scale require careful planning. Maciej Ryś, who founded HackYeah and has worked on over 100 hackathons worldwide, studied 48 events across five different roles and identified the common pitfalls. In his book *Sparks for Innovation*, he found that poorly defined challenges, unclear judging criteria, and a failure to consider participant well-being were among the most frequent causes of hackathon failure.[14]

Hackathons vs buildathons

A close cousin of the hackathon has started to appear across software organisations in the last few years. A buildathon takes the same time-boxed energy and cross-functional teaming but swaps the open-ended brief and competitive format for something more outcome-focused. Instead of 'build whatever you want that fits one of these themes, and we'll pick a winner', the brief becomes 'build the thing this team has agreed it needs, in the time we have, together'.

The difference shows up in three places. First, the brief is narrower and the deliverable is agreed in advance, often a specific internal tool, a feature the team has prioritised but never had time to build, or a working prototype that will be picked up by the regular delivery process the following Monday. Second, the competitive element drops away. There is usually no judging panel, no prize, and no winner, because the goal is not to surface the best idea but to compress the work into a single intense session. Third, the team composition tends to be tighter. Where a hackathon mixes people who do not usually work together to surface fresh thinking, a buildathon uses the people who will own the result, because they need to be able to maintain it afterwards.

When to use hackathons and buildathons

The two formats sit alongside each other rather than one replacing the other. Reach for a hackathon when you need creative energy and a way to break people out of routine thinking to generate fresh ideas. They suit organisations that want to crowdsource ideas from their own talent or build a culture of innovation.

A buildathon makes more sense when you have a specific problem, and you want to leave the event with something closer to the final product. Plenty of organisations now run both, one to generate ideas and energise the culture, and the other to compress the build work into a single intense session.

Both formats are the wrong choice when you need deep, validated insights, because their discovery remains shallow unless real customers are involved.

What if you need a more structured approach to making a specific decision that has been validated by customers? Then it's worth considering Design Sprints.

DESIGN SPRINTS

In the early 2010s, Jake Knapp was a designer at Google working on products like Gmail and Hangouts. He noticed that teams would spend months debating ideas in meetings, only to discover later that customers did not want what they had built. Knapp began experimenting with a different approach. What if you could compress the best parts of Design Thinking and other discovery approaches into a single week?

The result was the Design Sprint. Knapp refined the method at Google Ventures, where it became a tool for rapidly validating which startup ideas were worth backing, and his 2016 book, *Sprint*, helped spread it to thousands of organisations.[15]

Sprint 2.0

The original Design Sprint spanned five days, with each day serving a specific purpose: Map on Monday; Sketch on Tuesday; Decide on Wednesday; Prototype on Thursday; and Test on Friday. The methodology has since evolved. AJ&Smart, a Berlin-based design agency, ran over 200 Design Sprints and, working with Jake Knapp, developed Design Sprint 2.0, the only update officially approved by Sprint's creator.[16]

The most significant change is that Sprint 2.0 takes four days instead of five. Getting busy executives and key stakeholders to commit five full days is a challenging ask. Cutting that by 20 per cent makes sprints dramatically easier to schedule.

You also only need the full Sprint team for the first two days. Subject matter experts, executives, and key stakeholders take part on Monday and Tuesday, then return to their regular work while a smaller core team handles the prototyping and testing. That makes Sprint 2.0 far more practical in large organisations, where freeing everyone for a full week is close to impossible.

The four-day structure

The best way to bring a four-day sprint to life is to picture one running on a real problem. Imagine a fintech team trying to decide whether to add a new automated savings feature to their mobile app. The customer research suggests there is sufficient demand, but the executives are not so sure, and three months of debate have produced no decision, so they decide to run a Design Sprint.

Day 1: Map and Sketch

Monday morning, the team frames the challenge by setting a long-term goal, 'help our users build savings habits without thinking about it', and listing the risks that could kill the project, like users not trusting an algorithm with their money. A simple map is drawn of how customers experience saving today. They interview two internal experts who have done customer research and one who runs the engineering platform, then pick one customer and one step in that journey to focus on. The whole afternoon is focused on sketching, but not in the way most workshops do it.

Instead of group brainstorming, which tends to be dominated by a few loud voices, each person sketches their own ideas through a short sequence of notes, ideas, Crazy Eights (eight quick sketches in eight minutes), and a final detailed solution. Working alone keeps the ideas diverse. The CFO ends up with a different sketch from the product manager, who ends up with a different sketch from the engineer. By the end of Monday, the team will have 8–10 distinct concepts on the wall.

Day 2: Decide and Storyboard

Tuesday is decision day. The team reviews every sketch through structured voting and critique rather than opening things up to lots of debate, because debating things is the part that can waste time and be unproductive if no one is willing to make a decision. A nominated decision-maker with authority over the project, in this case the head of product, makes the final call between the concepts that have the most votes. The chosen idea then becomes a step-by-step storyboard detailed enough to build from, frame by frame, like a comic strip of the user's journey through the new feature.

At the end of the second day, the executives and external stakeholders head back to their regular work, since their job is done. The core team then takes over for the rest of the week.

Day 3: Prototype

On Wednesday, the focus is on building. A prototype is constructed to what Knapp calls Goldilocks quality – rough enough to put together in a day but real enough for users to interact with. For a digital feature like the savings app, that usually means clickable screens stitched together in a tool like Figma, or for a physical product, a foam model. A service might be tested with a scripted roleplay where a team member acts out the customer interactions.

Day 4: Test

Thursday, five target customers come in one at a time, with the rest of the team watching from another room through a video link. Each customer interacts with the prototype while a facilitator gently probes what they are thinking. The team takes notes on what works and what is deemed to be confusing.

Five users sounds like a small sample, but research by Jakob Nielsen, co-founder of the Nielsen Norman Group, found that five users typically uncover around 85 per cent of

Figure 11.2 The four-day Design Sprint

usability issues.[17] After the fifth interview, the patterns are usually obvious. By the end of the day, the team knows whether to proceed, pivot, or abandon.

When five days still makes sense

The original five-day format remains valuable in specific situations. Teams running their first sprint benefit from the slower pace, because compressing Map and Sketch into a single day can feel overwhelming for people unfamiliar with the process. Complex problems with a large number of stakeholders may also need the extra time, and keeping everyone present through to Friday's testing session lets executives witness customer reactions first-hand, which is sometimes worth more than any deck the team could produce later.

For most teams, though, the four-day format delivers the same learning for less of everyone's time.

LEGO's revolution

In 2017, LEGO's internal digital agency faced a problem too big for incremental improvements. As Eik Thyrsted Brandsgård, who led the transformation, later explained, they needed a revolution rather than an evolution.[18]

They took a radical approach and stopped normal operations for an entire week. They used that time to run 10 Design Sprints simultaneously, with 150 people working in parallel teams on different challenges. Project managers were handed copies of the *Sprint* book on Friday and told they would be facilitating one starting Monday, preparing day by day while their teams worked through the exercises. The process was prescriptive enough that people could hit the ground running without months of training.

By the end of 12 months, LEGO had completed over 150 Design Sprints, and the first prototypes from those early sessions had started appearing on shelves. But the real success was not any single product. It was the fact that Design Sprints became the default method for kicking off projects with high uncertainty, and the company now holds meeting-free weeks each month where teams can run sprints without interruption.[19]

When to use Design Sprints

Design Sprints work best when you have a high-stakes decision to make and you want real user feedback on a prototype within a week. They suit a team stuck debating options for weeks that needs to break the deadlock, or one weighing a significant new direction before committing serious resources like the fintech team in the walkthrough above.

They are less useful when the problem is still vague, and you have not yet worked out what you're really trying to solve. A Design Sprint validates a direction, it does not find one for you. Two practical requirements are worth noting. You will need to recruit five target users who can test the prototype on the final day, and you will need a senior decision-maker with the authority to commit to whatever direction emerges from the sprint. Without that authority in the room, teams risk going through the entire process only to have their findings overturned the following week.

CHOOSING BETWEEN FRAMEWORKS

With so many event-based frameworks to choose from, it helps to see them side by side. Table 11.1 compares the major approaches we have discussed in this chapter across the dimensions worth weighing when deciding which one to choose.

Table 11.1 Comparison of the event-based frameworks

Framework	Duration	When to use	Key output	Discovery depth	Resources and facilitation
Design Thinking	4–8 weeks	When uncertainty is highest, and you need to understand the problem space deeply before committing to a direction	Validated problem definition and tested prototypes	High	Substantial. Often led by trained designers or an external agency. The most resource-heavy option.
Design Sprints	4–5 days	When you need a specific decision validated and want user feedback on a prototype quickly	Tested prototypes with user feedback	Medium	Moderate. A trained Sprint facilitator helps, especially the first time. You must recruit real users.
Hot Houses	2–3 days	When you need rapid alignment and want diverse stakeholders to leave with agreed solutions and delivery commitments	Agreed solutions with delivery commitments	Medium	High. Senior people and real customers, plus skilled facilitation and prizes.
Hackathons	24–48 hours	When you need creative energy and want to break out of routine thinking to generate fresh ideas	Working prototypes or proofs-of-concept	Low	Variable. Light facilitation but heavy logistics: venue, food, judges, and prizes. Can be run cheaply in-house.

(Continued)

Table 11.1 (Continued)

Framework	Duration	When to use	Key output	Discovery depth	Resources and facilitation
Buildathons	24–48 hours	When the team already knows what to build and wants to compress focused work into a single session	A working internal tool or prototype that the team will use	Low	Variable. Lighter than a hackathon. No judges, no prizes. The team itself owns the output.

Event-based frameworks deliver concentrated bursts of learning, but they cannot sustain a team's connection to customers over time. The question is, what happens in the weeks and months between sprints and workshops, and how do you keep your insights fresh once the energy of the event has faded? In the next chapter, we'll explore rhythm-based frameworks that make discovery an ongoing habit rather than a one-off event.

KEY TAKEAWAYS

- **Frameworks structure your discovery effort:** They tell you what to do and when, combining multiple techniques into a coherent approach.
- **Design Thinking prioritises empathy:** The Embrace infant warmer only succeeded because the team spent time in Nepal understanding the real challenge before building anything.
- **Hot Houses speed up decision-making:** Locking diverse stakeholders in a room with real customers and tight time constraints forces decisions that might otherwise take months of meetings.
- **Hackathons generate ideas but need follow-up:** Without clear ownership and a path forward, even the best concepts will be abandoned within weeks. Only 7 per cent of hackathon projects show any sign of continued work six months on.
- **Buildathons trade competition for outcomes:** When the team already knows what to build, the open-ended hackathon format gets in the way, and a focused build session is the better tool.
- **Design Sprints compress months into days:** Structured decision-making combined with rapid prototyping lets teams validate ideas before committing significant resources.
- **Five users reveal most problems:** You don't need large sample sizes to learn whether your prototype works.
- **Get decision-makers in the room:** Without someone who can commit to the direction that emerges, teams risk having their findings overturned later.

12 MAKE DISCOVERY AN ONGOING PRACTICE

'A discovery a day keeps the failures away.'

Paddy Dhanda

FAKE DOORS AT AN INVESTMENT BANK

A few years ago, I took on the role of head of Agile learning at a global investment bank. Within my first month, my manager, Gabby, set me the challenge of launching an Agile training curriculum for over 80,000 employees globally. The catch was that it had to be done within two weeks, with minimal budget and no team.

For the first couple of days, I was anxious. I had never done this before, and my biggest fear was letting Gabby down. My natural instincts kicked in, and I went straight into solution mode, obsessing over how to build the courses and what content they might include.

Thankfully, Gabby came to my rescue. What she saw, and what I couldn't at the time, was that I had skipped a fundamental question: what did our learners actually want to learn? When we're working in high-pressure environments, our rational thinking goes out the window, and I had wrongly assumed I knew what to build without actually validating my thinking.

That prompt helped me to step back and reframe the challenge. Instead of asking, 'How do I build these courses quickly?' I switched to 'How do I find out which courses are truly worth building?'

Rather than trying to build 15 courses from scratch, I did something far simpler and cheaper. Using my basic SharePoint skills, I built an intranet page listing the potential course titles, each with a button to register interest. We hadn't built a single course, and we hadn't promised to deliver any of them. The goal was purely to understand the demand.

The results became clear almost immediately. Out of 15 potential titles, 3 courses stood out, so those were the ones we rolled out to everyone. Over the three years I stayed in that role, we only ever created five courses from the original list. The rest simply didn't generate enough demand to justify the effort.

That experiment saved us from wasting months of time and resources, and it marked the beginning of what we called our Agile University, a learning platform that would eventually reach thousands of employees across the globe.

If you are an experienced product thinker, you will recognise this as a fake door test, which we covered in Chapter 10. But what I didn't realise at the time was that I had

Figure 12.1 Fake door test for training courses

stumbled on a way of thinking that had a name and was transforming how startups and product teams were working; it's called the Lean Startup approach, and we will see in a moment how it works.

The previous chapter looked at event-based discovery; another way of thinking of it is a time-boxed event. They typically help when a team needs to make a big decision quickly, such as through a Hot House or a Design Sprint. This chapter is about the frameworks that allow you to do ongoing discovery, not a one-time event.

The four approaches we are about to look at are often presented as rival methods that you have to choose between, and that framing causes a lot of confusion, because they actually operate at different levels and solve different problems. Try to think of them as complementary approaches that can be used alongside one another, depending upon your situation.

THE LEAN STARTUP

Most modern rhythm-based frameworks trace their roots to one influential book. Eric Ries' *Lean Startup*, published in 2011, fundamentally changed how we think about building products under uncertainty. Ries had first-hand experience of building products that nobody wanted. As co-founder of IMVU, a social networking site, he watched his team spend months building features based on assumptions that turned out to be completely wrong.[1]

The build–measure–learn loop

At the heart of the Lean Startup approach is a simple process: build, measure, learn. The goal is to minimise the total time through this loop. Rather than building a complete product and hoping it works, you build something small enough to tell you whether your assumptions are correct.

Build

Create a minimum viable product (MVP). This is one of the most misunderstood terms in product development. Many teams interpret it as 'build the smallest possible version of our product', but that misses the point entirely. Ries defines an MVP as 'that version of a new product which allows a team to collect the maximum amount of validated learning about customers with the least effort'.[2] The emphasis is on learning, not on building.

An MVP might be a landing page, a video demonstration, a paper prototype, or even a concierge service where you manually deliver what the product would eventually automate.

When Zappos founder Nick Swinmurn wanted to test whether customers would buy shoes online, he didn't build an e-commerce platform. He photographed shoes at local stores, posted the pictures online, bought them at full price when orders came in, and shipped them himself. The 'product' was manual and completely unscalable, but it validated the demand for the products.[3]

Measure

Define your success criteria before you run the experiment. It is worth being strict about this, because it's far too easy to look at ambiguous results and convince yourself they prove whatever you want to believe. Before you start, be clear about what would convince you to proceed and what would make you pivot or abandon the idea entirely.

Collect both quantitative data (did they click, did they sign up, how long did they spend on the page) and qualitative data (what did they say, where did they hesitate, what questions did they ask).

The numbers show you what happened. The conversations tell you why. A landing page might show a 2 per cent conversion rate, but only by watching people use it will you discover they couldn't find the sign-up button or misunderstood what the product actually does.

Learn

This is the equivalent of the Review Results step of the FEATR funnel we covered in Chapter 10. Based on the results, decide whether to persevere with your current approach or pivot to a different strategy. Persevere means the evidence supports your assumptions, and you should continue in the same direction. Pivot means something fundamental needs to change, whether that's the customer segment you're targeting, the problem you're solving, or the solution you're building.

The important thing to remember here is that you're making decisions based on evidence rather than opinion. It changes the conversation from 'I think customers want this' to 'We tested with 50 customers and here's what they did.'

This sounds obvious, but in practice it's a big cultural shift for most organisations. It means accepting that the most senior person in the room doesn't automatically have all the insights because they can only go by their own set of limited experiences.

What makes Lean Startup different

Lean Startup asks whether your product or initiative should exist at all. This makes it particularly suited to high-uncertainty situations, whether that's a whole new venture or a major initiative inside an established business.

If you're unsure whether anyone will pay for what you're building, or whether your distribution channel will work, or whether your pricing makes sense, the Lean Startup treats those assumptions as testable hypotheses.

Ries' approach also introduced the concept of the pivot as a deliberate strategic decision. When your experiments reveal that customers don't want what you're building, you don't necessarily have to abandon the idea. You can change direction based on what you've learned, perhaps targeting a different customer segment, solving a different problem, or using a different business model.

Much of the vocabulary we now take for granted in product work, including terms like MVP and validated learning, was popularised here. Lean Startup gave us the foundations for modern product discovery, but it was written for founders weighing up whether to proceed with launching a startup or initiative when uncertainty is high. Designers working inside established product teams needed a more tailored version that fit the work they were being asked to do, like defining interfaces and creating better user journeys. That adaptation came to be known as Lean UX.

LEAN UX

For decades, user experience design was measured by the size of specification documents: the bigger they were, the more thorough the work appeared to be.

I say this because I, too, have fallen victim to this trap when I was managing a large IT programme. One of my business analysts would produce large, comprehensive documents with every possible type of diagram you could think of. Everything from sequence diagrams to data flows, process charts, and many more. These artefacts looked impressive, but the development teams used a tiny fraction of the content to actually build the product.

Jeff Gothelf, author of *Lean UX*, who had worked at agencies, startups, and enterprises, observed this behaviour repeat itself throughout his career.[4] Teams would invest enormous effort into producing specifications that stakeholders approved enthusiastically, only to see the real products evolve into something completely different. The deliverables had become the goal in themselves, rather than a way to achieve something meaningful for users.

That led Gothelf to question everything he had been taught about UX practices. Working with Josh Seiden, they began applying principles from Eric Ries' Lean Startup to design work, and the result was Lean UX, a framework that replaced heavyweight deliverables with lightweight experiments and shifted the focus from outputs like specifications and prototypes to outcomes like changes in customer behaviour that create business value.

PayPal Lean Engineering

By 2011, PayPal had a problem that anyone who has worked in a large organisation will recognise. Making even a small change to their platform could take as long as six weeks before customers could use it. They worked sequentially, from the business, which wrote the requirements, to the designers, who produced a specification, and then over the wall to the engineers, who built it. Each handover was described as a wall, even by PayPal's own teams, and once a release finally shipped, the group that made it would break up and reform around the next project, which meant they carried all of the learning they had just gained away with them. That wall, and the large specifications passed across it, was exactly the deliverables culture that Lean UX had been created to dismantle.

When David Marcus took over as president in 2012, he set a charter for faster innovation and handed Bill Scott, newly arrived from Netflix to lead user interface engineering, a small team and a daunting brief. The challenge they were given was to rebuild their checkout capability, then responsible for around $3.5 billion of PayPal's annual revenue. Marcus, who thought like a founder, gave them six weeks to launch it.[5]

They could either work a little more efficiently while sticking to their current processes, or abandon them and try something different. They chose the latter.

Product, design, and engineering worked together in a single room from a shared understanding of the problem, sketching on whiteboards and turning ideas into working prototypes in the browser rather than passing documents back and forth. A version of the new checkout flow that the old way of working would have taken weeks of handoffs to reach was ready to be tested in three days, and the redesigned checkout launched inside the window Marcus had set.

The team had applied Lean UX. The cross-functional team and the shared understanding it built were two of Gothelf's founding principles, and so was their approach to replacing traditional specifications in favour of a rough working prototype. Bill Scott called this Lean Engineering, a way of building software designed to remove the things that were causing them friction.

The wider benefit was that the interface had become something the team could change cheaply and safely, which let them keep experimenting on it long after the launch, treating the design as a living thing to be tested and improved rather than a deliverable to be signed off and finished.

This is an example of the outcomes-over-outputs idea at the centre of Lean UX, because the team came to judge its progress by what customers actually did rather than by what it had managed to ship. Within a year, most of the original interface had been rebuilt as the team learned what customers genuinely liked, which in the old six-week model would have been unthinkable.

How to practise Lean UX

The hypothesis statement sits at the centre of Lean UX, and rather than starting with requirements that tell the team to 'build this feature', teams start with assumptions about what might work and why. This subtle shift changes everything about how design decisions get made, because it forces you to articulate not just what you want to build but what you expect to happen as a result.

Step 1: write hypothesis statements

You will recognise the hypothesis statement from earlier in the book, where it served as the Theory in our TEST framework. Lean UX uses the same idea, with one difference worth noting. It writes the measurable signal straight into the statement, rather than holding it back as a separate Thresholds step: 'We believe that [this capability] for [this type of user] will achieve [this outcome], and we will know this is true when we see [this measurable signal].' So instead of 'Add a search filter to the product listing page', you might write: 'We believe that adding category filters for mobile shoppers will increase conversion rates, and we will know this is true when we see a 10 per cent increase in purchases from users who interact with filters.'

Step 2: identify your riskiest assumptions

Every hypothesis contains multiple assumptions that you are treating as facts, and in the example above you're assuming mobile shoppers want to filter by category rather than by price or rating, that they can actually find the filters in the interface, and that filtering will lead to purchases rather than endless browsing. List all your assumptions out, then prioritise them by asking which assumptions would kill the whole idea if they turned out to be wrong, because those are the ones you need to test first.

Step 3: design the smallest possible experiment

Create an MVP that tests your riskiest assumption. This might be a paper sketch you show to five users, a clickable prototype built in an afternoon, or a simple A/B test on a single page. Similar to Lean Startup's definition, Gothelf emphasises that the MVP should be 'the smallest thing you can make to learn whether your hypothesis is valid', because the goal at this stage is learning rather than launching.

Step 4: run the experiment and measure

Put your MVP in front of real users and define your success criteria in advance so you know what would make you confident enough to proceed and what would make you pivot to a different approach. Watch what users actually do rather than relying on what they say they would do, because the gap between stated preferences and actual behaviour is often enormous.

Step 5: learn and iterate

Based on the results, update your hypothesis and decide what to do next. If the assumption was validated, move to the next riskiest assumption on your list. If it was invalidated, pivot your approach and try something different.

This cycle typically runs in one- to two-week iterations, which makes it compatible with Agile sprint cadences, but unlike traditional UX approaches that front-load all the design work before development begins, Lean UX spreads learning across the entire product development process.

When to use Lean UX

Unlike many of the other discovery frameworks, Lean UX consists of guiding principles, prescribed techniques, and a clear process for putting them into practice. It draws from three core foundations: Design Thinking for its human-centred approach; Agile for its iterative delivery; and Lean Startup for its emphasis on validated learning.

Gothelf and Seiden organise their principles into three categories. Team organisation principles advocate for cross-functional, co-located groups small enough to move quickly. Culture principles emphasise outcomes over outputs, shared understanding, and 'permission to fail'. Process principles focus on removing waste and getting out of the building to talk to real users.

Prescribed techniques

The framework includes specific techniques rather than leaving teams to invent their own. Design Studio is a structured exercise where the whole team sketches solutions together. Proto-personas are lightweight user personas created quickly from assumptions when you don't have access to actual users, and then validated through research. The hypothesis statement template provides a consistent format for structuring your expectations before building.

Best fit

Lean UX is designed for teams where designers and developers work in short cycles together, so that you can put a prototype in front of users quickly. That agility allows you to change direction quickly based on what you learn.

Instead of the most senior person in the room deciding the outcome, the team agrees on what success looks like and measures whether the design achieves it.

Lean UX assumes that designers, developers, and product managers sit close enough to collaborate daily, so it can be difficult to implement in organisations where these functions report into separate departments or where work passes through formal handoff processes. It also requires access to real users on a regular basis, which may need senior support to ensure you have the right infrastructure in place.

Lean UX gives designers a disciplined way to treat each design as a hypothesis and test it cheaply. What it does not settle is how discovery and delivery actually run alongside each other, week after week, in a team that is also under real pressure to ship working software. That is the question Dual-Track Agile was built to answer.

DUAL-TRACK AGILE

Before getting into how Dual-Track Agile works, it's worth seeing what teams typically try first, and the pitfalls with these approaches. If you work in a Scrum team, you've probably asked yourself where exactly discovery is supposed to fit. Scrum, and a number of other Agile frameworks, are designed to optimise the shipping of high-quality code, and the two-week sprint cadence works beautifully when you already know what to build and can plan the work in short, predictable cycles.

However, discovery is a different type of work because it is really about learning, and learning is difficult to estimate or compress neatly into two-week iterations, because there is no obvious endpoint.

You can rarely say at the outset how many conversations it will take to get there, because you don't know which of them might answer your question or open up several new ones you had never thought to ask. A lot of it also sits outside of your control, since you depend on stakeholders being available when you need them and on them actually knowing the insights that you need.

Since delivery and discovery move at different speeds, I like to think of them a bit like a tortoise and a hare.

Figure 12.2 Speed of discovery and delivery

Over the years, I've watched teams try creative ways to incorporate discovery and analysis into their ways of working, often with very little success. If you have struggled with this dilemma in your own teams, then you are definitely not alone, and it is one of the most challenging parts of product development to get right. Let me share a few of my favourite anti-patterns to ensure you avoid these pitfalls.

The 'Sprint Zero' approach

This is where you dedicate the very first sprint, often referred to as Sprint Zero, as a preparation sprint that allows you to set up the architecture and tooling. But many teams also use it as a way of front-loading their discovery work.

The *Scrum Guide* is quite firm that every sprint should produce a usable, potentially releasable increment, and a discovery-only Sprint Zero goes against that philosophy; therefore, Sprint Zero isn't really a sprint at all. Mike Cohn argues that the real issue is the precedent it sets, because once a team accepts that some sprints need not deliver anything shippable, the discipline that makes sprints valuable starts to erode.[6] He suggests treating genuine setup work as a 'project before the project' rather than dressing it up as a sprint.

The 'phased mini-waterfall'

Part of the appeal here is that it lets you keep telling everyone you are working in sprints, even though the underlying pattern resembles a waterfall approach. You run one sprint for discovery, the second for design, and another for development.

Marty Cagan also observed that many teams are 'essentially doing little mini-waterfalls within their Scrum framework. The product manager does some kind of "requirements" work, and that is passed to a designer that does his designs and generates his artifacts (usually annotated wireframes), and then that is handed off to the delivery team to build and test'.[7]

I even saw one team introduce decimal numbering to their sprints whenever one of them was at risk of spilling over, such as sprint 1.1, 1.2, and so on. It's a great way to keep the leadership happy. Since you are still technically in sprint 1, they cannot say you are late. The only issue is, you might be there for a long time.

The 'squeeze it in' approach

In this one, we reserve the first two days of each sprint for discovery activities, and then switch over to delivery. In theory, this sounds Agile. In practice, two days are barely enough to organise any type of meaningful work. You end up doing such a light-touch discovery that it probably validated very little. More often than not, it becomes a box-ticking activity because that's what the playbook says to do.

What links all three of these patterns is a single underlying mistake, which is treating discovery as something you can merge into the rhythm of delivery. The two are very different kinds of work that answer different questions.

Delivery tries to turn a decision into working software, while discovery exists to work out whether that decision is worth making in the first place, which takes far longer to achieve. They therefore run at very different speeds. And things are only going to get worse with new AI coding platforms that enable features to be built in a matter of seconds. That means discovery needs to accelerate to be even faster.

When you force both into the same two-week window, the slower and messier work ends up being rushed, which can create all sorts of unforeseen problems. Analysts risk burnout, engineers become frustrated by gaps in the discovery, the quality of the work suffers, and we haven't even talked about the pushback from stakeholders when asked to give up their valuable time.

Origins of Dual-Track Agile

This approach started in the mid-2000s at Alias, a Canadian software company later acquired by Autodesk. Lynn Miller[8] and her colleague Desirée Sy were struggling to integrate user-centred design with the new Agile methods their teams were adopting.[9]

They learned that design work needed to run one cycle ahead of development, but the two tracks had to stay tightly connected through regular synchronisation points.

In 2012, Jeff Patton coined the term Dual-Track Scrum to describe this parallel structure, and Marty Cagan popularised it through the Silicon Valley Product Group. They reframed the approach around two explicit tracks with distinct purposes. As Patton explains, 'No matter how you approach it, creating digital products involves two kinds of work, discovering the right thing to build, and building it.'[10]

The core concept

The Discovery Track focuses on generating validated backlog items. This is where the product manager, designer, and lead engineer work together to explore problems and test assumptions before committing development resources. The output is not a specification document but a stream of ideas that have been validated enough to justify building them.

The Delivery Track focuses on building, testing, and releasing validated solutions. Its output is releasable software. This follows the normal sprint process in Scrum. Engineers spend most of their time here, but they should regularly participate in discovery activities to maintain context and contribute ideas.

The keyword is 'parallel'. Discovery is not a phase that ends when delivery begins. While the delivery team is building sprint 5's features, the Discovery Track is validating concepts that might become sprint 7 or sprint 8's work. This creates a healthy discovery pipeline that runs ahead of delivery, continuously de-risking ideas.

Making it work in practice

The elegance of the concept can obscure the discipline required to execute it well. Teams that succeed with Dual-Track Agile typically follow several principles.

First, nothing enters the delivery backlog until it has been validated. This is the fundamental rule that separates Dual-Track from traditional Scrum. Validation might mean customer interviews or prototype testing, but some form of evidence must support the decision to build.

Second, the tracks synchronise regularly: weekly refinement sessions where the discovery shares upcoming work with the delivery; daily standups where both tracks flag blockers and dependencies. Without these touchpoints, the tracks drift apart and the handoffs become just as painful as the old waterfall approach.

Third, teams define what 'sufficiently validated' means for their context. A consumer app team might require usability testing with five users. An enterprise platform team might need sign-off from compliance. The threshold varies, but having an explicit standard prevents endless discovery cycles.

Fourth, teams protect time for both tracks. Some organisations allocate roughly 70 per cent of capacity to delivery and 30 per cent to discovery. Others vary this based on the maturity of their product. The important thing is that discovery has dedicated time rather than being squeezed into the gaps between delivery commitments.

How BNZ Digital bank did it

BNZ Digital, the digital banking arm of Bank of New Zealand, runs over 20 product teams with more than 250 people practising Dual-Track delivery.[11] As an experiment to test the approach, one of their teams had been asked to develop a logging feature that stakeholders were convinced customers wanted.

They had sized it at around 12 months of development effort. But rather than diving straight into delivery, the team applied discovery discipline. They started with their biggest assumption: 'Our customers want this.'

They talked to actual customers and examined usage analytics. What they discovered was that nobody wanted it. It's a classic problem I see in many organisations, where we assume stakeholders are the experts who know exactly what the end-user needs. But the perceived problem did not exist in the way they had understood it.

The team cancelled the initiative before writing a single line of code. Agile coach Ant Boobier reflected on what would have happened previously: 'We would have focused on building this feature efficiently, releasing it in 11 months and then celebrated.'

Instead, 12 months of development effort were avoided through a few weeks of disciplined discovery work. The success of this experiment led BNZ Digital to create a product management playbook that embedded Dual-Track thinking across the entire organisation.

When to use Dual-Track Agile

Dual-Track Agile works best when you already have an established delivery team using Scrum or Kanban. Unlike event-based frameworks, which are ad hoc time-boxes of discovery for specific challenges, Dual-Track creates an ongoing rhythm where discovery and delivery run continuously in parallel.

This makes it particularly suited to mature product teams working on incremental improvements rather than entirely new initiatives. If you're exploring whether a product should exist at all, Lean Startup might be a better starting point. But once you have a product with users and a delivery cadence in place, Dual-Track helps you systematically de-risk what goes into your backlog.

The approach requires dedicated product management and design resources. Teams without these capabilities may find the overhead difficult to sustain. It also requires organisational maturity to accept that some discovery work won't result in features, since the whole point is to filter out bad ideas before they consume development effort.

While Dual-Track Agile provides a focus on discovery, it doesn't prescribe specific methods. Teams are free to use whatever techniques work best for their context, whether that's customer interviews, prototyping, data analysis, or experiments. Dual-Track Agile gives you the structure for keeping discovery a step ahead of delivery, but structure on its own does not keep you close to your customers. A team can run two perfectly tidy tracks and still only speak to its users on the rare occasions when it has something ready to show them. Turning that contact from occasional into regular, so that it becomes a steady habit rather than an event, is what Continuous Discovery is built around.

CONTINUOUS DISCOVERY HABITS

Teresa Torres spent years coaching product teams who understood the value of customer research but struggled to work out how to have regular contact with users. She observed that teams would treat research as a phase that happened before development rather than an ongoing practice. They would conduct a burst of interviews at the start of a project, generate insights, and then start building for months at a time, only to emerge with a product that wasn't quite what users needed.

Torres is famous for helping develop the Continuous Discovery Habits framework, captured in her 2021 book of the same name.[12] It's based on a very simple principle, to have weekly touchpoints with customers.

For most teams, weekly customer contact might feel like it's overkill, but Torres believes that occasional deep research isn't enough. This is because customer needs evolve, and your understanding becomes out of date over time if you don't actively refresh it. Weekly contact keeps you aligned with the daily challenges of your users.

The CarMax experiment

Torres worked directly with a product team at CarMax, the US used-car retailer, who were already conducting customer interviews and running experiments.[13] They would talk to customers once a week, but only when they had something to validate. They would run one experiment per month, trying to test multiple assumptions in a single large test.

After working with Torres, the team shifted to engaging with 2–4 customers every week, regardless of whether they had anything to show them. They also changed how they thought about experiments entirely. As Jake Mitchell, the team's designer, explained: 'A big aha moment was that an experiment doesn't mean just a live A/B test. We now see experiments as a method of gathering data that supports or challenges an individual assumption.'

Instead of waiting until they had a polished prototype to gather feedback, the team built customer conversations into their weekly schedule. And rather than trying to validate an entire feature in one large experiment, they broke their ideas into smaller assumptions and tested the riskiest ones first.

Torres helped them organise their thinking using an Opportunity Solution Tree, a visual map that connects customer opportunities to potential solutions and experiments. Victoria Lawson, the product manager, described the impact: 'We are more in tune with our customers than we have ever been before and are able to take their stories and needs into every decision we make.'

The underlying structure

The Opportunity Solution Tree is a framework that connects three essential elements: outcomes, opportunities, and solutions.[14] Torres uses the metaphor of the tree intentionally, as it shows how everything flows from a single desired outcome at the top, branches into the opportunity space in the middle, and finally reaches potential solutions at the bottom. Each week, the team conducts small research activities that inform one or more of these layers.

Keep the outcome in mind

Every team needs clarity on what they are trying to accomplish, not in terms of features to ship, but in terms of the impact they are trying to create. Torres makes a critical distinction between two types of outcomes that product teams often confuse.[15]

Business outcomes measure the health of the organisation and are typically financial metrics such as growing revenue, increasing market share, or reducing churn. These are lagging indicators, meaning that by the time you see a change in revenue, it's as a result of many different decisions made over a period of time. You can rarely pinpoint a single initiative that may have led to a positive business outcome.

Product outcomes, by contrast, measure a change in customer behaviour or sentiment that the product team can directly influence. These are leading indicators that give you early signals of what might happen to business outcomes down the line. For example, increasing the percentage of users who complete onboarding is a product outcome that the team can measure weekly and directly affect through their work.

The distinction is important because assigning a team a business outcome like 'increase revenue' gives them no clear direction. They don't know which lever to pull. But assigning them a product outcome like 'increase the number of users who return within seven days' gives them something specific to explore and improve. As Torres puts it, the goal is to find the connection between product outcomes (metrics the team can influence) and business outcomes (metrics that drive the business).[16]

Discover what customers need

The second activity involves continuously exploring what Torres calls the 'opportunity space'. She uses the phrase 'needs, pain points, and desires', which she collectively labels as opportunities.[17] Traditional product thinking focuses almost exclusively on solving problems, but Torres argues this framing is too narrow.

Think about social media or streaming services. They don't solve problems in the traditional sense. If anything, they create new problems around time management and distraction. But they satisfy deep desires for connection and entertainment, which is why we keep using them.

This reframing changes how teams conduct customer research. Instead of only asking 'What problems do you face?' teams should also explore what customers aspire to, what delights them, and what they wish existed. The opportunity space represents everywhere the team could potentially intervene in a customer's life in a positive way.

Torres recommends that teams map their opportunities visually, organising them into parent–child relationships where broad opportunities break down into smaller, more specific sub-opportunities.[18]

This structure helps teams avoid two common traps. First, it stops them from looking too narrowly at a single problem; and second, it prevents them from becoming overwhelmed by trying to address too many opportunities at once. By selecting one opportunity to focus on at a time, teams can make meaningful progress without losing sight of the bigger picture.

Discover solutions that address those opportunities

The third activity involves generating and testing potential solutions, but with an important rule: solutions should only exist in response to a clearly identified opportunity. This is where most teams usually go wrong. They live in what Torres calls 'solution world', jumping straight to features and ideas without first understanding which customer opportunity they are addressing.

If you cannot draw a clear line from your proposed feature to a specific customer need, pain point, or desire, you should question whether you should be building it at all.

Torres also advocates for generating multiple solutions for any given opportunity rather than falling in love with the first idea that comes to mind. Research on creative problem-solving suggests that the best ideas often emerge later in an ideation session, after the obvious solutions have been exhausted.[19] By working on at least three potential solutions simultaneously, teams avoid the trap of over-committing to an approach before they have explored alternatives.

But generating ideas is only half the battle. The real work comes from testing assumptions. You should identify the specific assumptions that need to be true for a solution to succeed, and then test those assumptions individually through small, rapid experiments.

How to interview every week

The weekly interview cadence sounds demanding, and in my experience it's the single biggest barrier teams face when trying to adopt Continuous Discovery. But the teams that build this habit consistently outperform those that don't, because they maintain the feedback loop that keeps them aligned with users.

Automate your recruiting

The other challenge is finding someone to talk to. One innovative way to do this is to embed a request directly into your product with a simple prompt: 'Do you have 20 minutes to share your experience with us?' Connect it to a calendar tool that lets participants self-select available slots. When Yury Oleynik's team at HiveMQ implemented this approach, they scheduled six interviews within the first week.[20]

Ground conversations in past behaviour

Most teams ask people what they want or what they would do. These questions feel natural but produce unreliable data, because people are notoriously bad at predicting their own future behaviour. A more effective approach is story-based interviewing. Instead, ask: 'Tell me about the last time you ...'. This simple structure focuses the conversation on what actually happened rather than what someone imagines they might do.

Pause and reflect

After each interview, take 15 minutes to map what happened and where friction occurred for the user. Capture the key moments, any workarounds the customer described, and the emotions they expressed. After every three or four conversations, step back and pause to look for patterns. Are multiple customers struggling with the same workflow? Do different users describe the same frustration using different language? These insights gathered across different interviews can reveal opportunities that no single conversation could surface alone.

BUILDING YOUR DISCOVERY STACK

Think of techniques as LEGO bricks. Each brick has a specific shape and purpose, but the real magic happens when you combine them. Every framework in this chapter and the one before is essentially a pre-designed LEGO kit, a proven combination of techniques that work well together for specific purposes.

Design Thinking is the kit for 'understanding problems deeply and creating human-centred solutions'. Design Sprints are the kit for 'making a major decision in one week'. Continuous Discovery is the kit for 'staying connected to customers over time'. Lean UX is the kit for 'integrating design into Agile development'. Dual-Track Agile is the kit for 'running discovery alongside delivery'.

Choosing the right kit

Choosing a rhythm-based framework depends on where you are as a team and what problem you're trying to solve. Table 12.1 presents a comparison to help you find the right fit.

FRAMEWORKS TO HUMAN SKILLS

At this point, we have covered some of the most useful discovery frameworks you can apply to your work. But just like a racing car requires a skilled driver, frameworks depend on the skills of the people using them.

You can follow a framework and still ask the wrong questions or run a workshop that gets sabotaged by the loudest person in the room. That is why the next part of the book moves from shifting your mindset and practising the techniques to the human skills that help you master discovery.

Table 12.1 Comparison of rhythm-based discovery frameworks

Framework	Level it operates at	When to use it	Key output
Lean Startup	New ventures or initiatives with high uncertainty	When you need to test assumptions quickly with minimal investment	Validated learning through experiments
Lean UX	Specific design and solution decisions	When designers need to test assumptions quickly within Agile sprints	Hypothesis-validated designs
Dual-Track Agile	Team workflow and process	When your Agile team needs to validate ideas before they enter the sprint backlog	Validated backlog items
Continuous Discovery	Ongoing product direction over time	When you want regular customer insight to guide what you build next	Continuously updated opportunity map

I introduced this idea in the preface because the phrase *soft skills* undervalues the work we do. Product discovery requires high amounts of judgement, curiosity, empathy, creativity, influence, and the ability to keep learning.

The World Economic Forum's *Future of Jobs Report* highlights a massive shift in the workforce.[21] With the acceleration of AI, employers are placing a premium on uniquely human and cognitive capabilities. They include many of the skills we will cover in the final part of this book.

We will begin with stakeholder collaboration, because nearly every discovery decision requires us to figure out ways to engage with our stakeholders, which can be one of the most challenging parts of the role. From there, we will look at different types of facilitation, because when we do bring people together, we have to skilfully work out how to ensure the conversation helps the group think clearly, challenge safely, and make better decisions. We will then move into powerful questions and presenting ideas with impact, before closing with building a discovery culture by introducing you to probably the most valuable skill of all: learning.

KEY TAKEAWAYS

- **Rhythm-based frameworks:** Unlike event-based approaches, rhythm-based frameworks create ongoing habits that keep you connected to customers.
- **Lean Startup treats every assumption as a test:** The build–measure–learn loop helps you validate ideas with minimal investment before committing further.

- **Lean UX treats designs as hypotheses to test:** Instead of spending months on specifications that may never get used, teams run small experiments to learn what actually works.
- **Dual-Track Agile runs discovery alongside delivery:** The two tracks run in parallel, with discovery continuously feeding validated ideas into the delivery backlog.
- **Continuous Discovery means weekly customer contact:** Occasional deep research isn't enough because your understanding becomes out of date over time.
- **Human skills are an essential part of discovery:** Analytical thinking, creativity, curiosity, resilience, empathy, influence, and self-awareness are the skills that help you use the frameworks well.

PART III
MASTERING PRODUCT DISCOVERY

13 READ STAKEHOLDERS AND NAVIGATE THE POLITICS

'Keep your difficult stakeholders close, but keep the quiet ones closer.'

Paddy Dhanda

ORIGINS OF THE STAKEHOLDER

The word 'stakeholder' has always intrigued me. When you say it slowly, 'stake holder', it sounds like someone from a Dracula film, with a sharp wooden spear, ready to do some damage. In the business world, we have all worked with people who seemed ready to sabotage our project at any moment, and that image isn't too far from the truth.

But that was never the intention behind the word. In the 18th century, a stakeholder was the person who held the money when a bet was placed.[1] The word entered the business world in 1963 as a deliberate play on the word 'stockholder', designed to make the point that companies owe something to more than just their shareholders. Two decades later, R. Edward Freeman defined a stakeholder as any group or individual who can affect or is affected by the achievement of an organisation's objectives.[2]

Yet the real horror story is not the stakeholders themselves, it's the way we have been taught to deal with them. We are encouraged to conduct stakeholder analysis where we plot people on grids and classify them as 'high power, low interest', as though we are cataloguing widgets rather than working with human beings who are emotional, unpredictable, and often under pressures we cannot see. These tools do have their place, as we will find out later, but they should never replace the hard work required to build the actual relationships.

I want to tell you about a stakeholder I will call David. He probably taught me most about how to build effective stakeholder relationships.

David was a senior director who was extremely busy and deeply frustrated. The breakdown in communication between him and the project team had got so bad that he had walked out of a project meeting halfway through because he felt the project manager was useless, and things had ground to a halt.

My colleague, whom I will call Asha, and I were brought in to see if we could help rebuild the relationship. Asha was a mature student on a summer internship with a background in sales. I was a software engineer, so I had more of a technical perspective. Before we explore what happened next, let's talk about why people are so complex and often so difficult to work with.

PEOPLE ARE MESSY

Think about the last decision you made that you knew was irrational, like buying something you did not need because it was on sale. If humans were rational, predictable creatures, the entire field of behavioural science would not need to exist. The field exists because humans are messy.

During a conversation I had with Robert Kerbeck, author of *Ruse: Lying the American Dream from Hollywood to Wall Street*,[3] who spent years working as a corporate spy, I got to learn about the methods he used to extract confidential information by exploiting our human blind spots.[4] He would call into major companies under false pretences and walk away with details of salaries and competitive strategies. Companies spend millions on cybersecurity, but the weakest point is always the humans who work for them. We have been conditioned to be helpful, so we respond to social cues even when those cues are being exploited by someone who is deliberately misleading us. If trained professionals in high-security environments will share confidential data because someone on the phone was polite and persistent, the idea that everyone in your next meeting will behave rationally when you present your feature priorities is, to put it gently, optimistic.

But the messiness cuts both ways. Your stakeholders are not the only ones prone to these effects – you are too. Think about what happens when you have a bad experience with a stakeholder. Maybe they came across negatively when you presented your ideas or failed to follow through on something they agreed to. Your brain jumps to judging them, rather than what they might be dealing with. 'They're resistant to change.' 'They don't get it.' 'They're political.'

Stanford psychologist Lee Ross refers to this as attribution error.[5] We overestimate the role of personality and underestimate the role of situation when explaining other people's behaviour. The stakeholder who seemed hostile in your meeting might have been dealing with a crisis at home that you knew nothing about. And the one who cancelled at the last minute might have had to let go of some of their team. We label people based on one or two interactions and then filter everything they do through that lens. The times they are reasonable go unnoticed, while the moments they are difficult confirm what we already believe. So before you try to read a stakeholder, it is worth asking whether you are approaching them with genuine curiosity, or whether you have already decided what kind of person they are.

STAKEHOLDER FORECASTING

We are all wired differently

None of this would be a problem if everyone thought the same way, but they do not. We all have genuinely different personality traits that impact the different ways we process information and respond under pressure. For decades, psychologists have been building tools to map those differences.

The most famous is the Myers–Briggs Type Indicator, which sorts people into 16 types and is taken by around 1.5 million people every year.[6] You might also have encountered the Big Five model, which measures personality across five traits: openness, conscientiousness, extraversion, agreeableness, and neuroticism. It has the strongest scientific backing of the lot, emerging from decades of research that started with two psychologists, Gordon Allport and Henry Odbert, identifying roughly 4,500 personality-describing words in the English dictionary back in 1936.[7] Unlike Myers–Briggs, which puts you in a specific box, the Big Five measures where you sit on a spectrum for each trait. Two people can hear the same discovery findings and walk away with completely different emotional responses, because their personality traits filter the information through different lenses.

For product practitioners, the challenge is that you will never have the luxury of sitting your stakeholders down and running a 40-minute personality assessment. You need a way to read people in the moment and adjust your approach on the fly, which is what this next section is designed to give you.

Reading the conditions

As a Brit, I know just how unpredictable the weather can be. I've learned that while you cannot control it, you can check the forecast and prepare yourself to get through the day. The same is true of the people you work with.

Over the years, I have noticed that stakeholder personalities tend to cluster around a set of recognisable patterns. Not everyone fits neatly into one, and the same person can shift depending on the situation, but learning to read the conditions helps you adapt your approach. I call the practice Stakeholder Forecasting, because the analogy captures five types of personality that are each represented by the weather. None of them is intended to represent bad weather, they each describe a very specific set of personality traits, which are broadly based on the Big Five model we looked at earlier.

Figure 13.1 Stakeholder Forecasting

Thundery stakeholders

Have you ever heard someone being described as loving the sound of their own voice? That is a thundery stakeholder. They are usually the most vocal person in the room, and other people either get talked over or simply get shut down.

Adam Galinsky at Columbia Business School found that people primed with a sense of power became measurably worse at taking other perspectives.[8] One of his most practical findings is that offering two options lowers defensiveness far more effectively than a single recommendation, because a single proposal becomes a yes-or-no challenge that they are wired to win, whereas two options become a conversation about preference: 'I have two approaches that could work here, and I'd value your view on which fits best.'

The other technique that works well is to acknowledge their position before introducing yours. Not to agree with it, but to show that you have heard it: 'You're raising something really important about speed to market, and I want to make sure we factor that in alongside what the customer research is showing us.'

When Asha and I first met David, his frustrations were loud and clear, and his default was to make his position known very loudly. Asha did not try to match his energy or push back. She told me to sit beside him rather than opposite, which changed the physical dynamic from confrontation to partnership.

Sunny stakeholders

This is the colleague who is always warm, approachable, and genuinely likeable. You leave every meeting feeling good about your progress. The problem is they don't always tell you when they disagree with you for fear it might come across as being negative.

You get three weeks into delivery and discover that concerns existed all along but were never raised. The cause is a psychological phenomenon called the Abilene Paradox, first described by management expert Jerry Harvey.[9] He told the story of a family who drove 50 miles to Abilene, Texas, for dinner that none of them actually wanted, because each person assumed the others were keen.

The skill with a sunny stakeholder is to make disagreement feel as safe as agreement. A good question to ask is, 'We covered a lot of ground today, and I'd find it really helpful to hear what could go wrong with this approach.'

After every meeting, Asha would call David to check on him. She would ask how he felt the session had gone, and she would share her honest feedback about our own failings. That was genuine empathy and not a tactic, and it was one of the reasons David trusted us enough to eventually share what was really on his mind.

Foggy stakeholders

Have you ever met someone and had no idea where they stood when it came to their thinking? That sums up a foggy stakeholder, because your visibility becomes blurred. Some people are masters at hiding their emotions and suppressing their body language, which makes them extremely difficult to read.

Other foggy stakeholders are not trying to be ambiguous intentionally. They prefer everything to be professional and formal, and conversations are efficient, factual, and stripped of small talk. Researchers Susan Fiske and Amy Cuddy found that when we meet someone new, we instinctively assess them on two dimensions: warmth and competence.[10] If you are like me, then I definitely lead with warmth. A cold, formal personality evaluates competence first, so if you try to build rapport before you have established that you know what you are doing, they read it as a lack of substance. Match their communication style, and once they trust your competence, they usually warm to you.

This is exactly what happened with David. When Asha and I took over writing the requirements specification, we did not ask David to change how he worked. We adapted to him. He was brilliant at providing business insights, but the laborious work of turning those insights into a structured document was not his strength, and forcing him to do it had been the source of the original breakdown. By taking that burden away and letting him focus on what he was good at, we earned his trust through competence, and not through our charm.

Windy stakeholders

Have you ever tried to plan a holiday with a group of your friends? I have a WhatsApp group for my holiday buddies, and whenever we attempt to arrange a trip, there is always one individual who struggles to make a decision. That is the windy stakeholder. Their priorities shift depending on who they spoke to that morning, or whichever direction the wind blows.

Psychologist Barry Schwartz identified two distinct patterns for how people make decisions. Satisficers choose an option once it meets their criteria and then move on, whereas maximisers keep searching even after they have found something good. Schwartz found that maximisers experience more regret and struggle to commit even when the evidence in front of them is strong.[11] The windy personality often operates from this perspective.

The problem is that people stop committing their effort fully in any direction because experience has taught them it will probably change again. They will also want constant reassurance that the direction is right, and you can get stuck in an endless discovery loop.

Try to ask a windy stakeholder to state what success looks like before any decision is made: 'What would need to be true for you to feel confident we are heading in the right direction?' Now there is a benchmark that you can measure against. When they revisit the topic a week later, you can review how far from or close to it you are.

Rainy stakeholders

Have you ever worked with someone who is constantly looking for a reason why everything will fail? They are the classic glass-half-empty personality, who we will refer to as the rainy stakeholder.

Every interaction is met with objections such as, 'We tried something like that before', or 'The business will never fund it.' None is unreasonable on its own, but the accumulation makes you dread seeing their name on the invite list.

The temptation is to dismiss their concerns as negative and ignore them, but that is the worst thing you can do. Psychologist Julie Norem calls this defensive pessimism.

Defensive pessimists set low expectations and mentally rehearse everything that could go wrong to help them prepare, and they perform just as well as optimists on the same tasks. But when Norem encouraged them to think positively, their performance actually got worse.[12] Telling a rainy personality to cheer up or look on the bright side isn't just unhelpful, it actively undermines the process they are using to engage with the problem.

So how do you channel that instinct? Having worked with many salespeople, one concept I have become familiar with is objection handling. They think through every reason a customer might say no and build the answers into their approach before they walk into the room.

You can do exactly the same thing with your discovery work, and the rainy personality is the best resource you have for doing it. Pull them into the conversation early and let them challenge your thinking while it is still easy to change direction. Every objection they raise at that stage is one you will not have to deal with in a steering committee six weeks later, in front of people with far less patience.

David had more than a hint of rainy about him too. The wider project team had made up their mind and labelled him as someone who wasn't just difficult, but impossible to work with, yet his scepticism about whether this time would be any different was entirely justified. We did not try to convince him otherwise; instead, we acknowledged what had gone wrong before and then showed him through our actions, week after week, that this time actually was different.

Checking the forecast

Table 13.1 summarises how to deal with each type of stakeholder.

Table 13.1 Stakeholder Forecasting

Condition	What you will observe	Practical tactics
Thundery	Dominant voice, strong opinions, wants control	Acknowledge their point first. Give them two options instead of one. Draw quieter people into the conversation.
Sunny	Warm, agreeable, avoids conflict	Do not assume they agree just because they are pleasant. Ask what could go wrong. Challenge your own idea first to make honesty feel safe.
Foggy	Reserved, gives little away, hard to read	Lead with facts and clarity. Ask specific questions, not broad ones. Test your reading of them by summarising what you think they mean.
Windy	Shifts position, reopens settled decisions	Agree on what success looks like before deciding. Write decisions down. Bring them back to what they said success looked like.
Rainy	Raises objections, focuses on past failures	Ask exactly what they think will fail. Acknowledge what happened before. Involve them early to pressure-test ideas.

When you read the conditions right

Dave Gauntley, a principal product manager, told me about a role early in his career where he was dropped into a large financial services organisation as a consultant.[13] He quickly found himself caught between two senior stakeholders who were, in his words, combustible.

The first was a new head of transformation who had been brought in to deliver results fast, and from the day she walked through the door, her job was on the line. Her counterpart was a head of service delivery who had spent 30 years working in IT and described herself as a bulldog, because she had learned long ago that if she was not fighting for her teams, nobody else would. Put the two of them in a room together, and the meetings usually ended with both of them shouting at Dave or at each other.

So Dave started reading the conditions. He would drop by their desks, have a coffee, and gradually build a picture of what was driving each of them. The head of service delivery was thundery. But the head of transformation was harder to pin down. She shifted priorities constantly, but underneath that was something closer to rainy. Every decision she made was based on one question, 'Will this help me survive the next six months?'

Once he understood what he was dealing with, Dave adapted. He started acknowledging the head of service delivery's concerns before introducing his own, and he reframed updates for the head of transformation in terms of the value they created for her specifically.

After one meeting that Dave thought had gone well, he got a phone call two miles down the road from his boss telling him the head of transformation wanted him removed from the site. Remember, I did say people are messy. She had sat through that entire meeting, engaged and positive, and made a completely different decision the moment Dave left the room. He went back the next day and worked on rebuilding their relationship, which was only possible because he had invested the time to understand what drove her.

The phone call happened because of pressures in her world that he could not see. While we can put our efforts into understanding people, there are always other dynamics at play, a darker side to business, better known as politics. That is where we go next.

THE POLITICS OF DISCOVERY

Only 9 per cent of the British public trust politicians to tell the truth, making them the least trusted profession in the country for over 40 years running.[14] So when you hear the word 'politics', it carries a lot of baggage, because for most of us we think of scheming or manipulating. Jeffrey Pfeffer at Stanford defines politics simply as the process by which people with different interests work things out.[15] It happens each day in every organisation where resources are limited, and more than one person has a view on how they should be used.

Figure 13.2 Unpopularity of politicians

As a product discovery thinker, you are the person who goes out, talks to customers, gathers evidence, and comes back with findings about how we should evolve the product. Sometimes those findings confirm what stakeholders already believe. But sometimes they contradict what a senior person has publicly committed to.

Nobody trains you for this

During my career, I have had to deal with many political situations. There was the time when I set up a product management team in my home city, Birmingham, for a global bank. I had to deal with office politics when our London colleagues refused to hand over their work so that we could continue to lead it. Then there was the stakeholder who was determined to sabotage the project, because their job was at risk if the IT platform went live.

But I was never trained to deal with many of those situations. There just isn't a certification in how to be a successful politician in the office. David Buchanan and Richard Badham studied the politics of organisational change and found that the change agent who is not politically skilled will fail.[16] Good ideas die inside organisations because the person presenting them did not understand the political environment they were operating in.

Mapping the power

The old saying 'knowledge is power' doesn't fully apply in a politically charged environment; instead, 'position is power' becomes more relevant. Pfeffer identified several sources of power that operate independently of job titles. Control of resources applies to the person who approves budgets or decides which teams get funding, while control of information gives power to the people who hold critical data that others depend on. Network centrality describes the people who sit at the intersection of multiple teams, which means they know what is happening across the business before anyone else does. These are often the people whose support you need most, and they are not necessarily the most senior.

A practical exercise I have used with teams is a simple power map. Before a significant meeting or initiative, draw a grid with two axes, influence on the horizontal and alignment on the vertical. Plot every relevant stakeholder. The ones in the top right, high influence and high alignment, are your champions. Those in the top left, high influence and low alignment, are the people you need to invest in to build a deeper relationship before you invite them to make a decision.

That map should change how you spend your time, because most people end up investing their energy in the people who are already supportive. When Lyndon Johnson was pushing the Civil Rights Act through the US Senate in 1964, he did not spend his evenings with the Northern liberals who already supported the bill. He spent them with the Southern Democrats who opposed it, particularly Senator Richard Russell, the most powerful opponent in the chamber. Johnson understood that the votes he already had were not the ones that needed his attention. The votes that could block him were.[17] The same logic applies to your stakeholder map.

POLITICS TACTICS

Building relationship tactics

Not every stakeholder will be involved in every project, and it's difficult to build meaningful connections if the first time you speak to them is the day you need their support. Your job goes beyond understanding their needs. You also need to build trust and show that you genuinely care about their challenges. The moment it becomes a box-ticking exercise, people sense it, and it feels transactional rather than a partnership.

The golden ticket

I used to tell my product teams, 'You have Willy Wonka's golden ticket.' What I meant by that is that you are in a unique position that enables you to speak to anyone in the organisation, including the CEO, and ask them pretty much anything. If they ask why, just say you are doing product discovery work, and it's your job to understand how things work.

At the home services organisation I introduced in Chapter 10, I needed to engage with our director of operations, who was responsible for the entire call centre. Rather than waiting to meet her during a project workshop, I offered to help her with some of her pet projects before she was sure whether they were big enough to be formalised. In reality, I was offering her free discovery in disguise, and she welcomed the extra help. At the same time, it meant that I had a strong supporter at the executive level for any future work we would do together.

Making deposits

Stephen Covey describes this using the metaphor of an emotional bank account.[18] Every positive interaction is a deposit. Every broken promise or missed follow-up is a withdrawal. The balance determines how much goodwill you have when you need it most.

You could share a useful article or a piece of data that is relevant to them. Take five minutes before a meeting to check what else is on their plate that week, so you can be sensitive to where their head is at. None of these are grand gestures. They are the small, consistent signals that tell a stakeholder you are willing to go the extra mile to help them.

Pre-wiring tactics

Psychologists who study decision-making have found that surprising negative outcomes produce a significantly stronger emotional reaction than expected negative ones.[19] A setback that arrives without any notice feels like an ambush, which is why it helps to pre-wire a stakeholder.

If you know your findings might challenge someone's position, go to that person privately and give them a heads-up: 'I have some findings that may contradict our current strategy, and I wanted to get your perspective before I share them more widely.' That framing positions the stakeholder as a collaborator rather than a recipient.

Protecting faces

Most political situations happen because someone was made to look wrong in front of their colleagues, and their instinct kicks in to protect themselves. Sociologist Erving Goffman found that we are all constantly engaged in what he called face-work, the effort to protect our own dignity and the dignity of others.[20] When someone's public image is threatened, they will go to extraordinary lengths to restore it. In a product meeting, it could lead them to attack the validity of your findings or shut the conversation down entirely.

William Ury, who co-founded the Harvard Program on Negotiation, described a technique he calls building a golden bridge.[21] When someone is backed into a corner, the worst thing you can do is push harder. Instead, you need to help them reframe and retreat from their position and move towards a better solution. Imagine your discovery research shows that the AI assistant a senior stakeholder championed is slowing customer service agents down. You could build a bridge: 'The work the team did on the AI model has given us a detailed picture of the most common customer queries. What if we used that insight to redesign a new solution?' The stakeholder is no longer being criticised for the failed project; instead, we have acknowledged that it's been invaluable in moving us in a new direction.

Shower them with kindness

As a last resort, there is a counterintuitive approach that I have found works better than any political tactic. When people are political or actively trying to undermine your credibility, just be relentlessly kind.

During my talk on influence, I sometimes set the audience a surprisingly difficult task: 'Think of one person that everyone in this room will probably like.' Then I put up a picture of Sir David Attenborough, who has an approval rating of 87 per cent, making him the most popular person in Britain.[22] Attenborough is not trying to sell anyone anything. He is an ordinary person who is passionate about his subject and treats his audience with respect. People sense that, and they warm to him.

Robert Cialdini, the author of the best-selling book *Influence*, states that we are far more easily persuaded by people we like.[23] In a study conducted with MBA students, a group told to treat a negotiation exercise as strictly business reached agreement 55 per cent of the time. Yet a second group, asked to find a similarity they shared before negotiating, reached agreement 90 per cent of the time, and the deals they struck were worth 18 per cent more to both sides.

Now, think about a stakeholder who is blocking your work. Your natural instinct might be to skip the small talk and keep interactions short and to the point, but Cialdini's research suggests that is the worst thing you can do. Start by finding out what they care about, what pressures they are under, and what success looks like from their perspective, because people who genuinely like you will find reasons to support you.

WHAT HAPPENED WITH DAVID

Going back to David, the frustrated stakeholder who had been labelled as unworkable eventually became one of our strongest supporters. David went out of his way to champion our work across the business. He helped me personally at several points in my career.

While we work with stakeholders on projects, we too are stakeholders in someone else's world, whether as a customer, a patient, or a parent at school. Now, what if you were told you were going to be managed? Yet, in product work, we believe we should be managing our stakeholders, when, in reality, we are kidding ourselves. Nobody wants to be managed. They want to be understood, involved, and treated as someone whose perspective counts.

That is the difference between managing stakeholders and collaborating with them. Asha did not manage David. She understood what drove him and adapted to his strengths. We made small wins that became deposits over time. The returns from that investment compounded into a lasting relationship.

FROM STAKEHOLDERS TO FACILITATION

Everything we have covered in this chapter has been about understanding stakeholders and building one-to-one relationships. But discovery requires you to bring groups of people together. You need the engineer who understands the technical constraints sitting alongside the designer who has spent time with customers. The insights that drive the best product decisions almost always emerge when we bring different perspectives together in the same room. That requires us to facilitate, which is what we will cover over the next two chapters.

KEY TAKEAWAYS

- **People are messy:** We are all irrational and will do things that are impossible to predict.
- **Learn to read the conditions:** Stakeholder Forecasting gives you five weather types based on a scientific personality model. Each one requires a different approach.
- **Map where the power sits:** Plot stakeholders on an influence-and-alignment grid. Spend your time on the high-influence people who are not yet on your side.
- **Build relationships before you need them:** Every positive interaction is a deposit. Every missed follow-up is a withdrawal. The balance determines whether a stakeholder will support your ideas.
- **Pre-wire the difficult conversations.** If your findings might challenge someone's position, share them privately first. Most political conflict happens in meetings because someone was caught off guard.
- **Protect faces, build bridges:** Be mindful of how you challenge someone in front of their peers.
- **Nobody wants to be managed:** Stakeholder collaboration means understanding who a person is and working with them on their terms.

14 FACILITATE TO BUILD TRUST AND EMPATHY

'Safety is the best policy in a workshop.'

Paddy Dhanda

THE UNIVERSAL DECLARATION

If you have ever tried to get a room full of stakeholders to agree on anything, you will know how hard it can be. Now imagine doing it with delegates from 58 nations who disagree on almost everything.

In December 1948, Eleanor Roosevelt stood before the United Nations General Assembly in Paris. For two years, she had chaired a committee charged with something many believed impossible, a universal declaration of human rights that the world could accept, while the Cold War hardened around them. She held no formal authority over anyone, and she was not a diplomat by training. Her position came from being the widow of a former president.

What she did with that position is the reason her name still appears in books like this one. Rather than impose her own views, she asked questions that helped opposing delegates understand each other. She also resisted forcing debates to a vote. Instead, she created informal spaces, private dinners, and afternoon teas, where adversaries could meet as people first. Over 85 meetings and countless drafts, she guided 18 delegates from rival nations to put their disagreements to one side.

On 10 December 1948, the Assembly voted, and 48 nations approved; not one voted against. The Universal Declaration of Human Rights went on to become one of the most translated documents in human history, into over 500 languages and dialects, and the

Figure 14.1 Eleanor Roosevelt bringing together multiple nations

foundation for treaties, constitutions, and laws across the world. It was reached through patient facilitation.

What Roosevelt understood is that the biggest breakthroughs rarely come from having the best idea yourself. They come from helping a group of people come together to share their collective ideas. That skill is the subject of this chapter and the next.

WHAT IS FACILITATION?

Facilitation is often confused with meeting management, project coordination, or simply being in charge of a workshop. But Sam Kaner, author of the definitive text on the subject, offers a more precise definition. A facilitator is someone who helps a group integrate the perspectives of all its members in ways that build shared understanding and commitment.[1]

Notice what this definition emphasises. It is not about driving the group towards your preferred outcome, ensuring the meeting ends on time, or being the person with all the answers. Instead, it is about helping diverse perspectives come together in ways that create something none of the individuals could have produced alone.

The word itself comes from the Latin *facilis*, meaning 'easy'. A facilitator makes things easier, not by doing the work for the group, but by removing the obstacles that get in the way of collaboration.

This is why Kaner distinguishes facilitation from chairing. A chairperson runs a meeting according to an agenda and keeps order in the room. A facilitator does something quite different. They help a group think together by creating conditions where the quiet person in the corner feels safe to speak, and the dominant personality learns to listen.

WHY DISCOVERY NEEDS FACILITATION

Think back to some of the discovery activities we explored in the FEATR funnel chapters. Stakeholder interviews require someone who can create the conditions for open and honest conversation. Opportunity prioritisation requires someone who can hold competing perspectives in balance without letting politics decide the outcome.

Without skilled facilitation, the value of these activities drains away. Imagine a team runs a workshop, follows the agenda, and notes the actions as they go. But the quiet people in the room never spoke up, and nobody challenged the team's assumptions. Was there any point in running it at all?

THE 4CS OF PRODUCT FACILITATION

If facilitation is the skill of helping a group think well together, then how do you build it into a skillset you can use for different situations? I have distilled the most common types of facilitation into four core capabilities. I call them the 4Cs: Connection, Care, Critical Thinking, and Cognitive Diversity.

Connection builds the safety that lets team members share openly and push back on each other. Care helps you uncover what users actually need and builds real empathy. Critical Thinking ensures you challenge assumptions instead of accepting them blindly. And Cognitive Diversity brings the mix of viewpoints you need to build products for everyone, rather than only for people who look and think like you.

This chapter covers the first two, Connection and Care, which are both about relationships and how we engage with the people in front of us. In the next chapter, we turn to Critical Thinking and Cognitive Diversity, which are about building the right intellectual muscles within the team. Let's begin with Connection.

CONNECTION: BUILDING DEEPER RELATIONSHIPS

You cannot simply walk into a meeting and say, 'It's safe to be vulnerable. Sarah, you go first.' You have to build safety intentionally. In Chapter 5, we saw how psychological safety, the shared belief that it is safe to speak up and admit mistakes, turned out to be the single biggest factor in how well a team performs. As facilitators, what's worth taking away from that insight is that safety does not happen by itself. It grows out of the quality of the relationships between the people on the team, which is what the rest of this section is about.

If people do not feel genuinely connected to their colleagues, they will not share half-formed ideas or raise unpopular opinions like, 'I think we are solving the wrong problem.' And if they don't do those things, you will never uncover critical insights.

The dysfunction that undermines everything

Patrick Lencioni spent years studying why talented teams fail to perform. His work identified five dysfunctions that build on each other like a pyramid. At the very bottom sits an absence of trust.[2] Without trust, teams avoid conflict, and when concerns don't get aired, people struggle to commit to decisions.

For facilitators, the useful question is, what does trust mean in this context? Lencioni distinguishes between predictive trust and vulnerability-based trust. Predictive trust is the confidence that someone will do what they say, and that they are reliable and competent. Vulnerability-based trust goes deeper. It is the willingness to admit 'I don't know', and to ask for help without fearing that others will use it against you.

Discovery work demands vulnerability-based trust. When we explore problems and test assumptions, we are working through uncertainty the whole time. If team members cannot admit what they don't understand, they will stop challenging product decisions and flawed hypotheses. The facilitator's job is to create an environment where the team can feel safe to openly talk about things, and that begins with how people relate to each other.

Why small teams discover more

Anthropologist Robin Dunbar's research looked at the relationship between brain size and social group size across primates. It revealed that humans can maintain stable social relationships with approximately 150 people, a figure now known as Dunbar's Number.[3] Within that number sit distinct layers. We typically have around 5 people in our closest support group and 15 in what Dunbar calls our sympathy group of close friends.

For product teams, this tells us that deep trust and real connection only happen in small groups, because every additional person increases the complexity of the relationships in the room.

A team of 5 has 10 possible communication pathways between members. A team of 8 has 28. A team of 12 has 66. This is one reason Agile frameworks recommend small team sizes, usually no more than 10. Beyond that threshold, communication becomes cumbersome and hard to coordinate. Picture a team of 20 people where every fresh insight has to be passed to everyone else. Multiply that across all the insights a team unearths in a typical week, and keeping everyone informed becomes a full-time job on its own.

I have facilitated discovery workshops with 20 or more people in the room, and the dynamic is completely different from a session with smaller numbers. In the larger group, the same three or four voices tend to dominate while the rest stay silent. Shrink the group, and there is nowhere to hide, and that visibility is exactly what makes people engage.

This doesn't mean you should never run sessions with larger groups. Sometimes you need the range of perspectives that only a bigger room can provide. When you do, you need techniques that break the large group into smaller conversations. The 1-2-4-All method, which we will come to shortly, exists for exactly this reason, because it recreates the intimacy of a small group inside a larger setting.

In person or virtual

Since the pandemic forced us all to work online, we seem to have developed a culture of virtual working. When it's for routine catch-ups and regular meetings, it seems to have become the norm for many people. But should we run discovery sessions virtually or in person?

Virtual collaboration is obviously cheaper and easier to arrange, but it has real limitations when you are searching for creative ideas. A study from Columbia and Stanford found that face-to-face groups not only generated around 20 per cent more ideas than virtual groups, but those ideas were also more creative.[4] The researchers suggested that physical spaces, with their objects and visual stimulation, spark connections in our minds that a video call cannot replicate. That might explain why some organisations have invested so heavily in interesting and colourful workspaces. My offices are all themed, and in some, you can be practising your golf putt while planning your roadmap (Figure 14.2).

My advice is to go for an in-person session when you want to maximise creativity in the early stages of ideation, where a more intimate session lets the team think deeply together. As you build on top of those early ideas, virtual working offers convenience and scales more easily to larger groups. I also find it easier to build a sense of connection when people are physically together, so you get some team-building almost for free.

Figure 14.2 QA Ltd St Katharine Docks Offices in London

How facilitators build connection

Keith McCandless, co-author of *Liberating Structures*, was facilitating a workshop in a hospital focused on stopping the spread of antibiotic-resistant infections.[5] During the session, one participant suggested that cedar oil might stop the bacteria from spreading. McCandless admitted he had to suppress his laughter because he knew enough about the science to understand that dangerous hospital superbugs would not be troubled by cedar oil.

Instead of dismissing the idea, the host he was training responded with curiosity. 'Well, how would we know if that idea would work?' Someone suggested putting cedar oil and the bacteria in a Petri dish to test them. Nobody actually needed to run the experiment. The idea had been taken seriously, the group had considered it for a moment, and then they moved on.

The cedar oil suggestion was never going to be the breakthrough in that meeting. But the next idea might have been, and that next idea only emerges if people believe their contributions will be heard rather than judged. When someone raises something, however absurd it may sound, thank them for it and ask a follow-up question to show you are taking it seriously: 'That's interesting. Can you tell us more about what you noticed?' That small step tells everyone in the room that speaking up is welcome here.

The SAFE signals

What other ways can facilitators help create a safe environment as they guide a discovery session? I want to share a simple tool I created to do exactly that. It's based on the acronym SAFE, which stands for Set the tone, Allow and acknowledge, Focus on the work, and End well.

Set the tone: People tend to decide whether it is safe to speak in the first few minutes. Open with warmth; psychologists call it emotional contagion, the way moods spread from one person to the next, and the mood you set at the start shapes how well a group cooperates and performs.[6] Invite the team to agree on a few simple working agreements, too, things like 'challenge the idea, not the person', because when the rules come from the group rather than from you, people own them. And show your own vulnerability first, sharing a small mistake and what it taught you, since people rarely open up until the person leading the room does.

Allow and acknowledge: Once people start to speak, your job is to make room for them and to reward the risk. When the room goes quiet after a question, resist the urge to fill the gap, because more often than not, people are simply thinking. Try saying, 'I can see you are thinking, take your time', and then wait. Silence, as someone once told me, is the sound of thinking. And the moment someone admits a mistake or raises an awkward concern, acknowledge it, even with a simple 'thank you for saying that', so the whole room learns that honesty is welcome here.

Focus on the work, not the person: When something has gone wrong, the words you choose decide whether people get defensive or curious. 'Why didn't you test that with customers?' puts one person on the spot, whereas 'What stopped us testing this with customers?' invites the whole team to look at what got in the way. In a reflection, drop the language of right and wrong altogether, and instead of 'What went well and what didn't?' ask 'What surprised us?' or 'What did we learn that we weren't expecting?'

End well: We remember endings most, so the last few minutes are important. Close by asking each person to name one thing a teammate did that helped them or that they admired. It ends the session on a human note, and because the final moment is the one people remember, it leaves them trusting the room a little more than when they walked in.

None of these signals is complicated, and that is the point. Building safety is less about grand gestures than about the small, repeated signals that tell people it is okay to be honest here.

How to facilitate for introverts

Safety also means recognising that not everyone shows up in the same way. Mentimeter's *State of Meetings Report* found that while 90 per cent of extroverts find traditional meetings effective, only 70 per cent of introverts feel the same.[7] Younger people increasingly identify as introverts and would rather contribute anonymously than speak up in front of the group. Traditional meeting formats can make it harder for some of your team's best thinkers to contribute.

The 1-2-4-All technique, which comes from the Liberating Structures movement, was designed to solve this.[8] McCandless explained to me that it works because it shifts control away from the facilitator and into the group.[9]

It runs in four stages. Individuals start alone, with one minute of silent thinking time to form their own ideas. People then pair up for two minutes, each sharing their thinking with one other person. Pairs combine into groups of four for four minutes, building on the best of what emerged. Finally, each group of four shares its strongest ideas with the whole room.

The short timings can feel uncomfortable, and that is deliberate. McCandless explained that the constraint does several things at once. It creates a productive confusion that disrupts our usual biases, like assuming the past will predict the future or hunting for information that confirms what we already believe. More voices get pulled into the mix because the pattern of interaction does more work than the content of any single step. And the rapid swapping forces recombination, where different ideas get swirled together until something new appears.

He compared this to traditional brainstorming, where you walk away with a long list of ideas and no real ownership of any of them. With 1-2-4-All, people feel their ideas get mixed with everyone else's, so they collectively own whatever comes out the other end. That sense of shared ownership is connection at work, turning a room full of individuals into a group that thinks together.

Rebalancing who speaks

We met David Marquet, the nuclear submarine commander, back in Chapter 5. A few years ago I went to the launch of his book, *Leadership is Language*, where he shared a tragic story that shows what I see in offices everywhere.

In 2015, the container ship *El Faro* sailed into Hurricane Joaquin and sank, with the loss of all 33 crew. When investigators recovered the ship's voice recorder, the transcripts told a story that is hard to read. For hours, members of the crew could see the storm strengthening on their instruments. The second mate raised the danger and suggested an alternative course. Others also voiced their concerns hoping the captain would listen to someone at least. He dismissed the early concerns with phrases like 'We're good' and 'It should be fine', and the officers did not feel they had the authority to press him any further.[10]

Even though they had warned the captain, no one could change his mind, because he was the most senior officer on the ship. The people who could see the danger most clearly were the ones with the least authority to act on it. For the families left behind, one of the hardest parts of the official reports was learning just how much the crew had seen coming, and how little their warnings counted.

When Marquet analysed the *El Faro* transcripts, they revealed something insightful about the dynamics between different levels of hierarchy in leadership. The proportion of words spoken by each person in a conversation is a reliable indicator of the seniority within a team. More senior people tend to dominate, while junior voices grow quieter and important information goes unsaid.

In product teams, this is known as the HiPPO effect, which stands for Highest Paid Person's Opinion. It describes what happens when the most senior person in the room takes over simply because of their seniority, rather than the quality of their idea.

As you facilitate, pay close attention to who is speaking and who is not. When I notice someone has gone quiet, I will create space for them by mentioning their name so there is no doubt who should speak next: 'We've heard several perspectives on this. Sarah, I'm curious what you're seeing from where you sit.' That signals their view is valuable and gives them explicit permission to offer it. In some sessions, I keep a rough tally in my head of who has been talking, and if the product director has spoken for 15 minutes while the engineers have barely said a word, that tells me something. The aim is never to silence senior voices, but to make sure junior people feel their insight is valued just as much.

Another technique is to name the dynamic out loud when you see it. If everyone is agreeing a little too quickly, I will say so: 'We seem to be converging fast here. Before we move on, let me ask a different question. What would have to be true for this assumption to be completely wrong?' This lets people disagree without anyone having to be the one who breaks ranks.

That brings the first C to a close. Connection is the foundation that everything else rests on, because a team whose members do not trust one another will never feel comfortable sharing their true perspectives or opinions. The second C builds on it and turns that trust outward, towards the people you are designing for.

CARE: THE ENGINE OF EMPATHIC UNDERSTANDING

One year, I travelled to 15 different countries. I was lucky enough to visit some incredible places, from Eastern Europe to India, Thailand, and the Philippines. Every time I met a stranger, I found myself full of questions about how they lived and how they saw the world.

The experience taught me a vital lesson about the second capability of facilitation. If you don't care about how other people experience the world, you will never develop the ability to truly empathise with them. Care and empathy are two sides of the same coin, and throughout this section I use them interchangeably. Where Connection is about the relationships inside your team, Care is about the relationship between your team and the people you serve.

The designer who became an old woman

In 1979, a 26-year-old industrial designer named Patricia Moore made a decision that changed how designers think about understanding users. Frustrated that her colleagues at Raymond Loewy, one of the most prestigious design firms in America, were ignoring the needs of older adults, Moore decided to experience their world directly. Over the next three years, she disguised herself as a woman in her eighties and travelled to more than 100 cities across the United States and Canada.[11]

Professional make-up artists aged her face with latex, and she wore clouded glasses to simulate cataracts. She bound her legs and torso to restrict her movement, and taped her fingers to stiffen her joints. When she hobbled down city streets with a cane, nobody recognised the young designer conducting research. They saw a vulnerable old woman struggling with everyday tasks.

Figure 14.3 Experiencing the world as an elderly person

Doors were too heavy for arthritic hands. Stairs became impossible barriers. Bus drivers pulled away before she could find a seat. Cashiers spoke to her companions rather than to her. In one frightening incident, she was mugged and beaten by teenagers who saw an easy target. She had felt what millions of older people live with every day, an experience most designers never bothered to understand.

Moore's work went on to shape products we now take for granted, from the lever-style door handles that replaced round knobs to the wide-grip peelers in every kitchen shop, and countless other ergonomic features in everyday objects.

I'm not suggesting you put on a disguise and spend three years pretending to be your users. But Moore's story shows something that gets lost in our data-driven world: the gap between knowing about your users and actually understanding them. What drove her was that she cared deeply about people whose needs were being ignored. That care allowed her to build a depth of empathy that led to design breakthroughs that would never have been possible otherwise.

Four attributes of empathic engagement

Researcher Theresa Wiseman studied how professionals in caring roles connect with the people they serve. Through her work, she identified four attributes that characterise empathic engagement in a professional context.[12]

Perspective-taking

When you actively try to see a situation from the other person's point of view, you are taking their perspective. This goes well beyond acknowledging that different perspectives exist. It asks for a genuine effort to step outside your own frame of reference and imagine how the world looks from where the other person is standing.

When a stakeholder pushes back on your product roadmap, perspective-taking means pausing to consider what pressures they are under from their own leadership, what promises they may already have made to customers, or what past experiences are shaping their reaction. Their resistance almost always makes sense once you understand their context.

Step into your customer's shoes

Kerry Nickols, Chief Mischief Maker at ShakerMakers Club, was running an Agile workshop with around 25 people spread across five tables.[13] One table kept raising a recurring issue with a particular customer. The conversations were transactional, and the team could not seem to build a real understanding. They were using an empathy map, which we looked at in Chapter 8, but it was not giving them the depth that they needed.

Rather than pressing on with the planned agenda, Kerry chose to intervene with a deeper empathy exercise drawn from her coaching practice. Instead of a broad customer group, she asked each participant to pick one specific customer to avoid forming stereotypes. They started by looking at the situation from their own perspective, but then Kerry asked them to physically move to a different place in the room and step into the customer's shoes, looking back at themselves as if they were that customer. Finally, they explored a third viewpoint, something like a fly on the wall or the perspective of someone who understands customer relationships especially well.

What made the difference was the physical movement. When we use regular empathy tools, we tend to rely on thinking and analysis, which keeps people inside their own heads. By moving around the room, the participants stopped treating empathy as something they filled in on a page and started to see the relationship differently. They came away with a more objective view of the situation and more thoughtful approaches they could take back into their conversations.

Before the exercise, the customer conversations had been functional and formulaic, built around questions like 'What are your problems?' and 'What can we improve?' Kerry described the whole dynamic as lacking a foundation, more tick-box than relationship. Afterwards, the team had a deeper appreciation of the person on the other side and a more human perspective.

Staying out of judgement

When we listen, our natural instinct is to evaluate what we are hearing, to decide whether we agree, whether the person is right or wrong. Wiseman found that real empathy means resisting that urge, at least at first. The moment we start judging, we stop listening properly.

Imagine a user explaining that they export data from your platform into a spreadsheet, reformat it by hand, and then import it into another system. Your instinct might be to think they are using the product wrong, or that they simply haven't found the integration feature you built. But if you judge their behaviour as incorrect, you miss the chance to understand why your integration doesn't meet their needs in the first place.

Recognising emotion

This is the ability to identify what someone is feeling, even when they haven't said it out loud. People often struggle to put their feelings into words, or may not fully realise what they are feeling. Good facilitators learn to read the signals in someone's tone and body language.

A sales team might tell you they need a faster quoting tool, but if you pay attention to how they describe their day, you might notice something deeper. The frustration in their voice when they mention chasing approvals, or the way they sigh when they describe month-end reporting, might tell you that the real problem isn't speed at all, but a lack of control over their own work.

Communicating understanding

Listening on its own isn't enough. Empathy grows when the other person actually feels understood. This means reflecting back what you have heard in a way that confirms you have grasped their experience, not only the facts but what those facts mean to them.

After listening to a customer describe their onboarding struggles, you might say, 'It sounds like you felt abandoned after the initial training, as though you were expected to figure everything out on your own.' When you get it right, you will often see relief wash over their face. They finally feel heard.

All four of these attributes start in the same place. You cannot take someone's perspective without first caring enough to wonder what it might be.

Empathy can be learned

The encouraging news is that empathy isn't a fixed trait you either have or you don't. Research at Stanford shows that empathy is a skill, and one that can be developed through deliberate practice. Their studies found that people who believe empathy can be improved are more likely to put in the effort to understand others, and more likely to succeed at it.[14] So, if empathy can be developed, how do you turn it into a consistent practice across your team?

Practical ways to empathise

Observe, don't interrogate

Have you ever tried to sleep with a ticking clock in the room? At first, it disturbs your sleep, but after a while you become numb to the sound because your mind focuses on something else. Dorothy Leonard and Jeffrey Rayport found something similar in their research on empathic design. People adapt to limitations until they stop noticing them as problems.[15]

In a user interview, if you ask people what they want, they will describe small improvements to the tools they already use. But if you watch them work, you will see the pain points and frustrations they have learned to live with or work around. They may not even think to mention them because they have come to accept them as facts of life, just like the ticking clock.

Running a day-in-the-life study

There is a powerful technique that happens to share its name with a Beatles track, the 'Day in the Life' study. It comes from anthropological research and involves following a user through their typical activities, and unlike interviews, which rely on what participants say, it focuses on what people actually do.[16] You don't need a full day. Even a few hours of watching someone work can reveal things that months of interviews would miss.

Arrive with a simple template divided into three columns: what the user did; what they said; and what you noticed. Position yourself where you can see the screen and their hands, but far enough back that they soon forget you are there. As you watch, look for the workarounds, where people copy data between systems or scrawl on a sticky note to track something the tool should be handling. Watch for the hesitations, the pause before a click, or the action undone a second after it was taken. And notice the shortcuts, the regular steps people skip, which usually point to work they have decided is not worth their time.

Afterwards, walk back through your notes with them. 'I noticed you copied that reference number into a notepad. Can you tell me more about that?' This brings out insights they would never think to mention in a normal interview, because so much of what they do has become automatic. They are on autopilot, and your job is to gently wake them up to it.

Create immersive experiences

Sometimes the best way to build empathy is to drop your team into an unfamiliar situation. IDEO uses a technique called analogous research, where teams experience situations similar to the ones their users face. When designing for operating-room safety, they observed NASCAR pit crews to understand high-pressure teamwork, and when designing a new voting system for Los Angeles, they took salsa lessons conducted entirely in Spanish, to feel what it is like working through an unfamiliar process in a language you don't speak.[17]

You can adapt this for your own work. If you are building for people under time pressure, have your team complete a task while being interrupted every 30 seconds. For users with accessibility needs, ask team members to complete a task with their dominant hand behind their back or wearing a blindfold. These experiences build a depth of understanding that no amount of reading or discussion can match.

Ask about behaviour, not opinions

Most of the time, you won't have the luxury of shadowing someone for a day, so the interview becomes your main tool. The trouble is that interviews make it dangerously easy to hear exactly what you hoped to hear. I have watched skilled, well-meaning people walk into a research session already in love with their idea, and walk out with a transcript full of evidence that they were right, none of which actually meant anything.

The reason is simple. If you ask someone whether they would use the thing you are about to build, they will almost always say yes. Saying no feels rude, and in the abstract, almost any helpful-sounding product is appealing. Erika Hall makes this point in her book *Just Enough Research*, where she argues that the job of user research is to understand what people actually do and why, rather than to gather opinions about what they think they might do.[18]

So I have trained myself to keep pulling conversations back to real behaviour. Rather than asking a parent whether they would use a meal-planning app, I might ask them to walk me through what they actually cooked last week and how each decision was made. The answers are far less flattering and far more useful. You hear about the four nights of takeaway because everyone was too tired to cook, the vegetables that rotted in the drawer when plans changed, the two apps they downloaded with the best intentions and abandoned within a week.

How you word these questions turns out to be one of the most valuable skills in all of discovery, and it is frighteningly easy to undo your good work with a leading phrase. There is so much to say here that I have given questioning a chapter of its own. We will explore it in more depth in Chapter 16, where I share the Question Compass and the traps that can ruin most discovery conversations. For now, hold on to the short version. Ask people what they did, not what they want.

In the next chapter, we turn to the intellectual side of facilitation, Critical Thinking and Cognitive Diversity. We will look at how a $500 million mistake could have been avoided if someone had simply asked the right question, and why Bic once managed to offend half the population.

KEY TAKEAWAYS

- **Facilitation is not the same as meeting management:** A facilitator helps a group integrate diverse perspectives to build shared understanding and commitment, rather than simply running through an agenda or keeping discussions on time.
- **The 4Cs are the core of product facilitation:** Connection and Care build the relationships inside the team and with users, while Critical Thinking and Cognitive Diversity (covered in Chapter 15) build the team's intellectual muscle.
- **Trust is the foundation of everything:** Discovery demands vulnerability-based trust, the willingness to say 'I don't know.' Role-model that openness yourself, because people take their cue from what they see happen when someone takes a risk.
- **Small groups discover more:** Deep trust and genuine connection are only possible in small groups, because relationship complexity rises sharply as teams grow. Break larger groups into smaller conversations with techniques like 1-2-4-All.
- **Rebalance who speaks:** Watch for the HiPPO effect, where senior voices dominate, and important information goes unsaid. Create explicit space for quieter people and name the dynamic when you see everyone agreeing too fast.
- **The SAFE signals:** Set the tone, allow and acknowledge, focus on the work not the person, and end well; these are the small signals that help set the right tone for a team to feel safe.
- **Empathy can be learned:** Care is a skill built through deliberate practice. Observe behaviour rather than asking people what they want, because users adapt to broken systems until they stop noticing the problems.
- **Ask about behaviour, not opinions:** What someone did last week tells you far more than what they say they would do in a hypothetical future. We go deeper on question design in Chapter 16.

15 FACILITATE SHARPER THINKING AND DIVERSE PERSPECTIVES

'Great minds think alike, which is exactly the problem.'

Paddy Dhanda

ZILLOW'S CRITICAL MISTAKE

In 2021, Zillow lost over half a billion dollars because it built a culture that prevented critical thinking.

The real estate giant had launched Zillow Offers in 2018, an 'iBuying' service that used algorithms to buy homes directly from sellers and resell them for profit.[1] Competitors like Opendoor and Offerpad had run a similar service for several years already. But Zillow had its famous AI Zestimate platform, which had been estimating home values since 2006, and the team believed that if anyone could predict future home prices accurately, it was them.

Under CEO Rich Barton's leadership, Zillow set aggressive growth targets, aiming to reach $20 billion in annual revenue.[2] To capture market share quickly, they instructed their algorithms to bid even higher than competitors to win deals. The strategy worked in terms of volume, and by 2021, Zillow Offers was buying thousands of homes a month across dozens of markets.

As volume grew, so did the pressure to keep the machine running. Then the post-pandemic housing boom began to slow down in mid-2021, and as a result, competitors adjusted their buying behaviour and became more cautious. But Zillow's leadership instructed its pricing experts to stop overriding the algorithm's valuations.[3]

Zillow soon found itself overpaying for homes it could not resell at a profit, and by the third quarter of 2021, they had to write down the value of their inventory by more than $500 million. In November, Barton announced that Zillow would shut down Zillow Offers entirely and lay off approximately 2,000 employees.[4]

What stands out about this example is how a fast-growing, well-resourced organisation deliberately removed the human judgement that had once acted as a safety net. The people at the very top making these decisions lacked the critical thinking discipline to question their own strategy. We will return to Zillow after each of the techniques in this chapter and ask how a well-run discovery session can help come up with better decisions.

In the previous chapter, we explored how effective facilitation begins with relationships. Connection and Care are the first two of the 4Cs, the relational dimensions that help us understand how to engage with our teams as well as our users.

A team can feel deeply connected and genuinely care about its users and still build the wrong thing, either because the difficult questions never get raised, or because leadership stops listening when they do. Zillow's team was full of smart, well-intentioned people who believed in their mission, but that on its own was not enough.

This chapter covers Critical Thinking and Cognitive Diversity, the last two of the 4Cs, which are the intellectual muscles a team needs alongside the relational ones. It shares practical techniques for building critical thinking into your discovery work, including a chair technique from the man behind Mickey Mouse, and it shows why cognitive diversity counts for more than expertise alone. We will draw lessons from some unlikely sources, including 18th-century pirates and Formula 1 pit crews.

CRITICAL THINKING: CHALLENGING ASSUMPTIONS

The phrase 'critical thinking' gets thrown around so much in business that it has almost lost its meaning, so let us start with a formal definition. According to the Foundation for Critical Thinking, it is 'the intellectually disciplined process of actively and skilfully conceptualising, applying, analysing, synthesising, and evaluating information gathered from observation, experience, reflection, reasoning, or communication, as a guide to belief and action'.[5]

For our purposes, critical thinking means questioning what we think we know before we act on it. When we are working to tight deadlines and are expected to deliver at speed, it can be difficult for teams to build this kind of questioning into their discovery work. But as we have seen throughout this book, when we rush to build things before fully thinking through the solution, we end up adding to the Failure Economy.

Without structured techniques, even smart leadership teams risk falling into the same trap as Zillow, so the facilitator's job is to make assumptions explicit and then create opportunities to test them.

The goal is not to kill ideas or create a culture of negativity, but to strengthen ideas by exposing their weaknesses early, while there is still time to address them. A flaw found in a discovery session costs almost nothing to fix, while the same flaw found after launch can cost millions. The techniques that follow are designed to make this feel less like personal criticism and more like a shared team activity.

Walt Disney's Three Chairs

It turns out that critical thinking is not a new concept, and the folks behind Mickey Mouse have been practising it for years. Walt Disney had a strange habit that puzzled his colleagues. When working on a new idea, he would physically move between three different chairs in his office. In the first, the dreamer, he let his imagination run wild, generating concepts without any constraints. In the second, the realist, he examined how those dreams might actually be built, weighing timelines, budgets, and logistics. In the third, the critic, he scrutinised the assumptions behind the ideas.

Robert Dilts, who we met in Chapter 8, later modelled this approach and named it the Disney Creativity Strategy.[6] I spoke with Jennifer Battan, the 'Out of the Box BA' and creative facilitator, about it.[7] She explained why the sequencing is so important. 'Everybody needs to dream together. That's the idea generation, think of anything that could be possible. Realist is how do we make it happen, how do we make this a reality? Critic is last, because this is where you start to put holes into some of these ideas.'

What Disney understood is that creative thinking and critical thinking work in completely different ways, and when we try to do both at the same time, we do neither well. The dreamer gets demotivated by the critic before ideas can fully form, and the realist never gets a chance to work out the details because the dreamer keeps adding new requirements.

Battan pointed to Disney's own track record as evidence that the method works. 'There are so many books and documentaries about the amazing things that they've done. They really realised that if there was something that didn't exist that they wanted to do, well then, let's build it. Let's figure out how to make it work. Why don't we all do that?'

In practice, I name which chair we are sitting in at any given moment. At the start of a session I write 'Dreamer' on the whiteboard so everyone can see it. When we have enough ideas on the wall, I announce that we are moving to Realist mode and update the board. Only after we have explored the practical considerations do I switch us into Critic mode, where we deliberately look for the flaws and risks. Making the transition visible gives people permission to think differently in each phase, which stops the Critic from killing ideas before they have a chance to develop.

Think back to Zillow for a moment. Leadership had no shortage of dreamers and realists pushing for growth, but nobody senior was formally sitting in the critic's chair, asking what would happen to all those purchases if the model was wrong and the market turned.

The Three Chairs technique separates modes of thinking so that each gets proper attention. But how do you build critical thinking directly into how your team works every day? That is where the Three Amigos come in.

The Three Amigos: healthy conflict

In Agile environments, the Three Amigos technique is another popular approach to critical thinking. Like the Disney model, it uses three separate perspectives, but it appeals to product teams because it builds critical thinking directly into their existing workflow rather than treating it as a separate activity.

The term was first used by software development coach George Dinwiddie around 2009, drawing inspiration from the 1986 comedy film of the same name.[8] Dinwiddie was performing acceptance test-driven development and noticed that bringing together three specific perspectives before work began dramatically reduced misunderstandings and the risk of building the wrong thing.

Three perspectives give the technique its name: a developer, who represents technical feasibility and implementation concerns; a tester, who represents quality, edge cases, and verification; and a business representative, such as a product owner or business analyst, who represents user value and business needs.[9] The concept is not limited strictly to three people, and you can include additional perspectives when relevant, but the core idea is to make sure these three viewpoints are always represented.

The power of the Three Amigos lies in what each perspective naturally questions. A developer asking 'How will we build this?' focuses on technical assumptions the business side may not have considered, and might point out that a simple-looking feature actually requires significant architectural changes. A tester asking 'What could go wrong?' surfaces the edge cases, error conditions, and integration points where users behave differently from the happy path the business had in mind. And a business representative asking 'Is this what users actually need?' challenges whether the solution genuinely addresses the underlying problem, and can question technical requirements that deliver no real value.

What I find valuable about the Three Amigos is that the critical thinking is built into how work flows through the team, and each perspective is expected to challenge the others as part of their normal role. When done well, this healthy conflict prevents assumptions from going unchallenged. According to the Agile Alliance, the meeting works best when scheduled one or two sprints before development begins, which leaves enough time to address any issues raised.[10]

The tester's question, 'What could go wrong?' was being asked by the pricing experts at Zillow, but not where it mattered, in the leadership team. Both the Three Chairs and Three Amigos help teams challenge assumptions in the moment. But what about raising risks that people are reluctant to voice at all? For that, we need a different approach.

The Pre-Mortem: imagining failure before it happens

Another powerful technique for challenging assumptions comes from psychologist Gary Klein, who has spent his career studying how people make decisions in high-stakes environments. In a 2007 *Harvard Business Review* article titled 'Performing a project premortem', Klein introduced a method that flips traditional risk assessment on its head.[11]

Most planning sessions include some version of the question 'What could go wrong?' But Klein noticed that this rarely surfaced genuine concerns. Team members are reluctant to criticise a plan their leader has endorsed, and the pressure to appear supportive overrides honest assessment of risk. People worry that raising concerns will make them look negative or difficult, so they keep their doubts to themselves and hope for the best.

The Pre-Mortem takes a different approach that overcomes these social barriers. Instead of asking what might fail in the future, you tell the team to imagine that the project has already failed spectacularly. You transport them mentally to a point in the future where the initiative was a complete disaster, and their task is simply to explain why it failed.

This shift from 'what might happen' to 'what did happen' changes how people think in ways you might not expect. Klein based the technique on research into prospective hindsight conducted in 1989, where researchers found that imagining an event has already occurred increases the ability to correctly identify reasons for that outcome by approximately 30 per cent.[12]

To run a Pre-Mortem, gather your team after they have been briefed on a plan or proposal. Tell them to imagine looking into a crystal ball that shows the project was a complete disaster, perhaps six months or a year from now, with the timeframe matching the realistic timeline of your initiative. Give each person 2–3 minutes of quiet time to independently write down every reason they can think of for why it failed so badly. Letting people work individually is important because it stops groupthink from taking hold before ideas are shared.

Next, go around the room with each person sharing one reason at a time while the facilitator records everything without judgement or discussion. Carry on until everyone has exhausted their lists, then review the full list together, prioritise the most concerning items, and discuss how to address them before moving forward.

At a Pre-Mortem run at Zillow in early 2021, with leadership in the room, asking why Zillow Offers had collapsed a year later, somebody would almost certainly have written down 'the market turned, and the algorithm kept buying'. That may have got them to rethink their whole strategy and possibly saved the company from disaster.

The technique works because it gives everyone explicit permission to voice concerns without appearing disloyal, and when the whole team is asked to imagine failure, criticism becomes a shared exercise rather than one person being singled out.

Sometimes you are pushed for time and need to work at speed. That is when you need a Devil's Advocate in the team.

The Devil's Advocate: a role with medieval roots

Deliberately arguing against a point of view to strengthen the final decision has surprisingly ancient origins. The Roman Catholic Church used to appoint an official called the Devil's Advocate, whose entire job was to argue against granting sainthood to a candidate.[13] His task was to look for holes in the evidence, challenge any miracles attributed to the candidate, and present every possible reason why the person should not become a saint.

It had recognised something important about how humans make decisions. When everyone involved wants a particular outcome, and there is social pressure to support the consensus, important concerns tend to go unspoken. So the Church created an official role whose only job was to challenge and criticise.

In product work, assigning a Devil's Advocate means designating someone to deliberately challenge the big ideas everyone thinks we should build, even if they personally agree with them. The role is not to be difficult for its own sake, but to highlight concerns the group might have missed.

Psychologists who studied disasters caused by groupthink, including the Bay of Pigs invasion and the attack on Pearl Harbor, found that formally designating a Devil's

Advocate was one of the most effective ways to combat premature consensus.[14] The key is that the role needs to be assigned, because when criticism comes from an official position rather than from someone simply being sceptical, it feels less like an attack and more like a valuable contribution.

There is one pitfall to avoid. Research found that the technique only works when the person genuinely engages with the arguments rather than going through the motions.[15] A half-hearted Devil's Advocate who raises weak objections can actually increase the group's confidence without meaningfully testing its thinking.

These four techniques, the Three Chairs, Three Amigos, Pre-Mortem, and Devil's Advocate, give you practical ways to build critical thinking into your discovery work. But what happens if everyone in the room thinks the same way?

Figure 15.1 The toolkit

COGNITIVE DIVERSITY: THE POWER OF DIFFERENT PERSPECTIVES

When a team shares similar backgrounds, experiences, and perspectives, they tend to share similar blind spots as well. This brings us to the fourth dimension of effective facilitation. In his book *Rebel Ideas*, Matthew Syed defines cognitive diversity as 'the ability to think differently about the world around us'.[16] It is not simply about demographic diversity, though that often contributes to it. It is about differences in perspective, insight, experience, and thinking style, and about deliberately bringing together people who see problems from different angles, so the gaps in one person's thinking can be filled by another's.

Syed argues that cognitive diversity counts for more now than it ever has. A few hundred years ago, most problems were linear and simple, whereas today's challenges are interconnected and complex. As he puts it, 'The more diverse the perspectives, the wider the range of potentially viable solutions a collection of problem solvers can find.'

Let's look at why teams that all think alike fail to build products that work for everyone, why expertise alone is not enough, and how facilitators can widen the range of perspectives in their discovery sessions.

The pirates who democratised the high seas

During the Golden Age of Piracy in the early 1700s, something unusual was happening on the ships that terrorised the Caribbean. While the British Royal Navy operated under rigid hierarchies where officers came almost exclusively from wealthy families and ordinary sailors faced brutal discipline, pirate ships ran on an entirely different model.

Pirate crews were unusually mixed for their time. According to the historian Marcus Rediker, who built his account from court records, demographic data, and survivor testimony, black sailors made up a substantial part of many crews and often served in the most trusted roles. On the pirate ship *Dragon*, more than half of one boarding party was black, and these were not captives but crew who shared in the plunder.[17] Some black pirates were freemen, while others had escaped slavery, and for many, piracy was an alternative to a life of bondage.

What made the model radical for its era was how these crews organised themselves. Under the pirate articles, captains were elected by a vote of the crew and could be removed if they lost the crew's confidence, and plunder was divided according to agreed shares rather than concentrated at the top. The economist Peter Leeson, who studied the hidden economics of piracy, points out that pirate ships adopted a form of constitutional democracy more than 50 years before the United States did.[18] On many ships, black pirates could vote, bear arms, and take an equal share of the booty, in an era when that would have been unthinkable in regular society.

The pirates were onto something that modern product firms are only now beginning to appreciate. When you bring together people with genuinely different perspectives and create conditions where all of them can contribute, you unlock capabilities that homogeneous groups simply cannot reach.

Why homogeneous teams build broken products

That pirate model might seem far removed from modern product work, but the same dynamics play out whenever teams lack diversity. When everyone in the room shares similar backgrounds and experiences, the result can be products that fail entire user segments. Caroline Criado Perez documented many examples in her book, *Invisible Women*.[19]

Look at car safety. Crash test dummies were modelled on the average male body for decades, and the result was that women were 47 per cent more likely to be seriously injured in a car accident, because the airbags and safety systems were optimised for bodies that looked like the test dummies rather than bodies that looked like nearly half the driving population.[20]

There was a viral video in 2017 showing a Nigerian Facebook employee testing an infrared soap dispenser.[21] When his white colleague put a hand under the sensor, soap dispensed perfectly, but when he put his own darker-skinned hand under the same sensor, nothing happened. The infrared technology detected light reflecting off the skin, and darker colours absorb more light than they reflect. As the employee, Chukwuemeka Afigbo, noted when sharing the video, 'If you have ever had a problem grasping the importance of diversity in tech and its impact on society, watch this video.'

The developers had missed this in testing, presumably because everyone on the team had similar skin tones.

These were not malicious decisions. Nobody sat in a design workshop and said, 'let's make sure this product doesn't work for women', or 'let's ensure darker-skinned users can't wash their hands'. The failures happened because teams built products that reflected their own experiences, and they never noticed what they were missing because there was nobody in the room to point it out.

Perhaps my favourite example of all, because of the absurdity and the reaction to its launch, was the *Bic for Her* pens. They came in pink and purple, supposedly designed to fit a woman's hand, and they were far more expensive than regular pens for no functional reason whatsoever. Ellen DeGeneres famously mocked them on her show, saying, 'they're just like regular pens except they're pink, so they cost twice as much'.[22]

Its Amazon reviews became legendary for their sarcasm, with one reviewer thanking Bic for finally letting her write without needing a man's help. The team had not only failed to include diverse perspectives but had also created something patronising that revealed how little they understood the audience they were aiming at.

There is a common theme across these examples. When product decisions are made by people who look and think alike, the result may work beautifully for people like themselves and fail for everyone else. But what if we bring experts into the room? Surely they should be able to avoid these mistakes?

The trap of expertise

A less obvious challenge to cognitive diversity is just as dangerous, and it is the assumption that expertise is always valuable and that bringing in the most senior people guarantees better outcomes.

Malcolm Gladwell famously popularised the 10,000-hour rule in his book *Outliers*.[23] The basic premise is that to master any skill, whether playing the piano or playing pickleball, you need to practise for at least 10,000 hours. The figure has been challenged over the years, but the principle still holds.

Take Serena Williams, who has won 23 Grand Slam singles titles. Her father coached her from the age of three with a single goal: turn her professional. The rules of tennis have barely changed over the decades. Courts are the same size, nets are the same height, and the shots are familiar, and in that kind of stable environment, expertise wins, because the skills you have developed stay relevant over time.

The world we work in is very different. We are constantly dealing with new technology, new regulations, new market trends, and shifting customer expectations, and in that environment, thousands of hours of expertise can become outdated very quickly.

There is another problem with expertise that the economist Tim Harford calls the God Complex.[24] It is the tendency for specialists to grow so confident in their knowledge that they dismiss ideas from outside their domain; doctors are particularly prone to this. For years, they assumed stomach ulcers were caused by stress or spicy food.

When two Australian scientists, Barry Marshall and Robin Warren, suggested that ulcers were actually caused by bacteria, the medical establishment mocked them because the doctors felt they knew better, and their experience seemed to confirm it.

Marshall eventually infected himself with the bacteria to prove the point and developed gastritis within days. As the Nobel Committee later noted when awarding Marshall and Warren the 2005 Nobel Prize in Physiology or Medicine, 'Thanks to the pioneering discovery by Marshall and Warren, peptic ulcer disease is no longer a chronic, frequently disabling condition, but a disease that can be cured by a short regimen of antibiotics.'[25] That extreme act was necessary because experts had let their ego get in the way of the science.

The takeaway for facilitators is to be wary of so-called experts dominating your sessions. Whoever is most senior in the room, or holds the most experience, is not always going to be right. Create space for junior voices and naive questions, because sometimes the person who knows least about how things have always been done is best placed to see how things should be done differently.

The wisdom of crowds

If expertise can be a trap, then what is the alternative? In 1906, Sir Francis Galton, a pioneer of statistics, attended a livestock fair in Plymouth, where nearly 800 people took part in a contest to guess the weight of an ox after it had been slaughtered and dressed. Galton, who was interested in the limits of democracy and suspicious of collective wisdom, gathered up all the estimates after the fair and analysed them.[26] What he found surprised him. While individual guesses varied wildly, some far too high and others far too low, when he averaged them together, the result was 1,197 pounds. The actual weight was 1,198 pounds, so the crowd was off by just one pound.

Galton had revealed what James Surowiecki later called the wisdom of crowds.[27] When certain conditions are met, groups can be surprisingly intelligent, often smarter than the smartest individuals within them, and those conditions include diversity of opinion and independence, meaning people are not pressured to agree with each other. Each person brings genuine knowledge to a problem, but they also bring biases and mistakes, and when you aggregate enough diverse guesses, the errors tend to cancel each other out, leaving behind a more accurate picture than any one person would reach alone.

But here's the problem. You almost never get a real crowd inside a company. Everyone in your discovery session probably shares a profession, often a similar education, the same company culture, and a reporting line that connects most of them. Two of the conditions the wisdom of crowds depends on, genuine diversity and genuine independence, are the two that your average product team has the least of. When the junior analyst defers to the more senior colleague, you do not have a crowd of independent team members, you have one dominant opinion with several people who feel obliged to agree, and that is better described as an echo chamber.

So the facilitator's job is not to pretend the daily standup is a Galton ox-weighing experiment. It is to protect the two ingredients that are usually missing. You protect independence by gathering views privately before opinions converge, and you protect diversity by deliberately widening the perspectives in the room, which is the subject of the rest of this chapter.

Looking in the corners

One of the most powerful ways to widen cognitive diversity is to look outside your own industry for inspiration, because the best ideas often come from the most unexpected places.

My wife teases me about the way I vacuum the house. Like a lot of people, I simply push the vacuum back and forth in nice straight lines, but anyone who really understands cleaning will tell you that the dust gathers around the edges and corners of a room. Whenever my wife wants to check whether I have done a good job, she never looks at the most visible part of the room, which is the middle. She goes straight to the corners.

The same principle applies to learning. Most of us look for inspiration in the obvious places, like a LinkedIn feed that curates content from like-minded people, or conferences full of fellow professionals. But the most valuable insights often come from the corners, the places outside our immediate field of vision, where other industries have already solved similar problems in unexpected ways.

Consider what happened when doctors at Great Ormond Street Hospital in London were struggling with a persistent problem. They were performing complex heart surgery on babies, but too many infants were dying, not during the surgery itself but during the handover from the operating theatre to the intensive care unit.[28]

One evening, after a long operation, two senior doctors were watching Formula 1 and noticed that a pit crew could change all four tyres in under two seconds with flawless coordination. They asked themselves a question that seemed absurd at first, which was what racing mechanics could possibly teach surgeons about saving babies. On a hunch,

Figure 15.2 The pit stop ICU

they reached out to Ferrari, and later Williams, and invited the teams to observe their handover process. The racing engineers were blunt, describing the medical process as shoddy, noisy, and uncoordinated, with no clear leadership and far too many voices competing for attention compared with the silence of their own pit stops.

Working together, the medical and racing teams redesigned the handover. They introduced clear leadership roles, with the anaesthetist directing the transfer until formally handing over to the intensivist, choreographed positions so people would not get in each other's way, and added checklists and structured communication. The hospital cut handover errors sharply, and the approach has since been adopted by medical centres around the world.[29]

BRINGING IT ALL TOGETHER

The four capabilities we have explored over these two chapters, Connection, Care, Critical Thinking, and Cognitive Diversity, are not separate skills to be practised in isolation. They are deeply interconnected, and each one reinforces and enables the others.

So how do you create conditions that bring all four to life at the same time? It begins with humility, with leaving your ego at the door. Eleanor Roosevelt, who chaired the drafting of the Universal Declaration of Human Rights, which we met at the start of the previous chapter, succeeded not because she was the smartest or most experienced person in the room, but because she understood that her role was to help others think. She asked questions rather than giving answers, created informal spaces where adversaries could connect as human beings, and made sure that voices from every region were heard, whether or not she agreed with their ideology.

Whether you are running a user interview, facilitating a discovery workshop, observing users in their workplace, or simply helping your team work through a difficult decision, the same principles apply. Your job is not to have the best ideas, it is to create the conditions where the best ideas can emerge from the collective intelligence of the group. And that brings us to a tool we use every day but have probably never been shown how to use well.

We will look at why questions are such a powerful discovery tool, why the best insights come from how we listen, and how to build a practical toolkit of questions that will improve your discovery conversations.

KEY TAKEAWAYS

- **Critical thinking means questioning assumptions:** It is the practice of questioning what we think we know before we act on it, and without structured techniques, teams let contradictory evidence slide past them.
- **Critical thinking has to start at the top:** Zillow's $500 million loss shows that a leadership team can have all the data and expertise, and still fail because it stops questioning its own assumptions.

- **Separate dreaming from critiquing:** Walt Disney's Three Chairs method shows that creative thinking and critical thinking are two different modes, and trying to do both at once means doing neither well.
- **Build critical thinking into the workflow:** The Three Amigos technique embeds assumption-challenging into how work flows through a team, with the developer, tester, and business perspectives each questioning different aspects of a proposed solution.
- **Imagine failure before it happens:** The Pre-Mortem overcomes the social barriers to honest assessment by asking a team to explain why a project has already failed, and it works best when everyone writes down their reasons privately before anyone speaks, so the loudest voice does not set the tone.
- **A token Devil's Advocate is worse than none:** A challenge raised half-heartedly so the team can feel rigorous leaves the group more confident, not less, so the role only works when the person genuinely engages.
- **Cognitive diversity catches the blind spots expertise misses:** When a team shares similar backgrounds and experiences, they share similar blind spots, and history from pirate crews to crash test dummies shows what happens when only one kind of mind is in the room.
- **You rarely get a real crowd inside one company:** Most teams share a profession, a culture, and a hierarchy, so a facilitator has to import outside perspectives and protect independence rather than assume the wisdom of crowds happens by itself.
- **Look in the corners for inspiration:** When the team at Great Ormond Street borrowed handover techniques from Formula 1 pit crews, they cut errors that years of medical expertise had not, because cross-industry perspectives reveal solutions that experts inside a field overlook.

16 ASK POWERFUL QUESTIONS

'To ask or to listen, that is the question.'

Paddy Dhanda

THE $1.85 BILLION QUESTION

In 2009, Walmart asked its customers a question: 'Would you like our stores to be less cluttered?' Unsurprisingly, they said yes. As a result, Walmart launched Project Impact, a multi-year initiative to transform its customers' shopping experience.[1]

Despite their proactive approach, things went drastically wrong. Within two years, Walmart had lost an estimated $1.85 billion in revenue. The executives behind Project Impact were fired. But what went wrong? Walmart had done exactly what the research told them to do. They delivered what customers said they wanted.

One of their biggest mistakes was clearing out the notorious 'Action Alley', which was a line of pallets filled with popular everyday items like bottled water and mayonnaise. COO Bill Simon later called the initiative a 'self-inflicted wound' and acknowledged that traffic declines in the remodelled stores were 'deeper than we projected'.[2]

The question 'Would you like our stores to be less cluttered?' contains its own answer baked into it, and that answer is obviously yes, because it assumes clutter is inherently bad. It's a bit like asking 'Would you prefer things to be better?' and the only polite response is to agree.

What Walmart failed to realise is that customers love to rummage through Action Alley, in the hope they might find a bargain. The clutter was, in fact, a feature, and one that triggered valuable impulse-buying.

Most of us ask Walmart-style questions every single day without realising it, and those questions shape what gets built and what ultimately ends up failing. Yet at one stage of our lives, we were experts in questioning. According to Harvard psychologist Paul Harris, children ask approximately 40,000 questions between the ages of two and five, roughly 100 per day.[3] But somewhere along the line, we lose that desire to be curious, just as we lost our ability to be creative.

QUESTIONABLE QUESTIONS

How many times have you greeted a colleague by asking, 'How are you?' and received the predictable reply, 'Fine, thanks.' Behavioural researcher Vanessa Van Edwards calls these 'autopilot questions' because they trigger scripted responses that reveal nothing about a person.[4]

It's just one of the traps that impact the quality of our conversations. In product discovery, there are other habits that we need to unlearn so that we can ask better questions. Let me share three of the most common types of, what I refer to as, questionable questions.

The leading trap

The first trap involves questions that influence the answer. These questions typically sound like 'Don't you think it would be better if ...?' or 'Wouldn't you agree that ...?' or 'Isn't the real problem ...?' Every one of them is really an opinion disguised as a question.

In 1974, psychologists Elizabeth Loftus and John Palmer revealed how much impact a single word can have on an answer, in their now-famous car crash study.[5] They showed participants a film of a traffic accident and then asked them to estimate how fast the cars were going, but they changed one word. Some participants were asked how fast the cars were going when they 'hit' each other, while others were asked how fast they were going when they 'smashed' into each other.

Participants who heard 'smashed' estimated the cars were travelling at about 41 miles per hour. Those who heard 'hit' estimated about 34 miles per hour. A difference of nearly 20 per cent based solely on a single word.

One loaded word dropped into a question can skew how people judge and describe what they see. Consider the difference between asking your team, 'How would you describe the checkout experience?' and asking, 'How are we failing customers at checkout?' The first invites honest feedback, while the second uses the word 'failing' to imply something is seriously wrong, even though it might be perfectly fine.

The easiest way to spot this type of questionable question is to ask yourself whether it contains a hidden assumption.

The prediction trap

Have you ever been certain you would go to the gym tomorrow, only to find yourself still on the sofa instead? Or bought a book with the intention of reading it, but never did? If so, you definitely aren't alone.

Questions like 'How often would you use this?' or 'What would you pay for something like this?' feel like they are gathering useful data, but people are unreliable when predicting their own future actions. Psychologists call this the intention–action gap, and it affects all of us regardless of how self-aware we think we are.

In one UK study, 89 per cent of consumers reported having ethical concerns about the products they buy, and when asked if they intended to purchase more ethical products, 30 per cent said yes. But when researchers tracked what people actually bought, only 3 per cent did.[6]

The people in the study weren't intentionally lying. They genuinely believed they would follow through, but when we imagine our future selves we picture a more optimistic version who has more willpower and fewer competing priorities.

Rather than asking people to just imagine what they might do, it's better to also ask them to connect with something they have already done, so they have a point of reference. Instead of 'Would you use this feature?' ask 'What do you currently do when you face this problem, and how well does it work?' Where you might have asked 'What would you pay for this?' try 'What are you already paying for similar services, and how does that compare with the value you get?' And rather than 'Would this solve your problem?' ask 'What have you already tried, and why didn't it work?'

The binary trap

The third trap involves questions that narrow our thinking too early; these are more commonly known as closed questions. These types of questions have a binary answer, usually yes or no. They include questions like 'Is this a problem for you?' or 'Do you like this design?' These questionable questions end conversations instead of opening them up to deeper exploration.

Closed questions are particularly bad at the early stages of discovery when we want to go wide, rather than deep. I often run a simple activity with product teams to show them this in action.

The lateral thinking puzzle

It's based on a classic lateral thinking puzzle, a type of riddle popularised by Paul Sloane in his 1992 book *Lateral Thinking Puzzlers*.[7] I give the group a statement: 'She was pushing her car and stopped outside a hotel, and became bankrupt.' They have two minutes to ask questions and figure out what happened. The only rule is that they can't ask me directly for the answer. What they don't know is that I'm secretly tallying how many of their questions are closed vs open.

Each time, I see a similar pattern. The vast majority of questions are closed: 'Did her car break down?' and 'Was she on her way to work?' Each one gets a yes or no from me, and each one only rules out a single possibility. But the few people who ask open questions, like 'What was she doing before this happened?' get much richer information that moves them closer to the answer.

A better strategy is to ask a few open questions first, then use closed questions to narrow down. 'Describe the scene to me' might reveal she was sitting at a table. 'What was on the table?' would uncover a board game. Then, to eliminate some of the other possibilities, we can use closed questions like 'Was she playing the game at the same time as she was pushing the car?' And then 'Was she playing Monopoly?' confirms it.

The fix is straightforward but requires discipline. Every time you catch yourself about to ask a yes/no question, pause and reframe it. Instead of 'Is this a problem for you?' say 'Tell me about a time when this became frustrating.' Or instead of 'Do you like this design?' try 'What's your first reaction when you see this?' Each version invites a story rather than an abrupt end to the conversation.

None of this means that closed questions are the enemy, because they are exactly the right tool when you need to confirm something specific or eliminate an option.

Figure 16.1 The question traps

WHAT 250 INTERVIEWS TAUGHT ME ABOUT QUESTIONS

I started podcasting in 2020 as an experiment to help me learn from other experts, and at the time I had no idea what I was doing. The whole thing began because I wanted to have conversations with smart people, and podcasting seemed like a great excuse to reach out to authors and leaders who would otherwise have ignored my emails.

My very first guest was David Marquet, the ex-US nuclear submarine commander and author we met in earlier chapters. He is every podcast host's dream guest because he is such a natural storyteller.

If you listen to the episode, you'll hear that I spoke for less than 10 minutes of the entire 30-minute runtime.[8] But when I listen now, it sounds rigid because I was so focused on my list of questions that I missed opportunities to follow up on interesting threads.

After recording over 250 episodes, I started to notice patterns. Certain types of questions consistently led to better conversations, and the type of question I needed to ask depended on what I was trying to achieve.

Sometimes I wanted to build a connection with my guest. At other times I wanted specific facts and figures, or personal stories that would bring a concept to life.

Questioning is just like any other skill. The more you practise it, the better you get. I have taken everything I learned through those hundreds of conversations and created the Question Compass to make it easier for you to apply these patterns to your discovery work, whether you are interviewing stakeholders or trying to understand problems in more detail.

THE QUESTION COMPASS

The Compass has four directions, and each one serves a different purpose depending on what you are trying to achieve in a discovery conversation. Connection questions build empathy and establish a relationship with the person you are speaking with. Reality questions move the conversation to focus on experiences or facts that you can actually learn from. Exploratory questions open up new possibilities and encourage creative thinking. Deeper questions help you get to the root cause or find the real motivations behind someone's thinking. The rest of this chapter takes you through each direction in turn.

Question Compass in action

Every discovery conversation takes you on a questioning journey, and the best conversations keep switching direction so you don't get stuck in one mode for too long. Let me show you the Question Compass in action during an everyday situation that most of us should be familiar with.

It's Saturday evening, and my son wanders in and announces, 'I'm hungry. Can we go out for dinner?' In my family, this is never straightforward because my wife loves trying new restaurants, my son is devoted to crispy chicken nuggets, my daughter is vegan, and I avoid most seafood. We must be the stakeholders from hell whenever we eat out.

Watch how simple questions move through the Compass to reach a decision.

> 'How's everyone feeling about going out tonight?' I ask the room. [CONNECTION]
>
> My wife nods enthusiastically, and my daughter looks up from her phone. 'Yeah, I could eat. But please, nowhere that just serves a bland salad as the vegan option.'
>
> 'Tell me about the last place that actually had good vegan choices', my wife says. [REALITY]
>
> My daughter replies, 'That Mediterranean place. They had proper falafels.'
>
> Just as I'm about to object, my son pulls a face. 'I don't remember them having chicken nuggets. What about that American diner?'
>
> 'What happened the last time we went there?' my daughter asks. [REALITY]
>
> He pauses, remembering. 'Oh yeah. The nuggets were soggy. Pretty bad actually.'
>
> 'Why do crispy nuggets mean so much to you?' I ask. [DEEPER]
>
> 'Because soggy chicken is disgusting. It's the texture. If it's not crunchy, I won't eat it.'

We seem stuck. The Mediterranean place works for my daughter, but not my son, and the diner failed him last time.

> 'What if we tried somewhere completely new that none of us have been to before?' my wife suggests. [EXPLORATORY]

My daughter enthusiastically jumps in and says, 'There's a Greek place that opened last month that I saw on TikTok. They have deep-fried chicken bites on the kids' menu and proper vegan food.'

'What are we waiting for?' my son asks.

The questions moved naturally from checking everyone was on board, to understanding what had worked before, to opening up new possibilities when we seemed stuck, and finally coming to an agreement that worked for everyone.

Using the Compass

The best discovery conversations use all four directions on the Compass to create a dynamic and natural dialogue. But since we are all wired differently, we tend to have a natural preference to focus too much on one and not enough on the others.

Some of us are drawn to gathering facts and evidence over connecting emotionally, while others are brilliant at building rapport but struggle to dig into the specific details. Neither approach unlocks the full potential of a conversation unless we are prepared to step outside our comfort zone and try other directions.

The Compass is not a sequence to follow mechanically from one direction to the next. You can use it as a prompt when a conversation feels stuck. The simplest thing you can do is ask yourself which direction you have not explored yet, as that will usually tell you exactly what to ask next.

CONNECTION: BUILDING TRUST AND RAPPORT

Connection questions are a great starting point for any discovery conversation. People won't share their real thoughts or genuine fears with someone they don't trust, and trust is something you have to build. Use them when you're building rapport with new stakeholders, at the beginning of user research sessions, or when someone seems defensive.

When I record a podcast, I never have a pre-call with the guest. I want the conversation to feel natural, as if two people meeting for the first time in an airport lounge are chatting before their flight. So when I finally speak to them, I dedicate a few minutes to small talk, and this is critical because without it, the whole conversation can feel awkward or bland.

I usually focus on an observation, such as an object that's visible in the background. It could be a picture on the wall or their library of books stacked behind them. Guests almost always light up when you show genuine curiosity about something they care about.

Chris Voss learned this principle during his years as the FBI's lead international kidnapping negotiator. In *Never Split the Difference*, he explains that skilled negotiators build rapport before making any requests, using what he calls 'tactical empathy'.[9] A simple request like 'Help me understand your perspective' is more powerful than any argument because it creates a connection before it seeks agreement.

It only takes one question

I was running a team of product owners, and I had a problem. The team I had set up in Birmingham was struggling to get support from our London colleagues, and I needed buy-in from the senior executives to change that.

During one of my visits to the London office, I happened to share the lift with our chief operating officer. Let's call him Charlie. I noticed he was wearing cycling gear and carrying a cycling helmet in his hand, and I asked a question that changed everything: 'What's your favourite bicycle?'

That one question led to a 30-minute conversation about cycling. From that moment on, every time I saw Charlie, he would strike up a conversation. Sometimes it was about his next cycling adventure. Other times, we would discuss his fastest personal best. But the common theme was always cycling.

Because of this relationship, I noticed a shift in how the wider leadership engaged with my team. It grew into something genuinely positive, and the fact that we had Charlie's support meant our team counted for something.

The funny thing is, I did not actually cycle. At the time, I didn't even own a bicycle. But Charlie never asked, and it never once crossed my mind to tell him.

What good looks like

The first question I asked Charlie worked because it had nothing to do with what I needed and everything to do with what he cared about, and the best connection questions work in the same way.

'What's your biggest priority right now?' shows that you care about their world and their pressures, not just your own agenda. 'What would be most helpful for you to get out of this conversation?' flips the dynamic from extracting information to collaborating, and it often surprises people who expect to be interrogated. 'What concerns do you have about this project?' invites honesty about reservations they might not otherwise share.

Sometimes, the most powerful connection question is simply 'What's been on your mind lately?' because it gives people the opportunity to lean on a colleague. As the famous saying goes, a problem shared is a problem halved.

Here are some more questions to try:

- What's the best thing that's happened to you this week?
- What would make this conversation most useful for you?
- How are you feeling about all of this?
- What's been the hardest part of this for you?

What to avoid

Starting with 'Let's jump right into the questions' tells the other person you just want to get down to business, signalling a transactional relationship. People are not vending machines that dispense information when you press the right buttons.

'I'm sure you're busy, so I'll try to be quick' sounds like you're being respectful of their time, but it actually sends the opposite message. It tells them this conversation is not really important, so they do not need to invest in it either.

Having said all of that, it's important that you understand your stakeholders' communication preferences. Not everyone enjoys small talk, and with senior stakeholders time is of the essence. But even if it's a very small amount of time, it is usually worth spending some time building rapport.

A useful test for whether you have created enough connection is to ask yourself, would this person feel comfortable admitting a mistake to me, or asking what might seem like a stupid question? If the answer is no, you have more connecting work to do before you move on.

REALITY: GROUNDING YOUR UNDERSTANDING

Once you have established rapport, you can move to reality questions. As product people, we often talk about the 'as is' process and the 'to be', and reality questions help build understanding of the current situation. For Walmart, reality questions would have revealed what customers actually liked and disliked about the current shopping experience.

Requests like 'Tell me about your last shopping trip to Walmart, and walk me through what happened from the moment you arrived to when you left' would have revealed insights into the way they hunt for bargains and the impulse purchases picked up from Action Alley.

The story invitations

As a podcaster, I publish key moments as short clips on social media. After analysing the performance of hundreds of these clips, I noticed patterns. The ones that do well are moments where guests share a personal story, whether an experience of failure or overcoming a challenge. This led me to look into why stories work so much better than direct questions. Researchers have been studying this for decades.

During World War II, psychologist John Flanagan was commissioned by the US Air Force to figure out what separated successful pilots from unsuccessful ones.[10] He found that asking pilots general questions about their performance produced vague and unhelpful answers. But asking them to describe specific incidents where something went right or wrong produced much richer and more detailed accounts.

Flanagan called this the Critical Incident Technique. The principle behind it explains why story-based questions work so well in discovery.[11] Significant events stick in our memory compared with regular experiences, and when people recall those events, they share information they would never think to mention if you simply asked for their opinion. My favourite way to unlock these stories is by simply asking, 'Tell me about a time when ...'.

I have found it useful to add constraints to story-based questions because they help the other person focus their response. If you're interviewing a developer about deployment issues, you might say, 'Tell me about the last time a release went wrong, and give me two things that contributed to the problem.' When you are speaking with a banking operations team about payment processing, you could try 'Walk me through what happened last Monday when you were reconciling the batch files, and tell me the biggest delays you encountered.'

Without these constraints, you can end up with a lengthy conversation that feels productive at the time, but becomes difficult to analyse afterwards. The key points get buried inside the narrative. If you think about it in terms of creating your own viral shorts, every discovery conversation is an opportunity to uncover a story. When we're intentional with our questions, those stories are far more likely to emerge.

What good looks like

'What happened next?' is one of the most underrated questions in discovery because it keeps the story moving without leading the person in any particular direction. It's a phrase that you can repeat multiple times as a gentle nudge.

Another technique I learned from coaching is even simpler. Just repeat the last few words someone said with an upward inflexion. Voss calls this mirroring.[12] If someone tells you, 'We ended up building a workaround in a spreadsheet', you simply respond with 'A spreadsheet?' and wait. The repetition signals that you want them to elaborate, and most people will automatically continue talking. Voss recommends waiting at least four seconds after mirroring to let the technique work.

Here are some more prompts to try:

- Tell me about the last time this happened.
- Walk me through exactly what you did, step by step.
- What did you see or hear that made you think that?
- What have you already tried, and how did that go?

What to avoid

Remember the binary trap? It applies here, too. 'Do you usually have problems with this?' invites a simple yes or no, and the word 'usually' lets them give a general answer rather than pinpointing a specific experience. You will get an opinion rather than a story, and as we have seen, opinions are far less reliable than accounts of what actually happened.

When someone says 'I usually just ...' or 'It generally works fine', that's a sign to push for specifics. Ask them to describe an actual example of the last time it happened.

EXPLORATORY: SPARKING CREATIVE THINKING

Chapter 9 looked at ways to boost creativity through team activities that incorporate play and constraints. Exploratory questions are another powerful tool because they create conditions for creative thinking, allowing people to open their minds and let their imagination run free.

Permission to dream

Warren Berger spent years studying how creative thinkers innovate, and he discovered that the natural cycle of problem-solving breaks down into three core types of questions.[13] 'Why' questions help us understand a problem or opportunity. 'How' questions help us narrow down and take action. But between understanding and doing, there is a stage that many discovery conversations skip entirely, and that is the 'What if' stage, where we explore ideas and brainstorm possibilities before committing to any particular direction.

'What if' questions help us to dream, and they do this by temporarily suspending the practical constraints that usually limit our thinking. As Berger puts it: 'It's about how human beings solve problems: first they understand, then imagine, then do.'[14]

A rubbish question

That might sound like a big creative leap, but exploratory questions are just as useful in ordinary working life. Sometimes they help us see a familiar problem from a different angle. Chris Thomason, founder of Ingenious Growth Limited, learned this lesson after buying an insolvent manufacturing company that made equipment for the chemical processing industry.[15] The company worked with composite materials that could survive highly corrosive environments in situations where customers required something stronger than stainless steel.

The materials were expensive to buy, and the waste was expensive to throw away. Offcuts of glass matting were classed as hazardous, which meant the company had to pay to dispose of them properly.

That frustrated Chris. As he explained to me, nothing annoyed him more than paying good money to throw away materials he had already paid even more good money to buy. So one day, he asked another business owner, 'Where do you dispose of your waste?' The answer took him by surprise: 'We don't have any waste.'

Chris could not believe it. How could a business working with the same kind of materials have no waste? The explanation was almost too simple. They took old resin drums and cut them into three different sizes. Large offcuts went into the large drum, medium offcuts went into the middle drum, and small offcuts went into the small drum. They then introduced one simple rule: Before anyone cut a fresh piece from the main roll, they had to check the drums and use the smallest offcut that would do the job.

Back at his own factory, Chris spent about £50 on a couple of old drums and copied the idea. From that day on, he no longer had the same waste problem that had been costing him a fortune.

But the real lesson wasn't the drums or the simplicity of the solution, it was the question. Chris had been asking, 'Where do we dispose of our waste?' Hidden within that question was an assumption he had not noticed. The word waste had already narrowed his thinking and had sent him looking for disposal companies.

The better question might have been, 'What if we stopped thinking about this as waste?' Chris no longer had to think only about disposal, he could start thinking about how the same material might be used differently. Exploratory questions are designed to loosen the constraints around the problem, giving us permission to imagine options we might otherwise dismiss too quickly.

Beginner's mind

In Zen Buddhism, there is a concept called 'shoshin', which translates to 'beginner's mind'. It refers to seeing things with an open mind, which experts can't always do. Zen teacher Shunryu Suzuki wrote, 'In the beginner's mind there are many possibilities, but in the expert's mind there are few.'[16]

You might recognise this in your workshops when experienced team members dismiss ideas with 'we tried that before' or 'that would never work here'. Their experience, which is usually an asset, becomes the thing that holds them back.

When my kids became CEOs

A few years ago, we were pitching to a large retail bank for a training contract. I knew we were up against serious competition and spent days trying to come up with something memorable. Then I had a moment of inspiration. What if we used the beginner's mind as our competitive advantage? I convinced my kids to record an interview answering the question: 'What would you change if you were the CEO of a bank?' We opened the pitch by playing the video. The energy in the room completely changed as the kids talked about tracking deliveries through your banking app, making branches more fun, and helping the planet through sustainable practices.

It was the beginner's mind taken to the extreme, but it showed how questioning can bring out the child in all of us, even in the boardroom. I can't say for certain how much the video influenced the final decision, but we won the contract.

Exploratory questions help recreate that beginner's mind by inviting people to temporarily set their expertise aside. When you ask someone, 'What would you do if you had to do things differently?' or 'If money were no object, what would you do?' it shifts the mindset so we can broaden our thinking.

What good looks like

In 1971, educator Bob Eberle developed a technique called SCAMPER to help children become more creative, and it has since become one of the most widely used ideation tools in business.[17] The technique is built entirely around questions. It works by challenging how you look at a problem from seven angles: Substitute, Combine, Adapt, Modify, Put to other uses, Eliminate, and Reverse.

'What if we reversed the process?' often produces the most surprising breakthroughs. On Black Friday 2011, while every other retailer was urging customers to buy more, Patagonia ran a full-page advertisement in the *New York Times* with the headline 'Don't Buy This Jacket'. The following year, their sales increased by 30 per cent.[18]

Here are some more questions to try:

- If money were no object, what would you do?
- What would you build if you only had a week?
- If we had to start again from scratch, what would we do differently?
- If this were a headline in the news next year, what would we want it to say?

What to avoid

There's an important distinction between exploratory questions and predictive questions, and it's easy to confuse them. 'Would you use this feature?' is not an exploratory question because it falls into the prediction trap we discussed earlier.

Asking exploratory questions and then immediately critiquing the answers defeats their purpose entirely. When someone shuts down an idea with 'That would never work ...' you have recreated the conditions that killed their creative confidence.

There is also a danger in pushing this too far the other way. Exploration without a clear purpose can use up valuable time in a workshop, so give it room, put a sensible time-box around it, and be clear about how you will bring the conversation back to something practical.

DEEPER: FINDING ROOT CAUSES AND REAL MOTIVATIONS

The previous three directions on the Compass help you build trust, gather facts, and open up new possibilities. But sometimes you need to dig deeper to find out the reasons behind the insights. That's where deeper questions come in.

Don't settle for the first answer

When you ask a question, people tend to give the answer they believe the interviewer wants to hear. Researchers call this social desirability bias.[19] Sometimes people genuinely believe the answer they are giving, even though it doesn't match their actual behaviour. Other times, people know the real answer but choose to say something different to make a good impression or avoid looking foolish.

Either way, when running discovery interviews, always try to go deeper on the first answer you hear. When users tell you they want 'improved search capabilities', what they often really mean is that they feel lost and frustrated. When a stakeholder says they need 'real-time data', what they often really mean is that they want to feel confident they are making good decisions.

The woman who rounded up her numbers

In 2004, Bank of America wanted to get more people to open savings accounts. Instead of just running more adverts, they sent a team of researchers to observe and interview families around the USA.[20]

One researcher was looking through the chequebook of a woman in Atlanta when she noticed something strange. Instead of writing the exact amount of each purchase, this woman rounded up all her numbers. A purchase of $22.73 was written down as $23.

The researcher probed a little deeper. Why do you round up the numbers like that? The woman explained that it made the maths easier. But there was more to it. By rounding up a little bit each time, she always had a small buffer at the end of the month. It was her way of saving without really trying.

This insight led to a service called Keep the Change that rounded up debit card purchases and put the difference into savings accounts automatically. Within a year, two million customers had signed up.[21] And it started because one researcher kept asking 'why?' about a small habit she noticed in a chequebook.

Five whys

Taiichi Ohno, an engineer at Toyota, developed a breakthrough for exploring root causes.[22] When something went wrong, he would ask why it happened, then ask why again about whatever answer he got. He kept asking why until he found something he could actually fix.

Imagine a product team notices that users of their workforce management platform are submitting timesheets late. Over 65 per cent of employees miss the Friday deadline each week. They could just send more reminder notifications, but instead, they decide to ask why.

- Why are users submitting timesheets late? Because they leave it until the end of the week and then forget.
- Why do they leave it until the end of the week? Because they cannot remember what they worked on each day by Friday afternoon.
- Why can they not remember? Because their work is spread across multiple projects, clients, and tasks that blur together.
- Why does their work blur together? Because there's nothing capturing the details about the work while it's being worked on.
- Why is there nothing capturing their work? Because the timesheet is completely separate from the tools where they actually do their work.

The root cause is not that they are forgetful, it is that the timesheet exists in isolation from the systems where work happens. The solution might be calendar integration or daily micro-prompts rather than another Friday morning notification.

Reflective listening

Another technique, called Motivational Interviewing, comes from therapists and counsellors.[23] Their approach is built around reflective listening. Instead of asking another question, you make a statement that reflects back what you think the person meant, then wait to see if you got it right. This lets people hear their own thoughts played back, which often prompts them to go deeper than they would with a direct question.

Here is how it might work in discovery. A user says, 'I wish the reports were more customisable.' Instead of asking 'What customisation do you need?' you might say, 'It sounds like there's a gap between what the reports show and what you actually need to communicate.' The user then responds, 'Yes, exactly. My director asks about trends over time, but the report only shows this month. So every Monday, I'm pulling data into a spreadsheet just to answer her questions. It makes me look like I don't know my numbers.' Now you have learned something you might not have discovered with a direct question, because the real issue is not extra flexibility or more features. It is credibility in front of leadership.

Research on Motivational Interviewing suggests using at least two reflective statements for every question you ask.[24] You don't need to hit that exact ratio, but the principle is useful.

What good looks like

The best deeper questions invite people to think without telling them what to think. Here are some examples that I have found useful over the years.

'Why is that important to you?' is the simplest, deepest question you can ask. Do not be afraid to ask it more than once in a row, just change the words slightly each time.

'What would happen if we did nothing about this issue?' helps you understand how important a problem really is. Sometimes what people describe as urgent turns out to be a minor annoyance. Other times, what they mention turns out to be the thing keeping them awake at night.

Here are some more questions to try:

- Why do you think that is?
- What caused that to happen?
- What's the cost of not fixing this?
- What would success look like?

What to avoid

A word of caution about the five whys. When someone asks you 'why', your brain immediately starts looking for a 'because'. It demands justification and puts people on the defensive, even when you didn't mean it that way.

Avoid using 'why' questions when you are focusing on someone's behaviour or past decisions. Asking 'Why did you do that?' triggers defensiveness if the action is loaded with emotion. When you want to understand someone's behaviour, simply replace 'why' with 'what' or 'how'. These words are neutral and observation-based. 'What was the goal when you clicked that?' feels like you are being curious, while 'Why did you click that?' feels like you are being judgemental.

Another phrase to use instead of the five whys is 'And what else?' Michael Bungay Stanier, author of *The Coaching Habit*, calls this 'the best coaching question in the world' because it assumes there is always more to discover beyond what has already been shared.[25]

But 'why' is exactly the right word in other situations. When you are trying to understand the strategic value behind a request, 'why' works well because you are asking about business priorities rather than personal choices.

Finally, do not go too deep too fast. Deeper questions work best after you have built trust with connection questions and gathered facts with reality questions. If you jump straight to 'What does this really mean to you?' before someone feels comfortable, they are unlikely to give you the real answer.

BEFORE YOUR NEXT CONVERSATION

The four directions of the Compass give you a simple framework for structuring your discovery conversations. Before any important conversation, whether that's a podcast interview or a client discovery call, I define the outcomes I want to achieve. I then work

Figure 16.2 The Question Compass

backwards to identify specific questions from the Compass that will help meet those outcomes. This preparation takes less than 15 minutes but can transform the quality of the conversation.

There is one caveat worth noting before we move on. Everything in this chapter assumes you are working somewhere that genuinely wants to learn and where good questions are welcomed. You can ask every question perfectly, uncover exactly the right insight, and still watch the decision go the other way because of budgets, politics, or someone more senior who has already made up their mind. If you missed the section on dealing with the messy politics, then take a look back at Chapter 13.

For now, let's assume all the hard work you put into asking the right questions paid off. If you can't present your ideas with impact, they'll never make it beyond a set of slides. Most product management training focuses on innovation techniques but rarely teaches us how to present our ideas or influence the people who control budgets.

The next chapter takes you through how to turn discovery insights into stories that get buy-in from decision-makers. We'll look at why attention is harder to capture than ever and how to structure your message so it lands in the first 60 seconds.

KEY TAKEAWAYS

- **Questions shape what gets built:** Walmart's $1.85 billion loss came from asking customers the wrong question.
- **Three traps undermine discovery conversations:** Leading questions influence answers, prediction questions ask people to forecast behaviour they can't reliably predict, and binary questions close down exploration when you need to go wide.
- **The Question Compass gives you four directions:** Connection questions build trust. Reality questions ground conversations in actual experiences. Exploratory questions open up creative possibilities. Deeper questions uncover root causes and motivations.
- **Connection questions build trust:** People share accurate information only after they feel respected and heard, a principle FBI negotiators rely on before making any request.
- **Reality questions anchor responses in actual experience:** Asking 'Tell me about a time when ...' uncovers specific incidents that stick in the memory and surface details people would never mention in response to direct questions.
- **Exploratory questions give permission to dream:** 'What if' questions temporarily suspend the practical constraints that usually limit our thinking and invite the beginner's mind back into the room.
- **Deeper questions uncover root causes:** Techniques like the five whys and reflective listening help you move past surface-level responses to find root causes and motivations.

17 PRESENT IDEAS WITH IMPACT

'A story is worth a thousand slides.'

Paddy Dhanda

THE DOCTOR WHO COULDN'T MAKE THEM LISTEN

In 1847, Ignaz Semmelweis, a Hungarian doctor, was working at Vienna General Hospital, where mothers in one ward were dying at six times the rate of mothers in the ward next door.[1] One ward was staffed by doctors and the other by midwives, and Semmelweis traced the cause to handwashing. Doctors were passing infections from the morgue to the delivery room with their unwashed hands. When he introduced handwashing with chlorinated lime, the death rate dropped from over 18 per cent to under 2 per cent within months.[2]

He had found the cause of childbed fever years before anyone else, and the medical establishment refused to listen. Doctors felt they were being accused of killing their own patients. Charles Meigs, one of the most senior obstetricians in America, summed up the reaction: 'Doctors are gentlemen, and a gentleman's hands are clean.'[3] Semmelweis was so upset that he wrote open letters calling his critics murderers, and the book he published was so hostile that it alienated even his supporters.[4] By 1865, his colleagues had him committed to an asylum, where he died at the age of 47.

His ideas were proven correct a few years later, when Louis Pasteur and Joseph Lister established germ theory.[5] But even with the evidence to back his claims, Semmelweis could not get doctors to listen, and thousands of women died.

Semmelweis' story is nearly 200 years old, yet I see versions of it in every organisation I work with. People put in the hard work to come up with great ideas, but struggle to convince others they are worth investing in. This chapter will help you rethink the way you pitch those ideas, so that the people who need to hear them actually do.

WHY THE OLD PLAYBOOK DOESN'T WORK ANYMORE

Competing with mobile phones

At the HumanX conference in Silicon Valley, one of the largest AI gatherings in the world, I watched a Ukrainian founder called Dima preparing to pitch to investors backstage. Before going on stage, he said something to the MC that stuck with me: 'The main competitor is actually mobile, not other startups. You're competing with mobile phones for attention. How do you make it almost like a show?'

Dima was a first-time founder whose second language was English, arriving from the UK just four days earlier, yet he had identified the real problem more clearly than most experienced professionals. We are competing for people's attention. The person you are presenting to is almost certainly not giving you their full attention. Managers spend a quarter of their week in meetings, and senior leaders at larger companies over 40 per cent.[6] Most arrive straight from a meeting that overran, already thinking about the next.

The 47-second attention span

We are living in an age of infobesity, surrounded by more information than ever before. Gloria Mark, a leading expert on attention, first measured our ability to stay focused in 2004. She found people spent an average of 2.5 minutes on a screen before switching to something else. By 2012, that had dropped to 75 seconds, and in her most recent research the average attention span has fallen to just 47 seconds.[7]

But the distractions are just a small part of a much larger problem. When you do get interrupted, it takes around 25 minutes to fully re-engage with the original task and get back in the zone.[8] So imagine your key stakeholder receives an important notification that they happen to check during your presentation. It could take them up to 25 minutes before they are fully focused again on your message.

How our tools trained us badly

Even the tools we use have trained us into bad habits. The phrase 'death by PowerPoint' was popularised in 2001, and I still hear it today. When you create a new slide, the default layout gives you a title and a set of blank bullet points, and so we feel compelled to fill them in. It is no wonder it results in reams and reams of text that no one has the time or mental capacity to absorb. When you schedule a meeting, the calendar defaults to an hour, and so the assumption is that one-hour meetings should be the norm. But if we lose people after 47 seconds, how do we expect them to cope with a whole hour?

FROM PRESENTING TO PERFORMING

Recently, I started to learn how to DJ. The first question a great DJ asks is who the audience is, so they can understand their taste in music; then they select the right tracks, much like the key messages we choose for a presentation. We can take the same inspiration from performers to think differently about how we engage an audience.

A stand-up comedian doesn't simply read from a script. They have thought about who is in the room, built in moments of surprise, and timed every punchline. What performers have in common is that they design everything for their audience, not for themselves.

If we are going to make our pitch more like a show, as Dima suggested, we need to stop thinking like presenters and start thinking like performers. That is a shift from sharing information to creating an experience that makes your audience feel something strongly enough to act. Table 17.1 shows the difference between presenters and performers.

Table 17.1 Presenter vs performer

	The presenter	The performer
Prepares by	Building slides	Designing an experience
Opens with	An agenda	A reason to care
Treats the audience as	Recipients	Participants
Designs around	Coverage	Contrast
Ends with	'Any questions?'	A call to action
Measures success by	What did they understand?	What did they feel?

SEND YOUR MESSAGE

Every presentation is different. Sometimes you are sharing a progress update, other times you are building a case for investment and need a decision. But regardless of the type, there is a core set of ingredients that every presentation needs. If you miss any of them out, your message won't land the way you intended. I have simplified them using the acronym SENND: Stakes and Stakeholders, Emotion, Numbers, Novelty, and Decision.

S: Stakes and Stakeholders

If you have ever scrolled through TikTok, you will have noticed that the best creators grab your attention in the first few seconds, with a hook that tells you exactly why you should care: 'Here's why your morning routine is ruining your productivity.' They have learned that you have 3–4 seconds before someone swipes away.

The same applies in a business presentation. Your stakes are the reason anyone should care, and if you don't establish them early, you lose people's interest.

Most presentations open with 'Today, I'd like to take you through some updates.' I call these predictive phrases. Your audience has heard them so often that they already know what's coming, and it probably isn't exciting. There are a few patterns that work better.

Cost of inaction

The first is what I call the cost of inaction, where you open with what the problem is costing the business right now. For example, 'When we total up the time spent in project meetings across the team, it is costing us £100,000 a week, and I want to show you how we can cut that in half', or 'This manual step in the process is costing the sales team 400 hours a month.' These work because they put a tangible cost on the table and create a sense of urgency about fixing it.

Opportunity of action

The cost of inaction focuses on the negative impact if we do nothing, whereas missed opportunities focus on the positive gains you could make if the room backs this idea. For example, 'If we reduce our report generation time from four hours to under ten minutes, our analysts could reinvest 15 hours a week into higher-value work', or 'Our research

Figure 17.1 SENND: five ingredients for presentations

shows that 40 per cent of users who complete their preferences during the sign-up process go on to become paying customers, and right now only half of them are doing it.'

Voice of the customer

Sometimes the most powerful way to set the stakes is to let someone else do it for you. If a long-term customer has told your account team they are looking at alternatives because your reporting is too slow, that feels far more likely to happen than if you simply present some data predicting it might. Or if 8 out of 10 users in your focus group said they would not recommend you to someone they know, that would instantly get the attention of senior leaders. Using quotes or insights directly from your customers carries a credibility that most other kinds of data cannot.

The paradox

The fourth pattern is often overlooked. A paradox opens with a contradiction between what should be happening and what is. At the HumanX Pitch Competition, Evan Smith, founder of the retail coaching tool Ethosphere, opened by saying: 'The greatest predictor of a high-performing retail store is a high-performing store manager. Ask any store manager what the most important thing they do is, and they'll say, it's coaching and developing my people. And in the same breath they'll tell you, I don't have the time to do it.'

Everyone in that room knew he was right. Store managers say coaching is the most important part of their job, and then they don't do it. That's what a paradox does. It puts a belief and a behaviour side by side and shows that they contradict each other. The audience can see that something is off, and they are curious how it can be true. That curiosity keeps them listening, because they want to know what you are going to do about it.

But for the stakes to land with your audience, we need to understand who is in the room. What lands with one person may not land with another, because every stakeholder looks at things through a different lens. A CTO is interested in technical feasibility, a CFO wants to know about the costs and benefits, and a product designer cares about user experience. The same discovery finding, presented to each of these stakeholders, needs a different set of stakes to make them care.

When I did not know my audience

I learned this the hard way at my first official public-speaking event. It was an IIBA conference in Romania, and I was presenting to a room of business analysts about moving into a product owner role. I was nervous, and one way I dealt with it was humour. Most of my bad jokes were mocking project managers. One was about what happens when a business analyst goes on holiday, where the project grinds to a halt, but when the project manager is away, work carries on as normal. It felt like I was in a safe space, and the laughs seemed to confirm it.

At the end, during the Q&A, one man who had looked increasingly uncomfortable stood up and told me directly that he did not appreciate the jokes. I apologised, assuming he had been a project manager at some point. But when he revealed he was the PMI president for Romania, I didn't know how to respond. The room went quiet, so I did what I would have done with a friend and offered to take him for a drink afterwards, and luckily, he agreed. It taught me an important lesson. I had made a sweeping assumption about the audience without ever checking who was in the room, and I paid the price.

E: Emotion

The stakes give your audience a reason to listen, but there's no guarantee they will care enough to act. In a presentation, feeling is what drives action. The retail industry has exploited this for decades. In supermarkets, everything from the layout to limited-time offers is designed to trigger an emotional response. Gallup found that around 70 per cent of purchasing decisions are based on emotional factors, with only 30 per cent rational.[9]

Science behind storytelling

But the most powerful tool for creating an emotional response is storytelling. Neuroscientists at Princeton used brain scans to study what happens when someone tells a story and another person listens. They found that when a story genuinely connects, the listener's brain activity begins to mirror the speaker's, almost in real time. The researchers described it as the brains becoming coupled, like two people dancing together.[10] And the stronger that coupling, the better the listener understands, remembers, and acts on what they have heard. When the story failed to land, the coupling vanished completely.

Stories that made money

One of my favourite examples is the Significant Objects project. In 2009, journalist Rob Walker and editor Joshua Glenn bought 100 cheap household items from thrift stores around New York, for about $1 each, and asked 100 writers to invent short stories, which they listed on eBay with the items.[11]

The one that stuck with me was an egg whisk. It was about a woman whose husband made extravagant ten-egg omelettes for his lovers, until his cholesterol got so high he needed bypass surgery. She comes home to find a mountain of eggshells in the bin and an egg whisk she has never seen before. 'A gift from a friend', he says. On her way out of the house for the last time, she takes the whisk because she knows it has sentimental value for him. That 25-cent whisk sold for $30.

The items had cost roughly $130 in total and sold for nearly $8,000, a whopping 6,000 per cent profit. Wrap an idea in a story and you create an emotional connection that increases the perceived value of whatever you are presenting.

Tell it as you would to a friend

There is a whole industry of books teaching storytelling arcs like the hero's journey and the Pixar formula. They work well for keynotes and TED talks, where you have the stage to craft a polished narrative. But in a business presentation they can feel forced, and when you have a 10-minute slot with an impatient group, trying to deliver an Oscar-worthy performance risks coming across as less than genuine.

So the approach I would recommend is to tell the story as if you were explaining it to a friend over coffee. You would not say, 'Once upon a time there was a product team.' Instead, you would say something like, 'So I was on this call with a customer last week, really lovely woman, and she offered to share her screen so I could watch her use the app. She's clicking through the order form, everything seems fine, and then she gets to the payment section and just stops. She stares at it for about 10 seconds, sighs, and says "I always get stuck here."' The friend version feels more natural, and it doesn't feel out of place in a product meeting.

You also do not have to tell your entire story in one go. A technique called the story loop has you start a story at the beginning of your presentation, but hold off on finishing it. That example could be turned into a story loop by opening with: 'This week, one of our users tried a feature for the first time and discovered a use case we had never considered. I will come back to that at the end.' An open loop like that creates curiosity that keeps the audience interested throughout, because they want to know how it ends, which means they are paying closer attention to every detail.

N: Numbers

Why big numbers don't land

As product people, we love our data, but we have so much of it that we often end up showing statistics that don't connect. I have lost count of the presentations where someone puts up a slide packed with numbers, and everyone looks confused.

Chip Heath wrote a book on why most of us get numbers wrong. In *Making Numbers Count*, he and Karla Starr argue our brains were never built to process abstract numbers.[12] For most of human history, many languages did not even have words for numbers greater than five. If someone puts up a big number on a slide, a million users or a billion transactions, they assume people in the room will understand what they mean. But unless you are extremely wealthy, you will probably find it difficult to picture what those numbers look like in reality, and I used to work with numbers every day at a bank. David Landy, a psychologist at Indiana University, found that about half of his participants treated million, billion, and trillion as roughly the same distance apart.[13] If your audience cannot feel the difference between a million-pound problem and a billion-pound one, the data on its own is meaningless.

Anchoring to the familiar

The way to overcome this is to anchor your numbers to something your audience can relate to. Reuters did this brilliantly with plastic bottles. Their 'Drowning in Plastic' page shows the bottles sold worldwide piled up. After a single day, 1.3 billion bottles would make a pile half the height of the Eiffel Tower, and after a year, taller than the Burj Khalifa.[14]

The same works in a product presentation. If your research found users spending 25 minutes on a task that should take 5 minutes, don't just state it. 'Imagine your morning commute took four times longer every day. That is what our users go through every time they try to complete this process.' We have all had to commute at some point, and the thought of it taking four times as long puts your audience inside the problem.

The same applies when you are presenting drop-off rates. If 60 per cent of users are abandoning a process before completing it, you could show a chart. Or you could say, 'Imagine you own a restaurant and ten people walk through the door for dinner. Six of them sit down, look at the menu, and then leave before ordering.'

In both cases, the data on its own is just a set of figures. Our job is to give people a reason to care about the numbers, and the easiest way to do that is to connect them to something the audience can touch and feel in their own world.

N: Novelty

Three moments I still remember

What do the elastic in a pair of knickers, bare feet, and Bhangra dancing all have in common? My colleague and good friend Paul Wigzel once pitched his product and pulled out a pair of knickers as a prop. He held them up and said his product was like the elastic, not all that exciting to talk about, but absolutely critical to an organisation, and he handed a pair to everyone in the room.

A few years ago, I sat through a course where the instructor took off his shoes and socks and ran the whole session barefoot. And when I used to run training at an investment bank, I would spend the first five minutes energising the room with Bhangra dancing. All three are novel, and I am telling you about them years later because they stick. I cannot remember the content of those sessions, but the novelty is as vivid as if it were yesterday.

Your novelty is your signature

By novelty, I mean adding something unusual that becomes the thing people remember you for. Some people call me the Bhangra guy, and at work I am known as the doodler because I draw my ideas live. Your novelty doesn't have to be as bold as Bhangra dancing. It can start small and build as your confidence grows. Table 17.2 lists some examples, ordered by how much confidence each requires.

Table 17.2 Confidence levels for novelty

Confidence needed	Suggestion
Low	Wearing something distinctive that becomes associated with you, such as a colourful scarf, a wacky T-shirt, or an unusual accessory
Low	Using a prop to anchor a metaphor that you return to throughout the presentation
Medium	Handing out a physical object that reinforces your point and that people can take away
Medium	Drawing your main idea live on a whiteboard or canvas, rather than using pre-built slides
High	Asking the audience to do something physical, such as standing up, moving to a different part of the room, or writing on the wall
Very high	Performing something that breaks the pattern entirely, such as singing, dancing, or running a session barefoot

I have come to think of novelty as the most powerful of the five SENND ingredients, and the one most people leave out. We are taught to fit in, but if you want to be remembered, blending in is the worst thing you can do. Your novelty is your signature, and once you find it, you become unforgettable.

The pedagogy of the unexpected

There is a formal teaching approach in education called the pedagogy of the unexpected; the idea behind it is simple.[15] If you deliberately introduce an element of surprise into a lesson, students will remember what you taught them far more clearly. That element could be an unusual prop, an unexpected change of setting, or doing something the class is not prepared for. In the film *Dead Poets Society*, there is a scene where Robin Williams has his students stand on their desks to see the classroom from a different perspective. That is the pedagogy of the unexpected in action, and it is one of the most memorable moments from the film.

Our brains love routine and spend most of their time predicting what will happen next. When something disrupts that flow, the brain treats it as a signal to pay attention and releases dopamine, the same chemical it produces when we experience something rewarding. Scientists call this the novelty penumbra, and the effect is not limited to the unexpected moment itself but also extends to the things you were doing around it.[16] In practical terms, it means that even if your moment of novelty has nothing to do with your message, like my Bhangra dancing, it can still make the surrounding content more memorable.

How Santa sold a sales enablement call

The clearest example in a product context is a sales enablement call I ran a few years ago. I had to present some new learning products to over 200 salespeople on Teams.

Instead of opening a slide deck, I drew Santa Claus on a blank canvas. It was about 70 days before Christmas, nowhere near the festive season, which was what made it work.

I told a story about Santa getting ready for the big day and wanting to sharpen his product skills. First, he needed better product management, because running a global gift operation with billions of customers and zero budget for returns is no small feat, and that introduced our product management course. Then I drew a conveyor belt, because his elves had no idea who was building what, so they went on a Kanban course. And finally Santa had lost so much weight in the gym that he needed a new belt, which introduced our Lean Six Sigma Green Belt course.

The real test came five days later, when I asked a few salespeople what they remembered. Nearly all recalled the whole story almost word for word. Our usual calls were the same slides and bullet points, and the content always faded. The Santa story stuck because it broke the pattern.

D: Decision

Why stakeholders defer decisions

Most presentations end with 'Any questions?' but marketing follows a different rule, where every communication ends with a call to action. In *This Is Marketing*, Seth Godin writes that you have not made an impact until you have changed someone.[17] The same is true of a product presentation. You can present brilliantly, but if nobody knows what to do next, nothing has changed.

The challenge is that stakeholders rarely like to decide on the spot, especially in front of an audience. Saying yes feels risky, because it closes off other options and commits them to a direction that might turn out to be wrong. Behavioural scientists call this decision aversion, and it is why you hear 'Let me think about it' or 'Can you send me the slides?' The mistake most presenters make is sharing one recommendation and hoping for approval. If you want them to act, make saying yes feel less risky than saying no.

The Goldilocks Principle

A more effective approach is what I call the Goldilocks Principle. Instead of one option, present three. The small one is low-cost and takes minimal effort, the medium one balances cost and impact, and the large one goes further but needs more investment. In practice, the small one might be a two-week pilot and the large one a full launch across every region. Showing all three makes clear you have weighed the trade-offs.

This works for two reasons. The first is psychological. In 1989, Stanford professor Itamar Simonson ran experiments that revealed the compromise effect. Given three options, people strongly prefer the middle one.[18] He and Amos Tversky confirmed it across dozens of categories, from cameras to cars.[19] Extremes feel risky. The smallest feels like too little, the largest like too much, and the middle feels just right.

Offering three options also changes the conversation, from 'Should we do this?' to 'Which one should we do?' One word of caution. The three need to be real alternatives, not the same idea with slightly different budgets. If the audience senses you have engineered the choice, you lose credibility.

HOW TO CREATE A WINNING STRUCTURE

The serial position effect

There's a famous saying: first impressions last. It reminds us to pay attention to how we come across when we first meet someone, but it overlooks the ending, which leaves just as strong an impression. When people are asked to remember a sequence, whether a list of words or a presentation, the beginning and the end stick, and everything in the middle becomes slightly blurred. Psychologists call this the serial position effect.[20]

Quentin Tarantino built his career on the principle that a story does not have to be told in the order it happened. In films like *Pulp Fiction* and *Kill Bill*, he deliberately breaks the chronological order, often showing the most dramatic moments right at the start or bringing the ending back around to where the story began. Critics have credited his non-linear approach with reshaping modern cinema.[21] The plot happens in the middle, but the beginning and the end are the most iconic scenes that audiences remember.

The same applies to your presentation. Your middle still has a job, because it is where you build your argument. Yet most presenters spend their preparation there and treat the two ends as an afterthought. Flip that balance, put far more of your effort into the opening and the closing, and your message will land much harder.

A portfolio strategy I structured differently

A few years ago, I was presenting a portfolio strategy to my executive team. We had all been given a template, and most colleagues stuck to it. They opened with revenue figures, walked through the current state of their portfolios, and ended with general recommendations. The leadership team had sat through that dozens of times, and you could feel attention fading by the second speaker.

I tried something different. Before building my deck, I was honest about what I actually wanted from the meeting. I had four or five asks, but one outweighed all the others combined. The executive team needed to back a significant investment in sales enablement, the biggest lever for growing the portfolio. So I surveyed my sales colleagues, the ones who had to sell the products, because their perspective was missing from the template.

I opened with the most negative finding. Beforehand, I had asked the sales team to rate, from one to five, how confident they felt selling our products, and the score came back around a two. That number went up on a slide with no context, and I paused. It was uncomfortable, and meant to be, because I wanted the room to picture a problem to fix.

At the end, I came back to the survey and shared the team's comments in their own words, people on the front line saying exactly what they needed and why. The decision I was asking for moved from one of several budget items to the executive team's top priority that quarter. My content was not dramatically different from my colleagues'. What differed was where I placed the most impactful material.

There is no fixed formula for where the SENND ingredients belong. Where your audience is analytical, lead with stakes and numbers and close on the decision. If you need to build empathy, open with a story and end on a provocation. The point is to design the experience deliberately, rather than sharing your work in the same predictable format as everyone else.

BUILD THE HABIT

From shy kid to keynote speaker

If you've got this far and are thinking that presenting fills you with dread, then you are not alone. In years of hosting my podcast and speaking at conferences, I have met hundreds of presenters and interviewed some of the world's leading communication experts, including Matt Abrahams from Stanford, who wrote the playbook on spontaneous speaking.[22] The one thing they all tell me is that presenting does not come naturally to most people. It is a learned skill, and it gets better with practice.

I know this because I used to be the shy kid who sat at the back of the classroom. When I was younger, I told everyone I was a professional introvert, and I said it as though it were a badge of honour rather than what it actually was, which was a way of avoiding the thing I found most terrifying.

What changed was a series of small steps, each one pushing slightly further past the edge of my comfort zone, from an internal presentation to a small team, to a training session for a dozen people, to a conference talk for 50. And then came something I could never have predicted when I was that quiet kid, the chance to head up the Agile learning for a global bank, a role that sent me around the world to train over 1,000 people. When I tell people now that I am addicted to conversation, they assume I have always been that way, but I have not, and that is the most important part of this story.

Communication improves through practice, not theory. One of the most useful things I ever did was a course where the trainer recorded me on video. There is nothing more cringeworthy than watching yourself back, but it forced me to see myself the way my audience saw me. I was using 'erm' between almost every sentence, my posture made me look like I didn't want to be there, and my tone was flat. None of it was obvious at the time, because when you present your attention is on the audience, not yourself. It gave me a clear checklist of things to work on.

From there, I intentionally started observing other speakers. I would analyse everything from the way they opened, their body language, and the jokes, whether good or bad, even looking across the room to observe the reactions from the rest of the audience. Today, you have more resources to learn from than ever, from TED Talks on YouTube to speakers you admire at work. When you start watching other presenters with the intention of improving your own skills, every talk becomes a mini training course.

Practise in small steps

The best way to build this skill is to practise in small steps. If you are apprehensive about presenting in front of an audience, then avoid taking a big leap straight into

Figure 17.2 Building your presentation muscles

a room full of senior leaders. That is like preparing for a marathon by only running marathons.

Instead, find a friendly audience like your immediate team, and ask to run a small activity at a meeting, an energiser, or a retrospective. Next time, try something harder, like sharing project updates. As your confidence builds, look for more opportunities, a show-and-tell, a community of practice, or a lightning talk at a meetup. Communities like Toastmasters exist for exactly this, a safe, structured place to present regularly with feedback from experienced speakers.

My favourite exercise came from Brenden Kumarasamy, a communication coach I interviewed on my podcast.[23] You pick any word and improvise a 60-second story around it with no preparation. When Brenden tried it live, I gave him the word 'speaker', and he built it into one of the most compelling pieces of improvisation I have witnessed. As he admitted, the first 100 attempts won't be great. You are building the ability to think on your feet, and the more you do it, the more natural it becomes.

THE SEMMELWEIS TRAGEDY

I recently travelled to Budapest for the first time, and one place I made sure to visit was the statue of Ignaz Semmelweis. It stands in front of Szent Rókus Hospital, where he once worked, created by the sculptor Alajos Stróbl in 1906, and shows Semmelweis alongside a grateful mother and child. In Hungary, he is remembered as the saviour of mothers, whose ideas would eventually save millions of lives.

But standing there, what struck me most was how long it took for his work to be recognised. The tragedy was that he never seemed to understand how his message was being received. None of us was in Vienna with him, but it almost came across as if he was judging his medical peers, when in fact he was simply trying to educate them. Being made to feel they had caused thousands of deaths put the doctors on the defensive, and once that happened, no amount of evidence was going to change their minds.

We live in a very different time now. Behavioural science has given us a deeper understanding of how people think, and throughout this chapter I have given you techniques to apply those insights, so your audience feels heard and genuinely engages with what you have to say. The only thing stopping you is the courage to try something different in your next presentation.

This brings us to the final chapter. Until now, the focus has been on building your own skills. Now you step into a different role, becoming a leader of product discovery in your organisation, with practical strategies to scale the discovery practices you have learned and spread them across your teams.

KEY TAKEAWAYS

- **Attention spans are shrinking:** The average person now switches tasks every 47 seconds, so your audience is distracted before you have even started.
- **The old engagement methods are outdated:** Hour-long meetings and text-heavy slides are still the norm, so shift from presenting to performing.
- **SENND gives you five ingredients:** Stakes, Emotion, Numbers, Novelty, and Decision are the building blocks of a memorable presentation. The proportions shift with your audience, but the ingredients stay the same.
- **Stories create connections that data cannot:** When a story genuinely lands, the listener's brain activity begins to mirror the speaker's.
- **Novelty is your signature:** We are taught to fit in, but doing the unexpected is what makes you memorable.
- **The opening and closing are what people remember:** The beginning and end leave the biggest impression, yet most presenters treat the ends as an afterthought.
- **Presenting is daunting for all of us:** Very few people are born great presenters. It is a learned skill, and small, consistent practice builds the muscle.

18 BUILD A DISCOVERY CULTURE

'Discovery culture eats uncertainty for breakfast.'

Paddy Dhanda

A WEBSITE THAT NEVER STOPS LEARNING

When was the last time you booked a holiday online? It's more than likely you used Booking.com, and if so, you would have taken part in an experiment without realising it. Everything you saw on the screen, from the price to the order of the photos, the wording of the button you clicked, even the little message designed to nudge you towards a purchase, was an opportunity to test an idea.

Booking runs around 25,000 controlled experiments a year, with roughly 1,000 of them running at the same time on any given day.[1] Anyone in the company can launch a test, from a copywriter changing a single word on a button through to a product manager rolling out a new feature. Every change is tested with real customers before it goes live, and after years of running these experiments, 2–3 times more people who visit Booking go on to make a reservation, compared to the average travel website.

I got to hear first-hand about the experimentation culture at Booking from Evie Brockwell, who worked there as a product manager.[2] She was inducted into it before she had even started her job, when Booking sent her a set of real scenarios from the site, each asking how she might go about testing it, and her first day rolled straight into two days of training on the statistical methods behind the tests.

When I asked Evie what an average week looked like, she told me she would have somewhere between 10 and 15 experiments running at any one time, most of them small, like a tweak to a single line of copy. A dedicated team of experimentation specialists owned the in-house tooling, ran the training and shared the lessons across the company when something interesting worked, or when something everyone expected to work quietly tanked. Within each squad, the team would sit down once a week and walk through every experiment that was running.

What surprised me most was when Evie revealed that around 80 per cent of the experiments Booking runs don't produce a positive result. Unlike many companies, Booking doesn't fixate on the success rate. For them, the point is the insight they get from every experiment about how their customers actually behave.

Booking is extraordinary because it has built a culture of learning into everything it does, from the pre-work before people even join, all the way through to the daily experiments.

WHY LEARNING HAS BECOME THE CRITICAL HUMAN SKILL

The traditional approach to learning in the workplace was built for a time when things didn't move at anything like the pace they do today. Most organisations still operate this way. Each year, your employer sets aside enough budget for one or two courses or a conference, so learning becomes an annual event, a bit like a birthday, and you had better choose wisely.

That model works fine if the knowledge you rely on only changes once or twice a year, like a plumber catching up on the latest building regulations. But most of us are knowledge workers in an environment that is changing almost all the time, especially in the superfast world of AI. Yet research shows that the average knowledge worker spends just 1 per cent of their week on formal learning, which works out to roughly 24 minutes.[3]

To get a sense of the pace, look at how fast AI itself is moving. SWE-bench is a coding benchmark where language models are asked to fix a real software bug from an open-source project without any human help. The Stanford AI Index Report found that in 2023, the leading systems could solve just 4.4 per cent of those problems, and by late 2025 they were solving more than 80 per cent.[4]

So how should organisations deal with all this change? Peter Senge had already written about that very question decades before the modern product organisation existed. He popularised the term 'learning organisation' in his 1990 book, *The Fifth Discipline*, where he argued that the companies that would go on to lead their industries would be the ones that worked out how to tap into their people's capacity to learn at every level.[5]

The rest of this chapter walks you through how to build that kind of learning into the way you work, at three different levels. We start with you, because every learning culture grows from the personal habits of the individuals inside it. From there, we look at how teams can build a Discovery Factory, before turning to how you can scale that learning across the wider organisation through communities of practice.

INDIVIDUAL LEVEL: BUILD YOUR LEARNING HABITS

Of all the human skills I have covered in this book, the one I have struggled with most is the discipline of learning itself.

Growing up, I was never an academic child. When I left my high school, the UK government released school league tables for the first time, and unfortunately my school was almost at the bottom, which made it one of the worst-performing high schools in the UK. It's a bit ironic that I now work for one of the largest technology training companies in the world, advising the C-suite at some of the most well-known brands on the planet, and I am sitting here writing a chapter dedicated to learning. The point isn't to share a lesson in overcoming adversity. I want to suggest that learning is something you can get better at with practice, because nobody at my school ever mentioned any of this to me.

But why do so many of us struggle with the skill of learning? I posed this question to my friend Phil Black, who we first met in Chapter 11 with his Hot House events. Phil is co-founder of the learning company Cormirus and has spent the past several years researching how the brain learns.[6] His answer in almost every case is that we have been conditioned to learn in the wrong way. We were taught how to memorise things for exams and how to sit still while somebody at the front of the room explained the lesson, although the actual mechanics of how a human brain turns new ideas into something usable were never part of the syllabus.

When you say something out loud while you are learning, the idea has to pass through more of your brain than when you read in silence, because you are using your mouth and your ears in addition to your eyes. The more anchors your brain has, the harder it is to forget, so telling kids to sit silently and read independently is essentially asking them to learn with one hand tied behind their backs.

According to Phil, schools that have introduced proper learning-to-learn programmes have seen pupils' grades rise by a whole grade on average, and by two whole grades for the most disadvantaged children. The implication for the rest of us is that learning is a learnable skill rather than a fixed trait, and most of us have simply never invested in the meta-skill our work depends on.

Find the way you learn

The first step is to work out how you want to learn. Ask yourself a few honest questions. Do you take in ideas best from text, audio, video, or by doing the thing yourself? How much time can you realistically dedicate to learning on any given day? Do you prefer to build a broad understanding first, or go deep on one thing at a time?

Each format has its own strengths. Social media and newsletters work best as a radar, giving you an awareness of what is worth investigating further. The brilliant thing about audio is that you can take it in while you do something else, so the dog walk, the school run, and the morning commute become your most productive moments for absorbing new insights. Video comes into its own when you need to see somebody demo a tool or technique, while books and formal courses remain the deepest routes into a topic, although course content can become out of date faster than the providers can update it.

Getting creative about how you learn

In Chapter 16, I explained that I started podcasting because I wanted to learn from smart people. I call this creative learning. It's the process of coming up with imaginative ways to build knowledge.

Around the same time, I had a side project running after I became curious about the Raspberry Pi, a tiny computer that can be made to do almost anything. Since my son loves gaming, I decided to build a retro arcade machine with it, figuring out the hardware and the software and how to make the two work together, all of which were skills I would never have picked up from a book. For someone working in product, the equivalent is to take an idea for an app you have been mulling over, vibe code a version using one of the AI coding tools, and see whether anyone would actually pay for it.

I am not suggesting you go out and start a podcast or build an arcade machine. The most creative learners I know have all found a way of incorporating learning into something they would happily do anyway. It might be a newsletter you commit to writing every fortnight, a book club that forces you to finish the books stacked unread on your shelf, or a regular lunch with someone whose career you admire. The trick is to design your learning to fit your circumstances and your passions so that it is enjoyable rather than a chore.

Your learning schedule

Building a habit of continuous learning has to be a deliberate choice rather than something you keep hoping you will find time for. We can no longer treat learning like climbing a mountain, where once you reach the top, you are done. What you are dealing with now is closer to surfing an open sea, where new waves keep arriving, and your job is to keep riding them just to stay afloat.

Take a moment to look at your typical week and ask yourself what a personal schedule of learning could look like. Table 18.1 lays out the main formats, and the most useful place to start is the time column. Begin with the recurring activities in your week, things like the 20-minute commute or going to the gym, and identify opportunities to fit learning in. Then turn to the depth column and make sure you are not overloading on shallow formats while neglecting the deeper ones that build mastery. Treat the table as something to come back to every six months, because your circumstances will change.

Table 18.1 Ways to build learning habits

Format	Time	Depth	Best for
Social media	Short	Low	Spotting the latest trends
Newsletter or Substack	Short	Medium	Following credible experts on specific topics
Book summary	Short	Low	Deciding what to read, or refreshing what you have read
YouTube video	Medium	Medium	Visual how-to and tool demonstrations
Podcast	Medium	Medium	Passive learning during walks, commutes, and chores
Audiobook	High	Deep	Deeper learning while doing something else
Business book	High	Deep	Deep exploration of a topic
Formal course	High	Deep	Structured learning with peers and an instructor
Conference	Very high	Medium	Exposure to a diverse set of perspectives and networking
Community	Very high	Deep	Shared learning from peers

TEAM LEVEL: BUILD A DISCOVERY FACTORY

All the different ways of learning I have walked through so far will help you build your own habits, but how do you create a team that discovers and learns together effectively? That depends on how the team is set up to do its work. One of the best examples I have come across is what Deloitte's business analyst practice in the UK calls a Discovery Factory. I had the chance to talk it through in some depth with Tom Hitchings, who leads the practice and helped invent the model with his colleague, Emma Haslam.

The Discovery Factory

When Tom first walked me through what was going on in his team before the Factory existed, it was a familiar story. They were in a large central government department in the UK, designing solutions to an enormous number of use cases in a fast-moving environment riddled with political pressure. The traditional model, where one business analyst follows a single project end to end, just wasn't sustainable. They were producing roughly one discovery per analyst every three or four months while new problems were popping up every week.

Pace was only part of the problem. The same business problem could end up on the backlog multiple times, and the team might produce slightly different recommendations depending on who picked it up. As Tom put it, 'we couldn't afford to make the same mistake twice'. The team was effectively duplicating effort, with no system for moving what one person figured out into the next person's discovery.

Their answer was to organise a small team of business analysts around a shared production line, with discovery as the product. The Factory took high-level requirements from policy and operations teams and turned them into precise designs that engineers could pick up and start building from, and the downstream developers and testers were treated with the same care a normal product team would give its end-users. Its name came from the team itself, after people started saying things like 'you operate like a well-oiled team, you've got a good production line'. Tom and Emma leaned into it deliberately because once you call something a factory, you start thinking about your funnel and your flow.

One of the key success factors behind the Factory is having the right people, and they don't necessarily have to be the most experienced. They are analysts who love problem-solving and can adapt quickly when priorities change. Tom is most proud that the Factory has become one of the best environments in his practice for graduates and apprentices.

After 18 months of working this way, the team completed over 100 discoveries, and the typical duration of a single discovery fell by two-thirds to just two or three sprints. The programme they were supporting decommissioned a legacy system that had been costing £12 million a year, and it realised that saving as a direct result of the Factory's pace.[7]

Figure 18.1 Key elements of a Discovery Factory

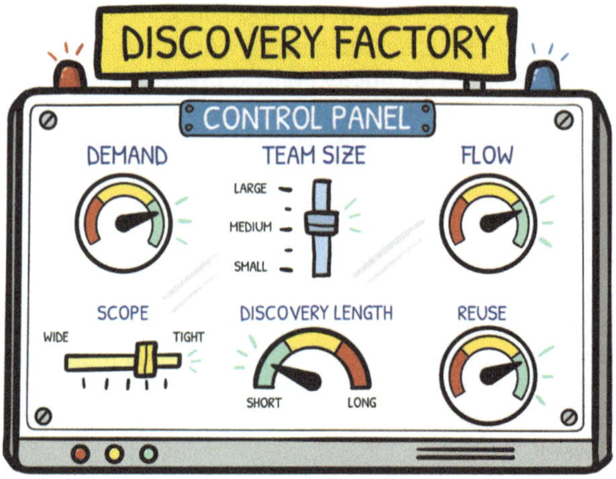

Inside the production line

Tom walked me through five practices that, taken together, hold the Factory's learning culture in place. They are also a useful starting point if you are trying to build a similar model for your own team.

1. Flex the team size

The Factory ran with about 6 or 7 analysts most of the time, flexing up to 10 when demand was high and down to 5 when it was lower. As Tom explained, 'once you've got it established, you can flex the size of it quite easily'. That elasticity is one of the reasons the model survived the political swings the team faced, so build the flexibility in from day one, or you will end up fighting for funding every time demand falls.

2. Control the front door

Work entered the Factory through a single front door. The product owner brought items into the backlog using a template the Factory had designed, and the team applied a deliberately strict scope test before accepting anything. In Tom's case, the test was tied directly to the programme's aim of decommissioning the legacy platform, so anything outside that goal was politely declined regardless of who had asked for it.

3. Put product first

Once a discovery was accepted, an analyst was assigned based on capacity and domain fit, with most running two or three discoveries in parallel. The team produced a plan on a page using the same template, starting with the problem itself, working through root causes rather than symptoms, and then opening up the menu of products and services already in its toolbox before considering anything new. Tom is clear about why this principle is important. His team would solve a problem once and then reuse the solution again and again across business areas, rather than running parallel discoveries that produced multiple answers to the same underlying need.

4. Keep discoveries short

The Factory had strong opinions about how long a discovery should take, with most running for two or three sprints, which is roughly 4–6 weeks. Keeping discoveries short is what kept the production line moving and the learning flowing into delivery. Treat the length of a discovery as a signal, and when something is dragging on, check the scope and look for ways to break it into smaller batches.

5. Standardise the exit

The team also standardised the way discoveries were handed over by using the same exit pack every time, covering the problem, the options considered and discounted, the chosen option, the wireframes, the assumptions and risks, the technical architect's commentary, and a yes-or-no sign-off. After hundreds of discoveries using the same template, the developers and testers downstream knew exactly what to expect.

The template itself was never fixed though, and everyone was encouraged to feed improvements back into the method. Partway through, the team introduced Figma app, which changed how they produced a lot of their outputs.

Is this approach right for you?

The Deloitte team built the Factory in response to a specific set of conditions, and they have been transparent about the fact that it works in some situations and not in others. It fits well when you are designing several digital products and services in parallel at pace, when consistency and reuse across solutions are essential, and when you want the team to build deep domain knowledge. The model fits less well when you are designing a single product and the requirements are staggered over many weeks, where a dedicated analyst is probably better suited.

If you decide to set up your own Factory, one piece of advice that is even more important than the operating practices is that you cannot do this independently. Tom needed buy-in from the developers, testers, technical architects, product owners, and the leadership of the wider portfolio, and some of those people were nervous at first that the Factory would skip things and make more work for them downstream, so the team had to earn that trust by delivering results. The reward is that learning flows across the team rather than staying locked inside individuals' heads, and because a typical discovery now runs two or three sprints instead of two or three months, the team finds out quickly whether their assumptions were correct.

ORGANISATION LEVEL: SCALE THROUGH A COMMUNITY OF PRACTICE

If you want to scale learning beyond one or two teams and across the organisation, then the most effective approach I have seen work is through communities of practice. In simple terms, a community of practice is a group of practitioners who actively develop their craft together over time. It is also the vehicle that turns Peter Senge's idea of the learning organisation into something you can actually build.

Scaling learning across an organisation is harder than it looks, but you can find some useful inspiration just by looking inside your kitchen cupboards. If you have ever spread strawberry jam on your toast, you will know it has lumpy bits, unlike raspberry jam, which is smooth and almost fruitless. The consultant Jerry Weinberg used that as a metaphor to describe two laws that are useful for anyone trying to scale a discovery practice across an organisation.[8]

His Law of Raspberry Jam stated that the wider you spread it, the thinner it gets. Most of us have seen this first-hand when a new leader comes into the organisation armed with lots of ideas, although none of them stick because very few people champion them. The opposite is true of Weinberg's Law of Strawberry Jam. As long as the jam has lumps in it, you can never spread it too thin. We can think of the discovery teams as the strawberries in our jam, and a community of practice is the jar that brings those lumpy bits together.

The idea of starting your own community can feel like a big ask, especially while you are also doing your day job. I have been there, and I want to show you that it is more achievable than it looks.

Five of us against 80,000

Throughout the book, I have shared some of my experiences at the global bank where I worked as the head of Agile learning. Probably the most satisfying of all of them was the legacy my team left behind.

We were a team of just five people, set up to spread new ways of working across product and engineering in a bank that had over 80,000 employees in multiple countries. At first, we tried various approaches, although what changed everything was setting up the Agility Guild. We built it as a community of practice for everyone in the bank trying to work in a more product-led way, regardless of their role, seniority, or location. Within three years, the Guild had grown to roughly 5,000 members, spread across many parts of the business that our small team would never have reached on its own.

The single best thing the Guild did was the Agile Awards. We aligned the categories with the values we were trying to embed, and almost overnight 80 applications came in from teams across the bank who were already doing this work in pockets we had no visibility of. The Awards gave leadership 80 documented case studies of new ways of working they had not known existed, which changed how senior people talked about the transformation, and they gave members the recognition that made the Guild feel like a valuable initiative to join.

What is a community of practice?

Before we get into how to start one, it is worth reflecting on what a community of practice is not. I have lost count of the number of times a client has shown me an intranet page and called it a community of practice, yet I see very little activity or collaboration happening on it. That is not a community of practice, it is just a website.

The term itself was coined in the early 1990s by the social learning theorist Etienne Wenger and the anthropologist Jean Lave, who spent years studying how apprentices learned their trades and found that learning rarely happened through formal instruction, it came from taking part in a shared practice.[9]

Wenger later distilled their thinking into three elements that a community of practice needs to have.[10] The first is a domain. There has to be a shared interest that brings the members together, whether that is product discovery, Agile, vibe coding, or some other topic they are all passionate about. The second is the community itself, meaning members who engage with each other and build relationships. Finally, there is a practice. Over time, the group develops a shared set of practices and expertise in the form of stories, tools, templates, and ways of working that members draw on and contribute to.

To see what the third element adds, think about Trekkies, the global community of Star Trek fans who attend conventions in their tens of thousands every year. They have a clear domain and a flourishing community, yet their gatherings are not oriented around making each member measurably better at a craft, which is why Wenger would call them a community of interest. In the business world, the whole point is to get better at the work you do, so that what you take away from the group makes you more effective the next time you sit at your desk.

How to launch a community of practice

Over the years of helping organisations set up professional communities, as well as my own, I have turned everything I have learned into a step-by-step blueprint I call COMET. It represents the five steps you need to launch a community, which are Clarify, Organise, Mobilise, Evolve, and Thrive.

Ruth is the director of AI at a global animal health company with people working across the United States, Brazil, Israel, Ireland, and a long list of other countries. We first met after she came to a talk I had given on communities of practice, and over the months that followed we worked through each stage of COMET together to launch what became the AI Champions community.

Figure 18.2 COMET: five steps to launch a community

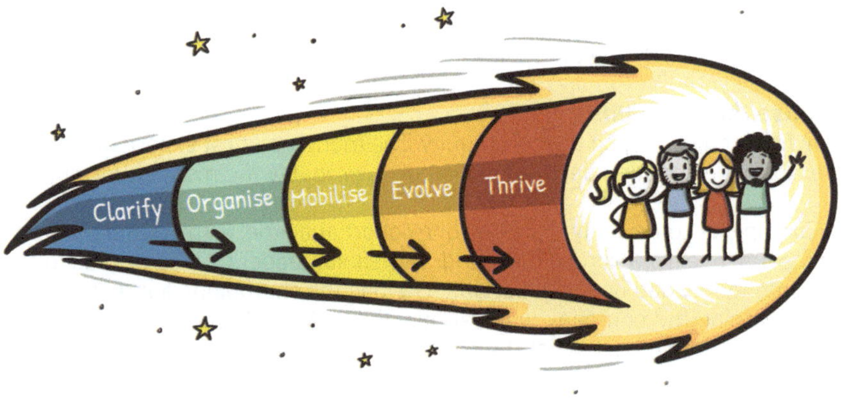

C: Clarify the core purpose

The first stage is the one most people skip, which is defining why the community actually exists. A community for product managers at one organisation might exist to spread modern product practices across teams that have spent years in a waterfall environment, while at another the same community might focus on helping teams adopt new AI-assisted tooling. Both are legitimate, although they would create very different experiences. The important thing is to make the reason compelling enough for members to connect with personally, rather than feeling like just another corporate initiative.

In Ruth's case, she painted a vision of the company as a group of islands, rich in knowledge, with some people still standing on the shore, some paddling around between the islands, and a few already strong swimmers moving easily between the islands and the mainland. The AI Champions, she said, would be the swimmers. They would know the waters and help others across safely.

We came up with this metaphor together because it was simple and easy for everyone to visualise. A vision like that usually starts with a short visioning workshop, where the sponsors and a handful of the community leaders look at the strategic priorities of the wider organisation alongside the skills members are trying to develop, and search for the overlap between the two. What comes out is a single vision statement that everybody can get behind.

O: Organise the foundations

The second stage is where we establish the ways of working and the roles by defining a charter. It can sound a little formal, although it is designed to set some basic ground rules on how the community will operate. I usually create it through a short workshop where the community leaders co-create the values and behaviours that will guide how members treat each other, how often the group will meet, and how the success of the community will be measured, all summarised in a one-page charter you make available to everyone.

In Ruth's case, we organised the community into two tiers, starting with a motivated group of champions who could each go back and build smaller communities inside their own function or site. Each champion was given a clear expectation of their time, around four hours upfront and two hours a week, with their manager's approval. We had expected somewhere between 20 and 30 people to step forward when the call for champions went out. By the time the window closed, over 70 had signed up.

M: Mobilise the community

Next, we focus on launching the community. The members' first experience determines whether they keep coming back, so this stage is probably the most important of all.

The AI Champions community launched one cohort at a time, with around 25 champions joining the first one from across the world. Two senior leaders joined the call to speak to why the community had been set up, which helped the champions appreciate they were joining something the company was serious about. A good amount of the launch was dedicated to reflecting back what the champions had told us about themselves in pre-work, covering who they were, how far along they were with AI, and what they hoped the community would help them achieve. Bringing these insights into the open turned out to be one of the most powerful moments of the session, because they started to feel they were joining a community shaped by them.

Whatever shape your launch takes, end it with a call to action. If you let members leave without making a commitment to do something, it can feel like they don't have skin in the game.

E: Evolve the value

Now we have to deliver the value we have promised through a variety of community events and initiatives. I usually approach this like I would a product roadmap, and get together with the community leads to map out a rolling calendar of events for the next quarter. It helps to have a regular cadence for an all-hands event where you bring everyone together and showcase success stories from the community. This amplifies the value, but equally creates a sense of FOMO (fear of missing out) for the other members, who feel compelled to make a contribution for next time. Alongside this, run sessions like external guest speakers, book clubs, hackathons, or spotlights showcasing a tool or a technique from other members.

When I led the business analyst community of practice at the bank a few years ago, one memorable initiative began life as a simple internal newsletter, sent to just over 2,000 business analysts. Over time, members began contributing more, the quality kept improving, and what had started as a newsletter slowly morphed into a quarterly professional publication that members took real pride in.

T: Thrive

The final stage is designed to ensure we keep the community healthy. Having worked with a number of community leaders, I have found that very few of them could quantify the value their community was delivering. An industry report that surveyed community leaders found that an alarming 30 per cent said it was hard to put a number on the value of their community.[11] The risk is that when an organisation decides to make budget cuts, the funding and time allocated tend to be among the first things to go.

The interesting part is that when I started looking for ways to measure the impact of a community, I found surprisingly few resources online. That led me to build my own community of practice healthcheck. It proved so successful that the team at Comparative Agility, the largest continuous improvement platform in the world, have published it for anyone to use.[12]

The healthcheck measures the value across five key dimensions, which are Purpose and Identity, Engagement and Participation, Knowledge Sharing and Collaboration, Leadership and Support, and Impact and Value. It shows the areas that are working well and reveals the biggest opportunities for improvement. Whether you use this healthcheck or create your own, the important thing is to seek feedback from your members at least quarterly, so you can keep listening, adapting, and earning their trust.

The biggest challenge is engagement

Before we finish, I want to share one of the biggest lessons I have learned working with communities. The hardest part is not setting them up, it is keeping people engaged once you have launched them. Research suggests that consistently engaging members is the top frustration that most community leaders share.[13] I like to think of it like a new relationship. Once the initial excitement of the honeymoon period is over, how do you keep people interested?

A useful way of thinking about engagement comes from work done by Jakob Nielsen, who we met in Chapter 11.[14] He called it the 90–9–1 rule, and it explains why most communities behave the way they do. Around 90 per cent of any community will be lurkers, who consume what is being shared but rarely contribute. Roughly 9 per cent are intermittent contributors, who post occasionally when something catches their attention. Just 1 per cent are heavy contributors who post regularly. Think about how often you write a review for the products you buy on Amazon. If you are anything like me, the answer is rarely, yet the vast majority of reviews you have ever browsed were written by a tiny percentage of customers.

So what does this mean for your community of practice? You don't need 90 per cent of your members to be active for the community to thrive. Far better to focus your efforts on the 1 per cent who are your biggest supporters and the 9 per cent who will contribute at some point. The hope is that, over time, the remaining 90 per cent also feel compelled to contribute.

IT STARTS WITH ONE PERSON

Everything we have covered might sound like a discovery culture only belongs in modern tech companies like Booking, where Evie and her colleagues run hundreds of experiments each week. But before we close, I want to leave you with a different kind of story, one that comes from healthcare in the public sector, where the pace is relentless and the bureaucracy heavy.

Christina Tan, president of IIBA UK, joined a large programme as the product manager for a suite of patient-centred data products.[15] She walked into an environment where the attitude was 'we don't have time for discovery, we just need to deliver'. They were making decisions without validating assumptions, and the team was constantly under pressure to deliver quickly. Does that sound familiar?

Christina told me, 'I knew pushing discovery as a process would fall flat.' So instead, she totalled up the number of hours the team had lost because of rework and the decisions that had been reversed due to unclear requirements. It feels ironic that she used her product discovery thinking to build the business case for product discovery itself, although as soon as the stakeholders saw the numbers, their attitudes started to change.

From there, Christina reframed discovery by using language that her stakeholders cared about, like reducing risk and protecting timelines, and introduced lightweight rapid discovery techniques that took a few hours rather than multiple weeks of effort. Making the insights visible and showing results quickly was what built her momentum.

Slowly, the way the team worked began to change. Engineers became more cautious, asking for clarity before rushing ahead with technical work. Analysts started validating user stories instead of rewriting them later, and senior leaders began reflecting on insights before making hasty decisions. The real turning point came when a senior stakeholder looked around the room and said, 'We can't make this decision until we've done discovery.' That was the moment Christina knew she had shifted the team towards embracing a learning culture.

Earlier, we used Weinberg's metaphor to explain why raspberry jam gets thinner the more you spread it, while strawberry jam doesn't because it has lumpy bits. Christina is one of those strawberries. She built a habit of learning in her team and then helped spread it across the entire programme. Booking and Christina look like opposites at first glance, with one running 25,000 experiments a year and the other fighting to get her first one taken seriously. But both share the same underlying belief, which is to learn fast so they can build the right things.

Behind everything in this book is one simple idea. Product discovery thinking is the willingness to learn about the people you serve, the problems they face, and the possibilities for solving them, before you act on what you think you know. The tools will keep changing, and AI will reshape almost every technique in these pages over the next few years, yet the teams that go on to thrive will be the ones who embrace a culture of learning, whatever tools they happen to be using.

As the brain coach Jim Kwik puts it, 'If knowledge is power, then learning is a superpower.' In the age of AI, that has never felt more true.

KEY TAKEAWAYS

- **Learning has become the critical human skill:** Formal training still has its place, although on its own it is no longer enough to keep you current in a field changing faster than annual courses can refresh.
- **Discovery cultures are built through everyday habits:** Booking.com works because experimentation is woven into the way people work, from onboarding and training through to weekly squad conversations and live customer tests.
- **Design a personal learning schedule that fits your routine:** Map the formats against the recurring moments in your week, balance shallow formats against deeper ones, and revisit the schedule every six months.
- **Build a Discovery Factory to help your team learn together:** A repeatable system with a controlled front door, short discoveries, and a standardised exit keeps learning flowing into delivery.
- **A community of practice needs a domain, a community, and a practice:** An intranet page is not enough. Members need a shared focus, real relationships, and practical things they can use in their work.
- **Use the COMET steps to launch and sustain a community:** Clarify the purpose, Organise the foundations, Mobilise the members, Evolve the value, and Thrive by measuring it, focusing your energy on the 1 per cent and 9 per cent who contribute.

FINAL WORD

'Be yourself, because everyone else sounds like AI.'

Paddy Dhanda

THE AGE OF PRODUCT SLOP

As I was walking the floor at the HumanX conference in Silicon Valley, which I mentioned earlier in the book, I spotted something strange about the exhibitor stands. Nearly every banner seemed to contain the words *agent* or *agentic*.

I stopped at a few of the stands and asked a simple question. What does your product actually do, and why should I care? Some of them confused me with AI jargon, while others reeled off a list of features that could have belonged to almost any product on the floor. Surprisingly, very few of them could tell me what problem they were trying to solve, or explain how their product differed from the dozens of others I had already seen.

Figure FW.1: Use human creativity to avoid product slop

As for the banners, I get it, you only have a few seconds to grab people's attention, and you have to sound like your products are cutting-edge. But as I kept walking around that floor, those responses confirmed the worrying trend I had been seeing for months in my own research. The whole industry has caught AI fever.

Just to be clear, AI is genuinely useful, and throughout this book we have seen plenty of places where it can amplify our work. The trouble is that when a tool makes something this easy, we stop putting in the effort to do it ourselves and outsource our thinking to technology.

Look at what satellite navigation has done to the way we travel. There used to be a time when I would study the route on a good old-fashioned map and arrive knowing how I got there. Now I follow the blue line on autopilot and rarely bother to remember the directions.

So how do we avoid becoming part of the slop? What if I told you the answer lies in a bucket of poo?

THE MOST CREATIVE CEO

A few years ago, I spoke to Terry Rich, who had spent most of his career in television out in Iowa.[1] Then, one day, he received a call for help from the state governor that changed the course of his life. The local zoo in Des Moines was losing $600,000 a year and was only weeks away from closing for good. The problem was that Terry had no experience of running a zoo.

He asked the experts what to do, and every one of them gave him the same answer. Build an impressive new exhibit, they said, or raise two million dollars from a wealthy donor. Terry didn't have two million dollars, and he didn't have a wealthy donor either. So instead of going with the obvious answers, he sat down with the keepers who knew the animals individually by name and asked them a different question. What is already here, right under our noses, that people might be willing to pay for?

The first idea came from a keeper who pointed out that the zoo was full of children by day but did not offer anything for the grown-ups. So they started opening the gates after dark for adults only, with the animals out under the lights and cold beer on tap. They called it Zoo Brew, and it became a date-night fixture that now sells a quarter of a million dollars' worth of beer every year.

Somebody else noticed that the local deer, who were forever wrecking nearby gardens, would stop the instant they caught the scent of a predator. So the zoo started offering tiger poo and selling it by the bucketload as a deterrent. That one idea raised another $20,000 in a single summer.

Within a few years, Terry and his team had cleared the debt and saved Blank Park Zoo for generations of families to come. The place that had once been on the verge of closing is now one of the most-visited attractions in the entire state.

What saved it was the keepers themselves, whose experiences with the animals and the families who visited them let them spot connections nobody else had thought to make.

YOUR BUCKET OF POO

You have your own version of that lived experience. Only you have ever lived it, and that makes it the most valuable thing you can bring to your work in a world drowning in product slop.

So go and see more of the world, and speak to as many people as you can. Read the books that nobody else in your team would think to read, and go on the walks that nobody else would take. Remember, the most original ideas do not always come from a polished prompt. Sometimes they turn up in a bucket of poo.

KEEP DISCOVERING

If you have made it this far, congratulations. Now the real work begins, which is why I want to point you to my website, where I keep exploring the human skills behind great product work.

You will find my podcast featuring conversations with practitioners from across the industry, along with templates, resources, and a regular newsletter to help you build on the ideas in this book.

Visit www.PaddyDhanda.com and let's keep discovering together.

ENDNOTES

CHAPTER 1

1 Clifford Nass and Byron Reeves (2003). *The Media Equation*. CSLI Publications.

2 *Time* (2013). 'The 50 worst inventions'. content.time.com/time/specials/packages/completelist/0,29569,1991915,00.html

3 Joseph D'Souza and Rohan Jambhale (2026, 26 March). 'Microsoft 365 statistics by downloads, subscribers, revenue and facts'. ElectroiQ. electroiq.com/stats/microsoft-365-statistics

4 Pendo.io (2019). 'The 2019 feature adoption report'. pendo.io/resources/the-2019-feature-adoption-report

5 asavoia (2014, 2 September). 'The law of market failure'. Jama Software. jamasoftware.com/blog/law-market-failure

6 Elizabeth Culliford (2021, 18 April). 'Clubhouse closes new round of funding that would value app at $4 billion – source'. Reuters. reuters.com/article/technology/clubhouse-closes-new-round-of-funding-that-would-value-app-at-4-billion-source-idUSNIKBN2C50LA

7 *The Economist* (2025, 8 May). 'Why so many IT projects go so horribly wrong'. economist.com/business/2025/05/08/why-so-many-it-projects-go-so-horribly-wrong

8 UK Government (2011). 'Universal Credit: Welfare Reform 2011 – impact assessment'. assets.publishing.service.gov.uk/government/uploads/system/uploads/attachment_data/file/220177/universal-credit-wr2011-ia.pdf

9 Child Poverty Action Group (CPAG) (2023, 27 June). 'Digital universal credit system breaches principles of law and stops claimants accessing support'. cpag.org.uk/news/digital-universal-credit-system-breaches-principles-law-and-stops-claimants-accessing-support

10 The Trussell Trust (2019). '#5weekstoolong: why we need to end the wait for Universal Credit'. cms.trussell.org.uk/sites/default/files/wp-assets/PolicyReport_Final_ForWeb.pdf

11 Rajeev Syal and Rowena Mason (2015, 25 June). 'Labour says Universal Credit will take 495 years to roll out as costs rise £3bn'. *The Guardian*. theguardian.com/society/2015/jun/25/labour-says-universal-credit-will-take-495-years-to-roll-out-as-costs-rise-3bn

12 Patrick Forth, Tom Reichert, Romain de Laubier and Saibal Chakraborty (2020, 29 October). 'Flipping the odds of digital transformation success'. Boston Consulting Group. bcg.com/publications/2020/increasing-odds-of-success-in-digital-transformation

13 Melissa Perri (2018). *Escaping the Build Trap.* O'Reilly Media.

14 John Cutler (2016, 17 November). '12 signs you're working in a feature factory'. Medium. medium.com/@johnpcutler/12-signs-youre-working-in-a-feature-factory-44a5b938d6a2

15 Sheena S. Iyengar and Mark R. Lepper (2000). 'When choice is demotivating: can one desire too much of a good thing?' *Journal of Personality and Social Psychology*, Vol. 79, No. 6, pp. 995–1006.

16 James Ryseff, Brandon F. De Bruhl and Sydne J. Newberry (2024, 13 August). 'The root causes of failure for artificial intelligence projects and how they can succeed: avoiding the anti-patterns of AI'. RAND Corporation. rand.org/pubs/research_reports/RRA2680-1.html

17 Maxwell Zeff (2025, 18 February). 'Humane's AI Pin is dead, as HP buys startup's assets for $116M'. TechCrunch. techcrunch.com/2025/02/18/humanes-ai-pin-is-dead-as-hp-buys-startups-assets-for-116m

18 Hostinger (2026, 10 March). '26 low-code trends for 2026: key statistics and insights'. hostinger.com/tutorials/low-code-trends

19 Andrej Karpathy (2025, 2 February). 'There's a new kind of coding I call "vibe coding", where you fully give in to the vibes, embrace exponentials, and forget that the code even exists'. Posted on X. x.com/karpathy/status/1886192184808149383

20 Laura Cress (2025, 6 November). '"Vibe coding" named word of the year by Collins Dictionary'. BBC. bbc.co.uk/news/articles/cpd2y053nleo

21 Skye Jacobs (2025, 3 April). 'Microsoft CTO predicts AI will generate 95% of code by 2030'. Techspot. techspot.com/news/107411-microsoft-cto-predicts-ai-generate-95-percent-code.html

22 Paddy Dhanda (2026, 17 March). 'My 13-year-old built a 3D game in a week using vibe coding (no coding skills required)', Product Powers. superpowers.school/p/vibe-coding-for-kids

23 Axios (2025, 14 October). 'Exclusive: AI writing hasn't overwhelmed the web yet'. axios.com/2025/10/14/ai-generated-writing-humans

24 Nicholas Quah (2025, 10 September). 'Who wants slop for your ears?' Vulture. vulture.com/article/inception-point-ai-podcasts-slop.html

25 Nilesh Christopher (2025, 12 December). 'Podcast industry under siege as AI bots flood airways with thousands of programs'. *Los Angeles Times.* latimes.com/business/story/2025-12-12/ai-podcasting-is-changing-industry

26 Earth.Org (2023, 21 August). '10 concerning fast fashion waste statistics'. earth.org/statistics-about-fast-fashion-waste

27 Martin Fowler (2019, 21 May). 'Technical debt'. martinfowler.com/bliki/TechnicalDebt.html

28 CB Insights (2026, 5 March). 'The top 9 reasons startups fail'. cbinsights.com/research/report/startup-failure-reasons-top

29 Museum of Failure (n.d.). museumoffailure.com

CHAPTER 2

1 Karen E. Adolph et al. (2012). 'How do you learn to walk? Thousands of steps and dozens of falls per day'. *Psychological Science*, Vol. 23, No. 11, pp. 1387–1394.

2 Neil Rackham (1988). *SPIN Selling*. McGraw-Hill.

3 Chris Orlob (2018, 5 February). 'Elements of effective sales conversations'. Gong Labs. gong.io/blog/elements-of-effective-sales-conversations

4 Wikipedia (n.d.). 'SOCRATES (pain assessment)'. en.wikipedia.org/wiki/SOCRATES_(pain_assessment)

5 David Spiegelhalter (2019). *The Art of Statistics: Learning from Data*. Penguin.

6 Wikipedia (n.d.). 'Primum non nocere'. en.wikipedia.org/wiki/Primum_non_nocere

7 NASA (2024). *The Discovery Program: Celebrating 30 Years of Exploration*. NASA.

8 Howard E. McCurdy (2001). *Faster, Better, Cheaper: Low-Cost Innovation in the U.S. Space Program*. Johns Hopkins University Press.

9 Encyclopaedia Britannica (2026, 22 July). 'O.J. Simpson trial'. britannica.com/event/O-J-Simpson-trial

10 *New York Times* (1995, 18 August). 'The relevance of the detective's tapes'. nytimes.com/1995/08/18/opinion/the-relevance-of-the-detective-s-tapes.html

11 James Marshment (2025, 4 April). 'How Liverpool almost committed gargantuan Mo Salah blunder as blockbuster deal is "agreed"'. Team Talk. teamtalk.com/liverpool/how-reds-almost-committed-gargantuan-mo-salah-blunder-blockbuster-deal-agreed

12 William Durant (1926). *The Story of Philosophy: The Lives and Opinions of the World's Greatest Philosophers*. Simon & Schuster.

13 James Clear (2015). 'This coach improved every tiny thing by 1 percent and here's what happened'. jamesclear.com/marginal-gains

14 James Clear (2018). *Atomic Habits: An Easy and Proven Way to Build Good Habits and Break Bad Ones*. Penguin UK.

15 Astha Khandelwal (2026, 22 July). 'How does Amazon & Netflix personalization work?' vwo.com/blog/deliver-personalized-recommendations-the-amazon-netflix-way

CHAPTER 3

1 Barry W. Boehm (1981). *Software Engineering Economics.* Prentice Hall.

2 Jennifer A. Whitson and Adam D. Galinsky (2008). 'Lacking control increases illusory pattern perception'. *Science*, Vol. 322, No. 5898, pp. 115–117.

3 E.J. Langer (1975). 'The illusion of control'. *Journal of Personality and Social Psychology*, Vol. 32, No. 2, pp. 311–328.

4 Wikipedia (n.d.). 'Alfred Korzybski'. en.wikipedia.org/wiki/Alfred_Korzybski

5 AgileAlliance.org (2001). 'Manifesto for Agile software development'. agilemanifesto.org

6 Marty Cagan (2007, 24 September). 'Product discovery'. Silicon Valley Product Group. svpg.com/product-discovery

7 Marty Cagan (2018). *Inspired: How to Create Tech Products Customers Love.* Wiley.

8 Design Council (n.d.). 'The Double Diamond: a universally accepted depiction of the design process'. designcouncil.org.uk/our-resources/the-double-diamond

9 Steve G. Blank (2005). *The Four Steps to the Epiphany*. web.stanford.edu/group/e145/cgi-bin/winter/drupal/upload/handouts/Four_Steps.pdf

10 Teresa Torres (2021). *Continuous Discovery Habits: Discover Products that Create Customer Value and Business Value.* Product Talk Press.

11 PeopleCert (2023). *PRINCE2® 7: Managing Successful Projects.* PeopleCert.

12 Project Management Institute (2022). *Process Groups: A Practice Guide*. Project Management Institute.

13 Agile Business Consortium (2025). *Agile PM®: Agile Project Management Reference Book v3*, 2nd ed. Agile Business Consortium.

14 Scaled Agile, Inc. (2026, 13 February). 'Integrating product design competency'. Scaled Agile Framework. framework.scaledagile.com/product-development-flow-discipline/integrating-product-design-competency

15 International Institute of Business Analysis (n.d.). 'What is business analysis?' iiba.org/professional-development/career-centre/what-is-business-analysis

16 Debra Paul, James Cadle, Malcolm Eva, Craig Rollason and Jonathan Hunsley (2020). *Business Analysis*, 4th ed. BCS.

17 Mike Cohn (2004). *User Stories Applied: For Agile Software Development.* Addison-Wesley.

18 AZQuotes (n.d.). azquotes.com/quote/347988

CHAPTER 4

1 Alex Hern (2018, 15 January). 'Hawaii missile false alarm due to badly designed user interface, reports say'. *The Guardian*. theguardian.com/technology/2018/jan/15/hawaii-missile-false-alarm-design-user-interface

2 Marty Cagan (2017, 4 December). 'The four big risks'. Silicon Valley Product Group. svpg.com/four-big-risks

3 Andreessen Horowitz (2019, 16 September). 'Product–user fit comes before product–market fit'. a16z.com/product-user-fit-comes-before-product-market-fit

4 Clayton Christensen and Scott Cook (2006, 16 January). 'What customers want from your products'. Harvard Business School Working Knowledge. library.hbs.edu/working-knowledge/what-customers-want-from-your-products

5 John T. Gourville (2006). 'Eager sellers and stony buyers: understanding the psychology of new-product adoption'. *Harvard Business Review*, June. hbr.org/2006/06/eager-sellers-and-stony-buyers-understanding-the-psychology-of-new-product-adoption

6 Rita Gunther McGrath and Ian C. MacMillan (1995). 'Discovery-driven planning'. *Harvard Business Review*, July–August. hbr.org/1995/07/discovery-driven-planning

7 Gary W. Loveman and Leonard A. Schlesinger (1993). 'Euro Disney: the first 100 days'. Harvard Business School Case 693-013. hbs.edu/faculty/Pages/item.aspx?num=22227

8 Don Norman (2013). *The Design of Everyday Things*, rev. ed. Basic Books.

9 Stewart Butterfield (2023). 'Mental models for building products people love'. *Lenny's Podcast*. youtu.be/kLe-zy5r0Mk

10 Fabricio Laguna (2026). Interview with Paddy Dhanda, unpublished recording.

11 Nick Statt (2019, 19 September). 'Why MoviePass really failed'. *The Verge*. theverge.com/2019/9/19/20872984/moviepass-shutdown-subscription-movies-helios-matheson-ted-farnsworth-explainer

12 Jenny Gathright (2019, 14 September). 'MoviePass has officially shut down, and we don't know if there will be a sequel'. NPR. npr.org/2019/09/14/760862605/moviepass-has-officially-shut-down-and-we-dont-know-if-there-will-be-a-sequel

13 Maria Yagoda (2024, 23 February). 'Airline held liable for its chatbot giving passenger bad advice: what this means for travellers'. BBC Travel. bbc.co.uk/travel/article/20240222-air-canada-chatbot-misinformation-what-travellers-should-know

14 Fast Company (2023). 'Tech companies often ignore "ethical debt": that could be a real problem when it comes to AI'. fastcompany.com/90884257/tech-companies-often-ignore-ethical-debt-and-that-could-be-a-real-problem-when-it-comes-to-ai

15 B. Wansink, J.E. Painter and J. North (2005). 'Bottomless bowls: why visual cues of portion size may influence intake'. *Obesity Research*, Vol. 13, No. 1, pp. 93–100.

16 Kate Payne (2024, 25 October). 'An AI chatbot pushed a teen to kill himself, a lawsuit against its creator alleges'. AP News. apnews.com/article/chatbot-ai-lawsuit-suicide-teen-artificial-intelligence-9d48adc572100822fdbc3c90d1456bd0

17 Jake Rossen (2024, 11 July). 'Kid lit: when LA Gear's LA lights sneakers created a frenzy'. Mental Floss. mentalfloss.com/culture/fashion-beauty/la-gear-light-up-sneakers-controversy

18 Paddy Dhanda and Tom Chatfield (2025, 8 May). 'When technology goes wrong: the 2020 A-level algorithm fiasco'. *When Technology Goes Wrong*. podcasts.apple.com/ca/podcast/when-technology-goes-wrong-the-2020-a-level/id1825138779?i=1000716184185

19 Geoffrey Hinton (2025, 28 December). Interview by Jake Tapper. CNN *State of the Union*. transcripts.cnn.com/show/sotu/date/2025-12-28/segment/01

20 Erik Brynjolfsson, Bharat Chandar and Ruyu Chen (2025, 13 November). 'Canaries in the coal mine? Six facts about the recent employment effects of artificial intelligence'. Stanford Digital Economy Lab. digitaleconomy.stanford.edu/wp-content/uploads/2025/08/Canaries_BrynjolfssonChandarChen.pdf

CHAPTER 5

1 Charles Duhigg (2016, 25 February). 'What Google learned from its quest to build the perfect team'. *New York Times Magazine*. nytimes.com/2016/02/28/magazine/what-google-learned-from-its-quest-to-build-the-perfect-team.html

2 Amy C. Edmondson (2018). *The Fearless Organization: Creating Psychological Safety in the Workplace for Learning, Innovation, and Growth*. Wiley.

3 Paddy Dhanda (2020). 'Leadership is language with David Marquet'. *The Peaky Agilist* podcast. youtube.com/watch?v=ldfJia3wtHY

4 Antoine Buteau (2005). 'Lessons from Ilkka Paananen'. antoinebuteau.com/lessons-from-ilkka-paananen/

5 Daniel Scrivner (2024, 31 December). 'Supercell founder Ilkka Paananen's game design lecture at BAFTA'. danielscrivner.com/supercell-founder-ilkka-paananen-game-design-lecture-at-bafta/

6 Ravi Arora (2019). *Innovation: The Tata Way*. Sage Publications.

7 Tata (2023). Dare to Try: Tata Innovista: the One Tata Way. tata.com/newsroom/business/tata-innovista-one-tata-spirit

8 Engineers Without Borders Canada (2008–2017). *Failure Report*. Engineers Without Borders Canada.

9 Denise Deby (2011, 1 December). 'How engineers without borders learned to embrace failure (and learn from it, too)'. *This Magazine*. this.org/2011/12/01/admitting-failure

10 Kathleen Elkins (2015, 3 April). 'The surprising dinner table question that got billionaire Sara Blakely to where she is today'. *Business Insider*. businessinsider.com/the-blakely-family-dinner-table-question-2015-3

CHAPTER 6

1 Henrik Kniberg and Anders Ivarsson (2012). 'Scaling Agile @ Spotify with tribes, squads, chapters & guilds'. Crisp. blog.crisp.se/wp-content/uploads/2012/11/SpotifyScaling.pdf

2 *Superpowers School* podcast (2025, 27 May). 'Are Agile teams dead? Henrik Kniberg on AI agents and the future of work'. superpowers.school/p/ai-agents-agile-teams-henrik-kniberg

3 Hengchen Dai, Katherine L. Milkman and Jason Riis (2014). 'The fresh start effect: temporal landmarks motivate aspirational behavior'. *Management Science*, Vol. 60, No. 10, pp. 2563–2582.

4 Matthew Rand, Elizabeth Goyder, Paul Norman and Robert Womack (2020). 'Why do new members stop attending health and fitness venues? The importance of developing frequent and stable attendance behaviour'. *Psychology of Sport and Exercise*, Vol. 51, art. 101771.

5 Filip Hendrickx (2026). Interview with Paddy Dhanda, unpublished recording.

6 Harpal Lidder (2026). Interview with Paddy Dhanda, unpublished recording.

7 Paul C. Nutt (1999). 'Surprising but true: half the decisions in organizations fail'. *Academy of Management Executive*, Vol. 13, No. 4, pp. 75–90.

CHAPTER 7

1 Russell L. Ackoff and Daniel Greenberg (2008). *Turning Learning Right Side Up: Putting Education Back on Track*. Pearson Prentice Hall.

2 Wikipedia (n.d.). 'Mo Money Mo Problems'. en.wikipedia.org/wiki/Mo_Money_Mo_Problems

3 Charles H. Kepner and Benjamin B. Tregoe (1965). *The Rational Manager: A Systematic Approach to Problem Solving and Decision-Making*. McGraw-Hill.

4 Mark Wilson (2023, 3 May). 'At. Freaking. Last. Airbnb is fixing its core design problems, says CEO Brian Chesky'. Fast Company. fastcompany.com/90890098/airbnb-fixing-core-design-problems-says-ceo-brian-chesky

5 Marketing Explainers (2025, 8 February). 'Anker's marketing strategy explained'. marketingexplainers.com/ankers-marketing-strategy-explained

6 YouTube (2015, 13 November). 'Day one: stories of entrepreneurship | Steven Yang, Anker Technology'. youtube.com/watch?v=UutELKH-chM

7 John Shook (2023, 20 June). 'How to go to the Gemba: go see, ask why, show respect'. Lean Enterprise Institute. lean.org/the-lean-post/articles/how-to-go-to-the-gemba-go-see-ask-why-show-respect/

8 Lauren Simonds (2004, 28 September). 'Intuit builds a quicker QuickBooks'. Small Business Computing. smallbusinesscomputing.com/software/intuit-builds-a-quicker-quickbooks

9 Geoff Colvin and Tom Ziegler (2014, 7 July). 'Brad Smith: getting rid of friction'. *Fortune*. fortune.com/2014/07/07/intuit-brad-smith

10 Paddy Dhanda (2023, 25 July). 'E104: Self-help – engagement 2.0. Virtual events to keep everyone hooked and involved – Lux Narayan (entrepreneur & author)'. *Product Powers*. superpowers.school/p/e104-self-help-engagement-20-virtual

11 George T. Doran (1981). 'There's a S.M.A.R.T. way to write management's goals and objectives'. *Management Review*, Vol. 70, No. 11, pp. 35–36.

12 Charles Goodhart (1975). 'Problems of monetary management: the U.K. experience'. In *Papers in Monetary Economics*. Reserve Bank of Australia.

13 Hasso Plattner Institute of Design at Stanford (2010). *'An Introduction to Design Thinking: Process Guide'*. Stanford University. web.stanford.edu/~mshanks/MichaelShanks/files/509554.pdf

14 Paul Adams (2016, 28 June). 'How we accidentally invented Job Stories'. intercom.com/blog/accidentally-invented-job-stories/

15 Min Basadur (1995). *The Power of Innovation*. Financial Times/Prentice Hall.

16 Colin Bryar and Bill Carr (2021). 'The Amazon Working Backwards PR/FAQ process'. Working Backwards LLC. workingbackwards.com/concepts/working-backwards-pr-faq-process

17 Building Slack (2024, 20 December). 'The death of Glitch, the birth of Slack'. buildingslack.com/the-death-of-glitch-the-birth-of-slack

18 Startup Archive (2024, 26 October). 'Ben Horowitz tells the story of Slack's pivot from a failed gaming app into a $28 billion company'. startuparchive.org/p/ben-horowitz-tells-the-story-of-slack-s-pivot-from-a-failed-gaming-app-into-a-28-billion-company

CHAPTER 8

1 Clayton M. Christensen, Scott Cook and Taddy Hall (2005). 'Marketing malpractice: the cause and the cure'. *Harvard Business Review*, December. hbr.org/2005/12/marketing-malpractice-the-cause-and-the-cure

2 Confucius (1893). *The Analects, Book 5:10*, trans. James Legge. Clarendon Press. Also available at: ctext.org/analects/gong-ye-chang

3 Susanne Krogh-Hansen (2026). Interview with Paddy Dhanda, unpublished recording.

4 Frederick E. Webster Jr. and Yoram Wind (1972). 'A general model for understanding organizational buying behavior'. *Journal of Marketing*, Vol. 36, No. 2, pp. 12–19.

5 David Ogilvy (1963). *Confessions of an Advertising Man*. Atheneum.

6 Filip Giorgi (2026). Interview with Paddy Dhanda, unpublished recording.

7 Wikipedia (n.d.). 'Desire path'. en.wikipedia.org/wiki/Desire_path

8 Kurt Kohlstedt (2016, 25 January). 'Least resistance: how desire paths can lead to better design'. 99% Invisible. 99percentinvisible.org/article/least-resistance-desire-paths-can-lead-better-design

9 Beatrice Nolan (2026, 24 January). 'Anthropic's head of Claude Code on how the tool won over non-coders—and kickstarted a new era for software engineers'. *Fortune*. fortune.com/2026/01/24/anthropic-boris-cherny-claude-code-non-coders-software-engineers

10 William Samuelson and Richard Zeckhauser (1988). 'Status quo bias in decision making'. *Journal of Risk and Uncertainty*, Vol. 1, pp. 7–59.

11 Albert Einstein, telegram to the Emergency Committee of Atomic Scientists, quoted in *New York Times* (1946, 25 May). 'Atomic education urged by Einstein', p. 13. nytimes.com/1946/05/25/archives/atomic-education-urged-by-einstein-scientist-in-plea-for-200000-to.html

12 Logical Levels Inventory (n.d.). 'Logical Levels model'. logicallevels.co.uk/pages/logical-levels-model-1

13 John Koetsier (2018, 5 April). 'Why every Amazon meeting has at least 1 empty chair'. Inc. inc.com/john-koetsier/why-every-amazon-meeting-has-at-least-one-empty-chair.html

14 Dave Gray (2017, 15 July). 'Updated empathy map canvas'. Medium. medium.com/@davegray/updated-empathy-map-canvas-46df22df3c8a

15 Hospital Management Asia (2024, February). 'Apollo Hospitals' emphasis on empathy for better patient-centred care'. hospitalmanagementasia.com/talent-skills/apollo-hospitals-emphasis-on-empathy-for-better-patient-centred-care

16 Nicolas Maechler, Kevin Neher and Robert Park (2016, 4 March). 'From touchpoints to journeys: seeing the world as customers do'. McKinsey & Company. mckinsey.com/capabilities/growth-marketing-and-sales/our-insights/from-touchpoints-to-journeys-seeing-the-world-as-customers-do

17 D. Kahneman, B.L. Fredrickson, C.A. Schreiber and D.A. Redelmeier (1993). 'When more pain is preferred to less: adding a better end'. *Psychological Science*, Vol. 6, No. 6, pp. 401–405.

18 Fabrice Robinet (2025, 23 March). 'Mind your language: the battle for linguistic diversity in AI'. UN News. news.un.org/en/story/2025/03/1161406

19 Yan Tao, Olga Viberg, Ryan S. Baker and René F. Kizilcec (2024). 'Cultural bias and cultural alignment of large language models'. *PNAS Nexus*, Vol. 3, No. 9, art. pgae346.

20 Maria Rosala and Kate Moran (2024, 21 June). 'Synthetic users: if, when, and how to use AI-generated "research"'. Nielsen Norman Group. nngroup.com/articles/synthetic-users

21 Jeff Sauro, Will Schiavone and Jim Lewis (2024, 2 April). 'Using ChatGPT in tree testing: experimental results'. MeasuringU. measuringu.com/chatgpt4-tree-test

CHAPTER 9

1 Gary Wolf (1996, 1 February). 'Steve Jobs: the next insanely great thing'. *Wired*. wired.com/1996/02/jobs-2

2 *Longman Dictionary of Contemporary English*. idea, n. ldoceonline.com/dictionary/idea

3 Blake Evans-Pritchard (2013). 'Aiming to reduce cleaning costs'. Works That Work. worksthatwork.com/1/urinal-fly

4 Mark A. Runco and Garrett J. Jaeger (2012). 'The standard definition of creativity'. *Creativity Research Journal*, Vol. 24, pp. 92–96.

5 George T. Ainsworth-Land, George Land and Beth Jarman (1992). *Breakpoint and Beyond: Mastering the Future Today*. HarperBusiness.

6 World Economic Forum (2025, 7 January). *Future of Jobs Report 2025*. WEF. weforum.org/publications/the-future-of-jobs-report-2025

7 Tom Kelley and David Kelley (2013). *Creative Confidence: Unleashing the Creative Potential Within Us All*. Crown Business.

8 Albert Bandura (1977). 'Self-efficacy: toward a unifying theory of behavioral change'. *Psychological Review*, Vol. 84, No. 2, pp. 191–215.

9 TEDx Talks (2012, 20 May). 'Transforming healthcare for children and their families: Doug Dietz at TEDxSanJoseCA 2012'. youtu.be/jajduxPD6H4?si=5L01oHDlLvyctKas

10 *Superpowers School* podcast (2022, 27 September). 'E47: Creativity: are people that do STEM subjects or arts more creative – Professor David Cropley (creativity researcher)?' superpowers.school/p/e47-creativity-are-people-that-do-142

11 Catrinel Haught-Tromp (2017). 'The Green Eggs and Ham hypothesis: how constraints facilitate creativity'. *Psychology of Aesthetics, Creativity, and the Arts*, Vol. 11, No. 1, pp. 10–17.

12 Stuart Brown and Christopher Vaughan (2009). *Play: How It Shapes the Brain, Opens the Imagination, and Invigorates the Soul*. Avery.

13 Frank R. Wilson (1998). *The Hand: How Its Use Shapes the Brain, Language, and Human Culture*. Pantheon Books.

14 Jungle Scrum (2019, 10 February). 'Jungle Scrum workshop, an epic Agile adventure: fun and engaging way to learn Agile for all!' YouTube. youtube.com/watch?v=el9FvlgDWcg

15 Brandon Griggs (2016, 4 January). '10 great quotes from Steve Jobs'. CNN Business. cnn.com/2012/10/04/tech/innovation/steve-jobs-quotes

16 Anthony W. Ulwick (2005). *What Customers Want: Using Outcome-Driven Innovation to Create Breakthrough Products and Services*. McGraw-Hill.

17 Strategyn (n.d.). 'Bosch enters competitive market with an award winning product'. strategyn.com/jobs-to-be-done/bosch-case-study

18 Anthony W. Ulwick (2016). *Jobs to be Done: Theory to Practice*. Idea Bite Press.

19 N. Kano, N. Seraku, F. Takahashi and S. Tsuji (1984). 'Attractive quality and must-be quality'. *Hinshitsu: The Journal of the Japanese Society for Quality Control*, Vol. 14, No. 2, pp. 39–48.

20 Phill Agnew (2026). Interview with Paddy Dhanda, unpublished recording.

21 Luke Hohmann (2006). *Innovation Games: Creating Breakthrough Products Through Collaborative Play*. Addison-Wesley.

CHAPTER 10

1 Ronny Kohavi, Diane Tang and Ya Xu (2020). *Trustworthy Online Controlled Experiments: A Practical Guide to A/B Testing.* Cambridge University Press.

2 Stefan H. Thomke (2020). *Experimentation Works: The Surprising Power of Business Experiments.* Harvard Business Review Press.

3 Jeff Gothelf and Josh Seiden (2013). *Lean UX: Applying Lean Principles to Improve User Experience.* O'Reilly Media.

4 Philip E. Tetlock and Dan Gardner (2015). *Superforecasting: The Art and Science of Prediction.* Random House.

5 Steve Krug (2010). *Rocket Surgery Made Easy: The Do-It-Yourself Guide to Finding and Fixing Usability Problems.* New Riders.

6 Michael Hallsworth, John A. List, Robert D. Metcalfe and Ivo Vlaev (2017). 'The behavioralist as tax collector: using natural field experiments to enhance tax compliance'. *Journal of Public Economics*, Vol. 148, pp. 14–31.

7 Douglas W. Hubbard (2014). *How to Measure Anything: Finding the Value of Intangibles in Business*, 3rd ed. Wiley.

8 Daniel Kahneman and Amos Tversky (1974). 'Judgment under uncertainty: heuristics and biases'. *Science*, Vol. 185, No. 4157, pp. 1124–1131.

9 Jonathan Baron and John Hershey (1988). 'Outcome bias in decision evaluation'. *Journal of Personality and Social Psychology*, Vol. 54, No. 4, pp. 569–579.

10 John Dewey (1933). *How We Think: A Restatement of the Relation of Reflective Thinking to the Educative Process.* D.C. Heath and Company.

11 Jeff Gothelf (2017, 8 May). 'Optimizing your team's velocity (of learning)'. Medium. medium.com/@jboogie/optimizing-your-teams-velocity-of-learning-700fd9ee10e4

12 Anita Williams Woolley, Christopher Chabris, Alex Pentland, Nada Hashmi and Thomas Malone (2010). 'Evidence for a collective intelligence factor in the performance of human groups'. *Science*, Vol. 330, No. 6004, pp. 686–688.

13 Lin Lu, Y. Connie Yuan and Poppy Lauretta McLeod (2012). 'Twenty-five years of hidden profiles in group decision making: a meta-analysis'. *Personality and Social Psychology Review*, Vol. 16, No. 1, pp. 54–75.

14 Scott I. Tannenbaum and Christopher P. Cerasoli (2013). 'Do team and individual debriefs enhance performance? A meta-analysis'. *Human Factors*, Vol. 55, No. 1, pp. 231–245.

15 Marilyn Darling, Charles Parry and Joseph Moore (2005). 'Learning in the thick of it'. *Harvard Business Review*, July–August. hbr.org/2005/07/learning-in-the-thick-of-it

16 Ben Hunt-Davis and Harriet Beveridge (2011). *Will It Make the Boat Go Faster? Olympic-Winning Strategies for Everyday Success.* Matador.

17 Ed Stuart-Bourne (2023, 3 August). 'How we launch new products at Monzo'. Monzo Blog. monzo.com/blog/2023/08/03/how-we-launch-new-products-at-monzo

CHAPTER 11

1 *Superpowers School* podcast (2022, 29 November). 'E65: Agile – how I led an Agile transformation at British Telecom – Phil Black (CEO)'. superpowers.school/p/e65-agile-how-i-led-an-agile-transformation-248

2 David Cliff (2008, 14 July). 'The Agile revolution'. Information Age. information-age.com/the-agile-revolution-3-24467

3 *Superpowers School* podcast, 'E65: Agile – how I led an Agile transformation'.

4 Interaction Design Foundation (2025). 'What is design thinking?' interaction-design.org/literature/topics/design-thinking

5 Kate Windsor (2024, 23 June). 'Method vs methodology: what are the key differences?' Listening.com. listening.com/blog/method-vs-methodology

6 John E. Arnold (1959). *Creative Engineering: Promoting Innovation by Thinking Differently*. Stanford University.

7 Robert H. McKim (1972). *Experiences in Visual Thinking*. Brooks/Cole Publishing Company.

8 *Superpowers School* podcast (2024, 24 September). 'What is product design? Eli Woolery – Stanford D.School lecturer E158'. superpowers.school/p/what-is-product-design-eli-woolery

9 Lukas McIntosh and Caroline Hardin (2021). 'Do hackathon projects change the world? An empirical analysis of GitHub repositories'. In: *Proceedings of the 52nd ACM Technical Symposium on Computer Science Education*. ACM.

10 Nick Turley (2025, 9 August). 'Inside ChatGPT: the fastest growing product in history'. *Lenny's Podcast*. lennysnewsletter.com/p/inside-chatgpt-nick-turley

11 ETH Zurich (2019, 15 May). 'HackZurich 2019: Europe's biggest Hackathon'. ETH Zurich Student Portal. ethz.ch/students/en/news/student-news/2019/05/hackzurich-2019--europes-biggest-hackathon.html

12 Giovanni Giuliani (2017, 18 September). 'Zurich backs the ZurichHack!' LinkedIn. linkedin.com/pulse/zurich-backs-zurichhack-giovanni-giuliani

13 Wikipedia Germany (n.d.). 'HackZurich'. de.wikipedia.org/wiki/HackZurich

14 Maciej Ryś (2025). *Sparks for Innovation: Why Hackathons Work and How to Organize One*. Columbia University Press.

15 Jake Knapp (2016). *Sprint: How to Solve Big Problems and Test New Ideas in Just Five Days*. Simon & Schuster.

16 AJ&Smart (2018, 9 July). 'The Design Sprint 2.0'. Medium. medium.com/inside-design/the-design-sprint-2-0-ba89b8713752

17 Jakob Nielsen (2000, 18 March). 'Why you only need to test with 5 users'. Nielsen Norman Group. nngroup.com/articles/why-you-only-need-to-test-with-5-users

18 Jonathan Courtney (2018, 11 May). 'How LEGO run Design Sprints at scale'. UX Planet. uxplanet.org/how-lego-run-design-sprints-at-scale-47bf56b785f7

19 Ben Linders (2019, 22 August). 'Design Sprints at LEGO: Q&A with Eik Thyrsted Brandsgård'. InfoQ. infoq.com/news/2019/08/design-sprints-lego

CHAPTER 12

1 Eric Ries (2011). *The Lean Startup*. Crown Business.

2 Eric Ries (2009, 3 August). 'Minimum viable product: a guide'. Startup Lessons Learned. startuplessonslearned.com/2009/08/minimum-viable-product-guide.html

3 Wikipedia (n.d.). 'Lean startup'. en.wikipedia.org/wiki/Lean_startup

4 Jeff Gothelf and Josh Seiden (2013). *Lean UX: Applying Lean Principles to Improve User Experience*. O'Reilly Media.

5 Bill Scott (2015). 'Lean Engineering: engineering for learning and experimentation in the enterprise'. Talk, Enterprise UX. slideshare.net/RosenfeldMedia/lean-engineering-engineering-for-learning-experimentation-in-the-enterprise-bill-scott-at-enterprise-ux-2015

6 Mike Cohn (2018, 31 October). 'Sprint Zero: a good idea or not?' Mountain Goat Software blog. mountaingoatsoftware.com/blog/sprint-zero-a-good-idea-or-not

7 Marty Cagan (2012, 17 September). 'Dual-track Agile'. Silicon Valley Product Group. svpg.com/dual-track-agile

8 Lynn Miller (2005, July). 'Case study of customer input for a successful product'. In: *Agile Conference*. IEEE Computer Society. research.cs.vt.edu/ns/cs5724papers/miller.agile.pdf

9 Desirée Sy (2007). 'Adapting usability investigations for Agile user-centered design'. *Journal of Usability Studies*, Vol. 2, No. 3, pp. 112–132.

10 Jeff Patton (2017, 10 May). 'Dual Track development is not duel track'. jpattonassociates.com/dual-track-development

11 Ant Boobier (2017). 'All Track Development: or how we created a collaborative product playbook by dropping the collective ego'. Agile Alliance. agilealliance.org/resources/experience-reports/all-track-development

12 Teresa Torres (2021). *Continuous Discovery Habits: Discover Products that Create Customer Value and Business Value*. Product Talk LLC.

13 Teresa Torres (2018, 12 September). 'Creating a sustainable Continuous Discovery practice at CarMax'. Product Talk. producttalk.org/carmax-case-study

14 Teresa Torres (2023, 6 December). 'Opportunity Solution Trees: visualize your discovery to stay aligned and drive outcomes'. Product Talk. producttalk.org/opportunity-solution-trees

15 Atlassian (2024). 'Using outcomes to guide product work'. atlassian.com/software/jira/product-discovery/resources/handbook/outcomes

16 Dan Lebrero (2024, 28 February). 'Book notes: Continuous Discovery Habits'. danlebrero.com/2024/02/28/continuous-discovery-habits-summary

17 Torres, *Continuous Discovery Habits*, p. 27.

18 Teresa Torres (2023, 2 August). 'Everyone can do Continuous Discovery – even you! Here's how'. Product Talk. producttalk.org/getting-started-with-discovery

19 Torres, *Continuous Discovery Habits*, ch. 8.

20 Melissa Suzuno (2024, 2 October). 'Tools of the trade: how HiveMQ automates customer interview recruiting with Orbital'. Product Talk. producttalk.org/2024/10/automate-recruiting-orbital

21 World Economic Forum (2025). *The Future of Jobs Report 2025*. World Economic Forum. weforum.org/publications/the-future-of-jobs-report-2025

CHAPTER 13

1 The word 'stakeholder' dates to 1708, originally meaning the person with whom bets are deposited when a wager is made. See Online Etymology Dictionary (n.d.). 'stake-holder'. etymonline.com/word/stake-holder

2 R. Edward Freeman (2010). *Strategic Management: A Stakeholder Approach*. Cambridge University Press.

3 Robert Kerbeck, *Ruse: Lying the American Dream from Hollywood to Wall Street*. Steerforth Press.

4 *Superpowers School* podcast (2022, 18 October). 'E53: Self-help: exploring the dark side of business: corporate spying – Robert Kerbeck (author of RUSE and former corporate spy)'. superpowers.school/p/e53-self-help-exploring-the-dark-565

5 Lee Ross (1977). 'The intuitive psychologist and his shortcomings: distortions in the attribution process'. In: Leonard Berkowitz (ed.), *Advances in Experimental Social Psychology*, Vol. 10. Academic Press, pp. 173–220.

6 The Myers–Briggs Company (n.d.). 'History reliability and validity of the Myers–Briggs® assessment'. themyersbriggs.com/en-US/Support/Validity-of-the-Myers-Briggs-assessment

7 Gordon W. Allport and Henry S. Odbert (1936). 'Trait-names: a psycho-lexical study'. *Psychological Monographs*, Vol. 47, No. 1, pp. i–171.

8 Adam D. Galinsky, Joe C. Magee, M. Ena Inesi and Deborah H. Gruenfeld (2006). 'Power and perspectives not taken'. *Psychological Science*, Vol. 17, No. 12, pp. 1068–1074.

9 Jerry B. Harvey (1974). 'The Abilene Paradox: the management of agreement'. *Organizational Dynamics*, Vol. 3, No. 1, pp. 63–80.

10 Susan T. Fiske, Amy J.C. Cuddy and Peter Glick (2007). 'Universal dimensions of social cognition: warmth and competence'. *Trends in Cognitive Sciences*, Vol. 11, No. 2, pp. 77–83.

11 Barry Schwartz (2004). *The Paradox of Choice: Why More Is Less*. Ecco Press.

12 Julie K. Norem and Nancy Cantor (1986). 'Defensive pessimism: harnessing anxiety as motivation'. *Journal of Personality and Social Psychology*, Vol. 51, No. 6, pp. 1208–1217.

13 Dave Gauntley (2026). Interview with Paddy Dhanda, unpublished recording.

14 Mike Clemence (2025, 9 December). 'Ipsos Veracity Index 2025'. Ipsos. ipsos.com/en-uk/ipsos-veracity-index-2025

15 Jeffrey Pfeffer (1992). *Managing with Power: Politics and Influence in Organizations*. Harvard Business School Press.

16 David Buchanan and Richard Badham (2020). *Power, Politics, and Organizational Change*, 3rd ed. Sage Publications.

17 Robert A. Caro (2012). *The Passage of Power: The Years of Lyndon Johnson*. The Bodley Head.

18 Stephen R. Covey (1989). *The 7 Habits of Highly Effective People*. Simon & Schuster.

19 Barbara Mellers (2000). 'Choice and the relative pleasure of consequences'. *Psychological Bulletin*, Vol. 126, No. 6, pp. 910–924.

20 Erving Goffman (1967). *Interaction Ritual: Essays on Face-to-Face Behavior*. Aldine Publishing.

21 William Ury (1992). *Getting Past No: Negotiating in Difficult Situations*. Random House Business.

22 Matthew Smith (2018, 7 November). 'David Attenborough is the most popular person in Britain'. YouGov. yougov.co.uk/entertainment/articles/21862-david-attenborough-most-popular-person-britain

23 Robert Cialdini (2026). *Influence: The Psychology of Persuasion*, rev. ed. Harper Business.

CHAPTER 14

1 Sam Kaner (2014). *Facilitator's Guide to Participatory Decision-Making*, 3rd ed. Jossey-Bass.

2 Patrick Lencioni (2002). *The Five Dysfunctions of a Team: A Leadership Fable*. Jossey-Bass.

3 Robin Dunbar (1992). 'Neocortex size as a constraint on group size in primates'. *Journal of Human Evolution*, Vol. 22, No. 6, pp. 469–493.

4 Melanie S. Brucks and Jonathan Levav (2022). 'Virtual communication curbs creative idea generation'. *Nature*, Vol. 605, pp. 108–112.

5 *Product Powers* podcast (2024, 3 December). 'Liberating structures facilitation tools for better meetings E168'. superpowers.school/p/liberating-structures-facilitation

6 Sigal G. Barsade (2002). 'The ripple effect: emotional contagion and its influence on group behavior'. *Administrative Science Quarterly*, Vol. 47, No. 4, pp. 644–675.

7 Mentimeter (2024). *State of Meetings Report.* Mentimeter.

8 Henri Lipmanowicz and Keith McCandless (2014). *The Surprising Power of Liberating Structures.* Liberating Structures Press.

9 *Product Powers* podcast, 'Liberating structures facilitation tools for better meetings'.

10 L. David Marquet (2020). *Leadership is Language: The Hidden Power of What You Say and What You Don't.* Portfolio/Penguin.

11 Patricia Moore and Charles Paul Conn (1985). *Disguised: A True Story.* Word Books.

12 Theresa Wiseman (1996). 'A concept analysis of empathy'. *Journal of Advanced Nursing*, Vol. 23, No. 6, pp. 1162–1167.

13 Kerry Nickols (2026). Interview with Paddy Dhanda, unpublished recording.

14 Jamil Zaki (2019). *The War for Kindness: Building Empathy in a Fractured World.* Crown.

15 Dorothy Leonard and Jeffrey F. Rayport (1997). 'Spark innovation through empathic design'. *Harvard Business Review*, November–December. hbr.org/1997/11/spark-innovation-through-empathic-design

16 Karen Eisenhauer (2023, 15 March). 'Day in the life studies: a unique method for gathering user context'. Dscout. dscout.com/people-nerds/day-in-the-life

17 IDEO U (2017, 19 December). 'Ways to grow your team's curiosity'. ideou.com/blogs/inspiration/ways-to-grow-your-team-s-curiosity

18 Erika Hall (2019). *Just Enough Research*, 2nd ed. A Book Apart.

CHAPTER 15

1 Naveen Gudigantala and Vijay Mehrotra (2024). 'When strength turns into weakness: exploring the role of AI in the closure of Zillow Offers'. *Journal of Information Systems Education*, Vol. 35, No. 1, pp. 67–72.

2 Patrick J. Kiger (2021, 9 December). 'Flip flop: why Zillow's algorithmic home buying venture imploded'. Stanford Graduate School of Business. gsb.stanford.edu/insights/flip-flop-why-zillows-algorithmic-home-buying-venture-imploded

3 Gudigantala and Mehrotra, 'When strength turns into weakness'.

4 Rachel Metz (2021, 9 November). 'Zillow's home-buying debacle shows how hard it is to use AI to value real estate'. CNN Business. cnn.com/2021/11/09/tech/zillow-ibuying-home-zestimate/index.html

5 Michael Scriven and Richard Paul (1987). 'Defining critical thinking'. Presented at the *8th Annual International Conference on Critical Thinking and Education Reform.* criticalthinking.org/pages/defining-critical-thinking/766

6 Robert Dilts (n.d.). 'Walt Disney: strategies of genius'. NLP University. nlpu.com/Articles/article7.htm

7 *Superpowers School* podcast (2024, 28 April). 'Creative brainstorming and fun games to boost innovation, Jennifer Battan, E141'. superpowers.school/p/creative-brainstorming-tips-to-boost-innovation

8 Robert Galen (2014, 20 May). '3 Amigos in Agile teams'. RGalen Consulting. rgalen.com/agile-training-news/2014/4/13/3-amigos-in-agile-teams

9 Agile Alliance (2023). 'Three Amigos'. Glossary entry. agilealliance.org/glossary/three-amigos

10 Agile Alliance, 'Three Amigos'.

11 Gary Klein (2007). 'Performing a project premortem'. *Harvard Business Review*, September. hbr.org/2007/09/performing-a-project-premortem

12 Deborah J. Mitchell, J. Edward Russo and Nancy Pennington (1989). 'Back to the future: temporal perspective in the explanation of events'. *Journal of Behavioral Decision Making*, Vol. 2, No. 1, pp. 25–38.

13 Wikipedia (n.d.). 'Devil's advocate'. en.wikipedia.org/wiki/Devil%27s_advocate

14 Irving L. Janis (1982). *Groupthink: Psychological Studies of Policy Decisions and Fiascoes*, 2nd ed. Houghton Mifflin.

15 Charles R. Schwenk (1984). 'Devil's advocacy in managerial decision making'. *Journal of Management Studies*, Vol. 21, No. 2, pp. 153–168.

16 Matthew Syed (2019). *Rebel Ideas: The Power of Diverse Thinking*. John Murray.

17 Peter T. Leeson (2009). *The Invisible Hook: The Hidden Economics of Pirates*. Princeton University Press. This book draws on the demographic and social history of Atlantic piracy compiled by Marcus Rediker.

18 Leeson, *The Invisible Hook*.

19 Caroline Criado Perez (2019). *Invisible Women: Exposing Data Bias in a World Designed for Men*. Chatto and Windus.

20 Criado Perez, *Invisible Women*.

21 Tom Hale (2017, 18 August). 'This viral video of a racist soap dispenser reveals a much bigger problem in tech'. IFL Science. iflscience.com/this-racist-soap-dispenser-reveals-why-diversity-in-tech-is-muchneeded-43318

22 Critical Media Project (2017). 'Bic Pens for Women, Ellen'. criticalmediaproject.org/bic-pens-for-women-ellen

23 Malcolm Gladwell (2008). *Outliers: The Story of Success*. Little, Brown and Company.

24 Tim Harford (2011, July). 'Trial, error and the God complex'. *TED Talk*. ted.com/talks/tim_harford_trial_error_and_the_god_complex

25 The Nobel Prize (2005, 3 October). 'Press release: the Nobel Prize in Physiology or Medicine 2005'. nobelprize.org/prizes/medicine/2005/press-release

26 Francis Galton (1907). 'Vox Populi'. *Nature*, Vol. 75, pp. 450–451.

27 James Surowiecki (2004). *The Wisdom of Crowds*. Doubleday.

28 Caroline Anne (2023, 5 May). 'The doctors who sought advice from Formula One'. Medium. medium.com/formula-one-forever/the-doctors-who-sought-advice-from-formula-one-3600cc0171df

29 Paul McClean (2016, 11 May). 'Hospital uses Formula One tactics to help newborn babies'. *The Irish Times*. irishtimes.com/news/world/uk/hospital-uses-formula-one-tactics-to-help-newborn-babies-1.2643664

CHAPTER 16

1 Pallavi Gogoi (2010, 31 March) 'Walmart's "Project Impact" craters sales, but the retailer persists'. Yahoo!Life. yahoo.com/lifestyle/2010-03-31-walmarts-project-impact-leaves-a-crater-in-sales-but-the-ret.html

2 Pallavi Gogoi, 'Walmart's "Project Impact"'.

3 Paul Harris (2012). *Trusting What You're Told: How Children Learn from Others.* Harvard University Press. Research indicates children ask 100–300 questions per day during peak questioning years (ages 2–5).

4 Science of People (2024, 13 February). '68 killer conversation starters so you can start a conversation with anyone, anytime'. scienceofpeople.com/conversation-starters-topics

5 Elizabeth F. Loftus and John C. Palmer (1974). 'Reconstruction of automobile destruction: an example of the interaction between language and memory'. *Journal of Verbal Learning and Verbal Behavior*, Vol. 13, No. 5, pp. 585–589.

6 Louise M. Hassan, Edward Shiu and Deirdre Shaw (2014). 'Who says there is an intention–behaviour gap? Assessing the empirical evidence of an intention–behaviour gap in ethical consumption'. *Journal of Business Ethics*, Vol. 136, pp. 219–236.

7 Paul Sloane (1992). *Lateral Thinking Puzzlers.* Sterling Publishing.

8 Paddy Dhanda (2020). 'Leadership is language with David Marquet'. *The Peaky Agilist* podcast. youtube.com/watch?v=IdfJia3wtHY

9 Chris Voss, with Tahl Raz (2016). *Never Split the Difference: Negotiating As If Your Life Depended On It.* Random House Business.

10 John C. Flanagan (1954). 'The critical incident technique'. *Psychological Bulletin*, Vol. 51, No. 4, pp. 327–358.

11 Maria Rosala (2020, 26 January). 'The critical incident technique in UX'. Nielsen Norman Group. nngroup.com/articles/critical-incident-technique

12 Voss and Raz, *Never Split the Difference.*

13 Warren Berger (2014). *A More Beautiful Question: The Power of Inquiry to Spark Breakthrough Ideas.* Bloomsbury.

14 *The Knowledge Project* podcast (2019). 'Warren Berger: asking the right questions [The Knowledge Project Ep. #26]'. fs.blog/knowledge-project-podcast/warren-berger

15 Chris Thomason (2026). Interview with Paddy Dhanda, unpublished recording.

16 Shunryu Suzuki (1970). *Zen Mind, Beginner's Mind: Informal Talks on Zen Meditation and Practice*. Weatherhill.

17 Bob Eberle (1971). *SCAMPER: Games for Imagination Development*. Prufrock Press.

18 The Brand Hopper (2025, 10 September). 'A case study on Patagonia's "Don't Buy This Jacket" campaign'. thebrandhopper.com/2025/06/07/a-case-study-on-patagonias-dont-buy-this-jacket-campaign

19 Allen L. Edwards introduced social desirability bias in 1953, showing how people's desire to appear favourable distorts self-reported data. Wikipedia (n.d.). 'Social-desirability bias'. en.wikipedia.org/wiki/Social-desirability_bias

20 Bank of America's 2004 ethnographic research, conducted with a design consultancy, led to the Keep the Change programme. This is Design Thinking (2018). 'Feeling in control: Bank of America helps customers to "keep the change"'. thisisdesignthinking.net/2018/09/feeling-in-control-bank-of-america-helps-customers-to-keep-the-change

21 Keep the Change attracted 2.5 million customers and 700,000 new checking accounts within its first year. Bloomberg Businessweek (2006, 19 June). 'Case study: Bank of America'. bloomberg.com/news/articles/2006-06-18/case-study-bank-of-america

22 Taiichi Ohno (1988). *Toyota Production System: Beyond Large-Scale Production*. Productivity Press.

23 William R. Miller and Stephen Rollnick (2013). *Motivational Interviewing: Helping People Change*, 3rd ed. Guilford Press.

24 Miller and Rollnick. *Motivational Interviewing*.

25 Michael Bungay Stanier (2016). *The Coaching Habit: Say Less, Ask More and Change the Way You Lead Forever*. Box of Crayons Press.

CHAPTER 17

1 Róza Gombos (2025, 15 September). 'Ignaz Semmelweis'. Science History Institute. sciencehistory.org/education/scientific-biographies/ignaz-semmelweis

2 Vanessa Ravel, Chandini Pandiyan and Krupa Chandran (2025). 'Ignaz Philipp Semmelweis (1818–1865): a public health visionary and champion of hand hygiene'. *GMS Hygiene and Infection Control*, Vol. 20. pmc.ncbi.nlm.nih.gov/articles/PMC12720402

3 WaterAid UK (2014, 22 September). 'Thank you, Dr Semmelweis'. Medium. medium.com/@WaterAidUK/thank-you-dr-semmelweis-f9249fef60b

4 H. Markel (2015). 'Wash your hands!' *Milbank Quarterly*, Vol. 93, No. 3, pp. 447–454.

5 Joseph Lister (1867). 'On the antiseptic principle in the practice of surgery'. *The Lancet*, Vol. 90, No. 2299, pp. 353–356.

6 Fellow (2024). *State of Meetings Report 2024*. fellow.ai/resources/state-of-meetings-2024

7 Gloria Mark (2023). *Attention Span: A Groundbreaking Way to Restore Balance, Happiness and Productivity*. Hanover Square Press.

8 Sandee LaMotte (2024, 15 May). 'If you think you can't focus for long, you're right'. CNN Health. edition.cnn.com/2023/01/11/health/short-attention-span-wellness

9 Ryan Pendell (2022, 6 September). 'Customer brand preference and decisions: Gallup's 70/30 principle'. Gallup. gallup.com/workplace/398954/customer-brand-preference-decisions-gallup-principle.aspx

10 Greg J. Stephens, Lauren J. Silbert and Uri Hasson (2010). 'Speaker–listener neural coupling underlies successful communication'. *Proceedings of the National Academy of Sciences*, Vol. 107, No. 32, pp. 14425–14430.

11 Rob Walker and Joshua Glenn (2009). 'About the Significant Objects project'. significantobjects.com/about

12 Chip Heath and Karla Starr (2022). *Making Numbers Count: The Art and Science of Communicating Numbers*. Avid Reader Press.

13 David Landy, Noah Silbert and Aleah Goldin (2013). 'Estimating large numbers'. *Cognitive Science*, Vol. 37, No. 5, pp. 775–799.

14 Simon Scarr and Marco Hernandez (2019, 4 September). 'Drowning in plastic: visualising the world's addiction to plastic bottles'. Reuters. reuters.com/graphics/ENVIRONMENT-PLASTIC/0100B275155

15 Sébastien Carle (2017). 'When the element of surprise fosters learning'. *Pédagogie Collégiale*, Vol. 30, No. 3, pp. 1–4.

16 A. Lorents, M.F.L. Ruitenberg and J. Schomaker (2023). 'Novelty-induced memory boosts in humans'. *Heliyon*, Vol. 9, No. 3, art. e14410.

17 Seth Godin (2018). *This Is Marketing: You Can't Be Seen Until You Learn to See*. Portfolio/Penguin.

18 Itamar Simonson (1989). 'Choice based on reasons: the case of attraction and compromise effects'. *Journal of Consumer Research*, Vol. 16, No. 2, pp. 158–174.

19 Itamar Simonson and Amos Tversky (1992). 'Choice in context: tradeoff contrast and extremeness aversion'. *Journal of Marketing Research*, Vol. 29, No. 3, pp. 281–295.

20 Bennet B. Murdock (1962). 'The serial position effect of free recall'. *Journal of Experimental Psychology*, Vol. 64, No. 5, pp. 482–488.

21 A.S. Pereira (2023). 'Beyond non-linearity: tracing *Pulp Fiction*'s structure and meaning'. *Journal of Science and Technology of the Arts*, Vol. 15, No. 2, pp. 192–197.

22 Matt Abrahams (2023). *Think Faster, Talk Smarter: How to Speak Successfully When You're Put on the Spot*. Simon & Schuster.

23 *Superpowers School* podcast (2022, 11 October). 'E51: Presentation – master public speaking with these essential presentation tips and training exercises – Brenden Kumarasamy (communication coach)'. superpowers.school/p/e51-presentation-master-public-speaking-051

CHAPTER 18

1 Stefan Thomke (2020). 'Building a culture of experimentation'. *Harvard Business Review*, March–April. hbr.org/2020/03/building-a-culture-of-experimentation

2 Evie Brockwell (2026). Interview with Paddy Dhanda, unpublished recording.

3 Josh Bersin (2018, 3 June). 'A new paradigm for corporate training: learning in the flow of work'. joshbersin.com/2018/06/a-new-paradigm-for-corporate-training-learning-in-the-flow-of-work

4 Stanford Institute for Human-Centered Artificial Intelligence (2026, April). *The 2026 AI Index Report*. Stanford University. hai.stanford.edu/ai-index/2026-ai-index-report

5 Peter M. Senge (1990). *The Fifth Discipline: The Art and Practice of The Learning Organization*. Doubleday.

6 *Superpowers School* podcast (2022, 1 December). 'E66: Agile – art of how to learn and why schools have failed to teach this fundamental skill – Phil Black (CEO)'. superpowers.school/p/e66-agile-art-of-how-to-learn-and-739

7 Tom Hitchings, Emma Haslam, Catrin Woodcock and Zara Ulrich (2025, 23 December). 'How a Discovery Factory can enable fast-flowing business analysis on an enterprise-wide scale'. Deloitte UK. deloitte.com/uk/en/Industries/defense-security-justice/perspectives/how-a-discovery-factory-can-enable-fast-flowing-business-analysis-on-an-enterprise-wide-scale.html

8 Gerald M. Weinberg (1985). *The Secrets of Consulting: A Guide to Giving and Getting Advice Successfully*. Dorset House Publishing.

9 Jean Lave and Etienne Wenger (1991). *Situated Learning: Legitimate Peripheral Participation*. Cambridge University Press.

10 Etienne Wenger (1998). *Communities of Practice: Learning, Meaning, and Identity*. Cambridge University Press.

11 CMX (2025). *The 2025 CMX Community Industry Trends Report*. Bevy/CMX. cmxhub.com/community-industry-report-2025

12 Paddy Dhanda (2025). 'Communities of practice healthcheck'. Comparative Agility. comparativeagility.com/capabilities/communities-of-practice-healthcheck-assessment

13 CMX, *The 2025 CMX Community Industry Trends Report*.

14 Jakob Nielsen (2006, 8 October). 'The 90–9–1 rule for participation inequality in social media and online communities'. Nielsen Norman Group. nngroup.com/articles/participation-inequality

15 Christina Tan (2026). Interview with Paddy Dhanda, unpublished recording.

FINAL WORD

1 *Superpowers School* podcast (2022, 21 June). 'E19: Entrepreneurship – get inspired by the most creative CEO – Terry Rich (Entrepreneur & CEO)'. superpowers.school/p/e19-entrepreneurship-get-inspired-ed2

INDEX